Neoliberalism, Media and

Also by Sean Phelan

Discourse Theory and Critical Media Politics (with Lincoln Dahlberg)
Scooped: The Politics and Power of Journalism in Aotearoa New Zealand (with Martin Hirst and Verica Rupar).

Neoliberalism, Media and the Political

Sean Phelan
Massey University, New Zealand

palgrave
macmillan

First published 2014 by
PALGRAVE MACMILLAN

Palgrave Macmillan in the UK is an imprint of Macmillan Publishers Limited,
registered in England, company number 785998, of Houndmills, Basingstoke,
Hampshire RG21 6XS.

Palgrave Macmillan in the US is a division of St Martin's Press LLC,
175 Fifth Avenue, New York, NY 10010.

Palgrave Macmillan is the global academic imprint of the above companies
and has companies and representatives throughout the world.

Palgrave® and Macmillan® are registered trademarks in the United States,
the United Kingdom, Europe and other countries

ISBN 978-1-349-45596-6   ISBN 978-1-137-30836-8 (eBook)
DOI 10.1057/9781137308368

This book is printed on paper suitable for recycling and made from fully
managed and sustained forest sources. Logging, pulping and manufacturing
processes are expected to conform to the environmental regulations of the
country of origin.

Transferred to Digital Printing in 2015

For my parents, Pat and Kathy Phelan

Contents

Acknowledgements

Different parts of this book have been published elsewhere. Thanks in each case for the permission to reuse and rework material here. Most of Chapter 4 was previously published as "Neoliberalism, Media, and the return of Brash" in the *New Zealand Journal of Media Studies* (2012) *13*(2), 4–17. The last two sections of Chapter 1 were adapted from a book chapter, "Critiquing neoliberalism: Three interrogations and defence", published in the Leah Lievrouw (2014) edited volume, *Challenging Communication Research* (Peter Lang). Parts of Chapter 3, Chapter 5 and the conclusion revisit material previously published as "The media as the neoliberalized sediment: Articulating Laclau's Discourse Theory with Bourdieu's Field Theory" (pp. 128–153), published in Lincoln Dahlberg and Sean Phelan (Eds., 2011), *Discourse Theory and Critical Media Politics* (Palgrave Macmillan). The discussion of discourse theory in Chapter 2 also takes direction from the introduction I co-authored with Lincoln in the same book.

Earlier versions of Chapters 4 and 7, and the final sections of Chapter 1, were presented as papers to the annual conferences of the International Communication Association in 2012, 2013 and 2014. A very early version of Chapter 5 was presented to the International Association of Media and Communication Research conference in Dublin in 2013. Thanks also to Chamsy el-Ojeili for giving me an opportunity to present an early version of Chapter 4 to the School of Social and Cultural Studies at Victoria University of Wellington; Ian Goodwin for inviting me to present some of the ideas developed in Chapter 1 to the School of English and Media Studies at Massey University, Wellington; and Aisling Gallagher and Russell Prince for inviting me to present a working version of Chapter 5 to their virtual seminar series "Government, Governance and the State".

Many people have helped make this book, and I will no doubt fail to thank them all. Chris Penfold and Felicity Plester at Palgrave Macmillan have been encouraging and supportive – and patient given my repeated haggling over deadlines. The financial support of the Massey University Research Fund was invaluable in giving me time to work on the book, and the School of Communication, Journalism and Marketing at

Massey has also been generous in its support. I am especially grateful to Elena Maydell and Chris Montgomerie for covering tutoring and marking responsibilities while I worked on the book. Thanks, too, to Nicky McInnes for her administrative support and good humour in the face of my periodic need to rant.

Different friends and colleagues have energized my work on the book, giving me opportunities to think aloud about the argument and reflect on the writing process. I single out in particular Judith Bernanke, Tim Corballis, Jeannie Fletcher, Shiv Ganesh, Mimi Hodis, James Hollings, Ingrid Horrocks, Ger Lane, Thomas Owen, Damian Ruth, Alan Samson, Fiona Shearer and Redmer Yska. And thanks to the members of Political Organisation Aotearoa for enabling a space to talk collectively about left politics.

I am very grateful to the different people who gave feedback on draft chapters, sometimes at short notice: Peter Berglez, Slavko Gajevic, Ian Goodwin, Peadar Kirby, Verica Rupar, Leon Salter and Murdoch Stephens. Their comments helped me refine aspects of the argument, though they can be reassured that I am claiming all the remaining errors as my own. Thanks also to the anonymous reviewer of the manuscript for the comments and feedback. And special thanks to Lincoln Dahlberg, who was kind enough to read most of the draft manuscript. More generally, thanks to Lincoln for his friendship and for being a reference point for intellectual rigour and commitment since I moved to Wellington in 2003.

I am indebted to Jennifer Carey for her copyediting work and for putting order on my chaotic bibliography. Much more importantly, thanks to Jennifer for her love, support and belief in me, despite my moments of self-preoccupation while working on the book.

Finally, thanks to my parents, Pat and Kathy Phelan, for always being there, even at a distance (my sister Elaine and brother Bryan too). They probably had not imagined a book dedication in their name, especially one titled *Neoliberalism, Media and the Political*. But I dedicate this book to them as an expression of love and gratitude.

Sean Phelan
May 19, 2014

Introduction: Disfiguring Neoliberalism

I started thinking and writing about neoliberalism in 1999 when I began graduate study at Dublin City University. Back then my understanding of it, and a whole lot of other things, was pretty unformed. I mainly had some hunches and intuitions. Perhaps my strongest one was that the power and authority of neoliberalism had something to do with how the social world was talked about in everyday media contexts – discourses that were deeply political and ideological, yet simultaneously trite and mundane. Much has changed since 1999. I was then writing about an Irish context that looks very different in 2014. And I moved to Aotearoa New Zealand in 2003, since engaging with its media and political culture. However, the argument here is essentially guided by similar intuitions, even if they are now articulated in a form that my earlier self would have been unable to formulate.

What has endured is my interest in understanding how people identify *and* disidentify with the thing called "neoliberalism".[1] The term has a lot more currency among left-wing academics and activist critics than among putative neoliberals themselves. Few people today would proudly claim the identity of neoliberal, though that does not mean the concept is nothing but the fanciful construct of paranoid academics and activists.[2] Two memories from the start of my graduate study – one specific, the other generic – capture this abiding interest in the politics of naming, or *not* naming, the social world as neoliberal. At a drinks reception for new students, I was introduced to an academic staff member and prompted to describe my plan to examine the influence of neoliberal assumptions in Irish media. The response to my laboured attempts to describe my project was not especially encouraging. I was told in a matter-of-fact way that we are now "post-neoliberal", the implication being that the neoliberal era was already over. The comment has stuck with me ever since as an exemplar of a more general tendency. It captures how the trajectory of neoliberalism has been entangled with claims about its dissolution and "post-ness", paradoxes evident in the

Irish social formation that backgrounded our conversation. Yet, side by side with my interlocutor's declaration of a post-neoliberalism, my return to university exposed me to a second kind of discourse, one with more authority and intellectual capital in the seminar room. Here it was often casually assumed that the world *is* neoliberal, the argument often made in a taken-for-granted way that necessitated no elaboration. If it did not explain everything, the term seemed to explain an awful lot. Within a critical milieu, neoliberalism seemed to be the go-to category when accounting for the present condition of the social order.

I recall these stylized memories because they capture two perspectives I have always found inadequate. The problem with the discourse of post-neoliberalism is that it binds the concept of neoliberalism to a fixed set of market-based policies and a political archetype that enacts its adoration for free-market capitalism. Change the policy or rhetoric and we magically enter a universe of post-neoliberalism, an eminently reasonable world free of the blinding effects of neoliberal ideology. The discourse of "neoliberalism explains everything" suffers from the inverse problem, because no matter what the policy or rhetoric, the social formation seems to be an essentially neoliberal one. The concept becomes a heavy-handed tool of social analysis that knows its answer in advance, determinedly tracing everything back to a neoliberal grand narrative. If the claim of post-neoliberalism can collapse into the lame assumption that ideology (and even politics) no longer matters, the neoliberal grand narrative can slide into an unreconstructed version of a "dominant ideology" thesis (Abercrombie, Hill & Turner, 1980; J. Gilbert, 2008): a world of people apparently colonized by neoliberalism.

My distinction simplifies. Nonetheless, it hints at an in-between space that centres the argument made in this book. The concept of neoliberalism should not be abandoned. However, we need to do more than invoke it as a "shorthand term for the ideological atmosphere" (Peck, 2010, p. xi), as if the term has such an obvious referent that it hardly needs to be accounted for at all. Neoliberalism needs, as Collier (2012) suggests, to become our "object of inquiry": posed "as a question rather than something that is taken for granted" (p. 184). This book links neoliberalism to two other grand objects: the media and the political. Taken together, the aim is to present a critical theoretical analysis that goes beyond a familiar narrative that casts the media as part of an ideological and political superstructure that reproduces neoliberal rule. That narrative surely has its basis and appeal: media practices are important in enabling and legitimizing the social reproduction of neoliberalism. The issue instead concerns its adequacy, as either a description or explanation of the relational dynamics between media, political and neoliberal logics. I find broad-stroke narratives of neoliberalism and media inadequate for various reasons that will hopefully become clear over the course of the book.

Disfiguring neoliberalism

My analysis takes different turns. But the spirit of my argument and approach is usefully captured by the metaphorical phrase "disfiguring neoliberalism". The metaphor is productive in four respects that intersect, but also trouble, each other. First, as an adjectival noun phrase, it signifies a social world disfigured by neoliberal policies and reason. Here we are on familiar critical ground. The metaphor signals the normative opposition to neoliberalism that structures most analyses of it (Birch & Mykhnenko, 2010; Harvey, 2005; Peck, 2010). Neoliberalism signifies how economic logics have colonized the logic of the social, rendering social, human and planetary life increasingly subordinate to the instrumentalist rationality of "the market". The story takes a familiar form across disciplines. It typically cites the 1980s rise of Thatcher in the UK and Reagan in the US as the most obvious symbols of a new ideological dispensation; the alignment of Chicago School economists with the 1973 Pinochet coup in Chile as a telling historical antecedent; the globalization of neoliberal political economy in the transnational architecture of the World Trade Organization, International Monetary Fund and World Bank in the 1980s and 1990s; the mutation of the ideologically confrontational neoliberalism of the 1980s into the softer third way neoliberalism of the 1990s and 2000s; and, most recently, the emergence of a hyper-neoliberal austerity politics, mocking earlier speculation about the "end" of neoliberalism. All told, neoliberalism represents the institutionalization of a more brutal form of finance-driven capitalism (Jessop, 2010): officially celebrated in the name of freedom, choice and empowerment, but without the protective social mechanisms of the "embedded liberalism" (Lacher, 1999) of the post-war era. Social life is disfigured by the material effects of neoliberal regimes, naturalizing a world of enormous income gaps between rich and poor, unaccountable corporate power, capitalist profiteering, structural adjustments, increased worker precarity, lives lived on credit, persistent unemployment, a weakened public infrastructure, environmental destruction, oppressive audit and surveillance regimes, narcissistic individualism and relentless commodification. The character of media and journalistic spaces is similarly altered, normalizing a culture of celebrity, personality, spectacle and aggressive opinionating that displaces a democratic orientation to the polity.

Our disfiguring metaphor also works as a verb, emphasizing how media and journalistic practices act on neoliberalism. Formulating an abstract conception of neoliberalism is one thing. But what happens to that conception – how is it disfigured? – when it is adapted to the everydayness of media spaces? (One could ask a similar question of other domains. We know much about the neoliberalization of the university. But what does neoliberalism look like when it is embodied as a managerial disposition at a school or university meeting? Whatever form it takes, we know it does not arrive in a T-shirt blazoned with the motto "up the neoliberals!"). This question is a key thematic concern of the book, approached from different angles and perspectives. But one suggestive answer is offered from within the corpus of neoliberal thought itself, in Frederick Hayek's (1960) reflections about the power and trajectory of ideas:[3]

> ...the influence of the abstract thinker on the masses operates only indirectly. People rarely know or care whether the commonplace ideas of their day have come to them from Aristotle or Locke, Rousseau or Marx, or from some professor whose views were fashionable among the intellectuals twenty years ago. Most of them have never read the works or even heard the names of the authors whose conceptions and ideals have become part of their thinking. So far as direct influence on current affairs is concerned, the influence of the political philosopher may be negligible. But when his [sic] ideas have become common property, through the work of historians and publicists, teachers and writers, and intellectuals generally, they effectively guide developments. This means not only that new ideas commonly begin to exercise their influence on political action only a generation or more after they have first been stated but that, before the contributions of the speculative thinker can exercise such influence, they have to pass through a long process of selection and modification (p. 113).

Reformulated in the theoretical vernacular of this book, Hayek's quote captures the logic of hegemony: how ideas that were once novel and contentious become naturalized and taken for granted. They become the "common property" of the people, as if Hayek was already intuiting the political victories of the future. Yet, by insisting ideas "have to pass through a long process of selection and modification", he also gives us cause to be sceptical of the image of a fully formed neoliberalism simply imposing itself on the social world. The quote suggests a slower process of cultural adaptation where, for neoliberal common sense to be politically effective, it needs to become imbricated in the common-sense assumptions of other domains. On the one hand, Hayek conjures up the image of a world of unintentional and unconscious neoliberals: people reproducing neoliberalism without knowing they are doing so – his own version of a critical theoretical argument about the ideological constitution of society. However, on the other hand, he captures an agented dimension where, in a sense, social actors make the abstract ideas their own through a dynamic process of selection and modification. Maybe Hayek helps us see the disfigured and fragmented character of our object of analysis, contrary to the one-dimensional image of a mainstream media colonized by a singular neoliberalism. Instead of imagining that journalists and others in the media reproduce neoliberalism because they are neoliberals, it might be more productive to explore how journalists reproduce neoliberalism by being journalists – by articulating a mode of neoliberal identification that is both specific to the journalistic field, generalized in a media posture that assumes authority over social fields (Couldry, 2003a), but, at the same time, not reducible to the concept of neoliberalism.

Our metaphor resonates in a second sense as a verb, this time through the image of the critical intervention as an act of disfiguring. It anticipates a critical engagement with the immanent rationality of neoliberal regimes: a mode of critique that parses their dynamic constitution and make-up (Fisher, 2009; Shore, 2008). It suggests a radical democratic mode of critique (Laclau & Mouffe, 2001) that wants to do more than simply oppose neoliberalism; if neoliberalism is a name for the given social order, that order needs to be reckoned with, and acted on, rather than simply denounced (Ferguson, 2009). Such an approach might seem inadequate to some, lacking the seeming clarity of purpose articulated in the demand for a total break from neoliberalism. Yet, it need not be "merely" reformist, so long as we bring into view the different constitutive elements that make neoliberal regimes possible. Here, as elsewhere in the book, Laclau (1990) is suggestive. He insists the "construction of an alternative project is based on the grounds created by [capitalist] transformations, not on opposition to them" (pp. 55–56). The key point: by disfiguring the internal composition of neoliberal social and media regimes, we might be able to better see the different sites and practices relevant to our problematic of neoliberalism, media and the political.

The final aspect of our metaphor concerns the question of ideology. If neoliberalism disfigures the social, ideology has historically been the master critical concept for describing the political disfiguring of society.

Marxists and others have theorized ideology in different ways, variously understood as an epistemological, ontological and sociological concept (Eagleton, 1991). Within critical media and communication studies, ideology critique has typically brought a "hermeneutics of suspicion" to the analysis of media and language (Scannell, 1998): inclined to see both as instruments that distort and obscure the real material condition of the social world. Ideology is a crucial concept in the book, central to my discussion of neoliberal identities in Chapter 2. However, my conception of ideology critique departs from the historically dominant one in some important respects. I do not tie the dualisms of representation/reality, surface/depth and false/true consciousness to how they have traditionally operated in ideology critique.[4] Nor do I regard political ideologies as inherently duplicitous and mystificatory: as Finlayson (2012) suggests, "ideology is a property of politics, not a malfunction" (p. 753); "ideologies can be creative acts" (p. 754). As a media researcher, I want to avoid slipping into a critical pessimism that casts the mainstream media as a space of unrelenting falsity and distortion. And, as a critical interpretative researcher, I want to avoid speaking over agents' own self-interpretations of the world (see Chapter 3), as if calling something neoliberal means it can be cursorily dismissed; as if calling something neoliberal is an argument clincher in its own right. I want to critically understand neoliberal media representations, not simply disparage them because they are neoliberal.[5]

About this book

This is most obviously a book about neoliberalism and media. But the category of "the political"– used as a noun – is also crucial. I do not offer a comprehensive overview of how neoliberalism is articulated in different media spaces and genres. Rather, I focus on the relational dynamic between neoliberalism, media and the political. If neoliberalism is most commonly identified as an economic ideology, I am most interested in its political rationality (Brown, 2003), though of course the discussion of politics cannot be separated from economy. I follow a recent trend in critical theory that, drawing on Laclau, Mouffe and others, distinguishes the concept of "the political" from "the domain of politics in a narrow sense" (Marchart, 2007, p. 1). The foregrounding of the concept speaks to the relative dearth of engagement with radical democratic theory in media and communication research (Karppinen, 2013). The concept encourages us to think of politics in expansive and radical terms: the entire social order, including the media, becomes a site of the political.

Marchart (2007) suggests the concept of the political points to "society's 'ontological' dimension", signifying how the "objective" social order is institutionalized in conditions that are always structurally vulnerable to contestation (p. 5). This "post-foundational" (p. 1) account of the social rejects the notion of society having an absolute foundation. Yet it also rejects the inverse image of a society with no foundations at all. Instead, the political becomes a social grounding that is always a provisional ground, because the very notion of society having a "final ground" is "impossible" (p. 7). Alongside a critical deconstruction of the existing social order, the concept focuses our attention on how a different kind of society might be reconstructed.

The concept of the political offers us much more than the glib thesis that "everything is political". On the contrary, many of those who insist on the distinction between the political and institutional politics argue that, in a neoliberal age, politics proper is a rare event (Laclau, 2005; Mouffe, 2005; Ranciere, 1999).[6] Contrary to everyday media representations that dramatize political conflict, the supposition is that the logic of the political is essentially repressed, obscured by routinized social practices that cannot see beyond the existing social architecture. How media and journalistic representations repress the logic of the political, either by consciously or unconsciously identifying with neoliberal logics, is a central concern of the book. I do not comprehensively explore the question of political and normative alternatives to a neoliberalized media and political culture, even if such analyses are necessary and already being done by others (see, for example, Couldry, 2010). Instead, rather than hardening the theoretical distinction between politics and the political (see Barnett, 2008; Oksala, 2010), I am primarily interested in identifying the potential sites of a cultural politics *within* the sedimented logics of neoliberal media regimes.

The rest of the book has eight chapters and a short conclusion. Chapters 1 to 3 provide the theoretical, historical and argumentative groundwork for what follows. We need to begin with general reflection on the concept of neoliberalism ahead of any substantive media analysis. Chapter 1 examines how neoliberalism is conceptualized in the existing critical media and communication studies literature, organized around a broad distinction between critical political economy, cultural studies and governmentality perspectives. I engage with debates about the usefulness of the category of neoliberalism, ending the chapter with a defence of the concept ahead of my own theoretical account in Chapters 2 and 3.

Chapters 2 and 3 note my debt to Laclau's discourse theory. Chapter 2 moves between a theoretical and empirical register. I discuss how different discourse theory concepts inform my account of neoliberalism alongside a historical overview of neoliberalism as a political-intellectual formation. I introduce an analytical distinction between two kinds of neoliberal discourse: the antagonistic neoliberalism of the early neoliberals and the third way neoliberalism of the 1990s and 2000s. Chapter 3 introduces the concept of neoliberal logics, drawing on Glynos and Howarth's (2007) theoretical and methodological reworking of discourse theory. I discuss my use of Bourdieu's field theory as a sociological supplement to discourse theory: a necessary supplement to the ontological-level orientation of Laclau's work.

Chapters 4 to 8 explore different argumentative trajectories grounded in substantive analyses of different empirical contexts. Chapter 4 examines a 2011 media-political event in New Zealand, exploring the discursive continuities and ruptures with the radical neoliberal formations in the New Zealand of the 1980s and 1990s. I show how contemporary media discourses naturalize the assumption that neoliberalism is something that happened in New Zealand's past, reinforced in the particular illustration by the mediated hostility to an overt neoliberal identity. Chapter 5 reflects on the relationship between neoliberalism and the journalistic habitus, supplementing the theoretical discussion with an analysis of how a particular Irish journalist has represented austerity policies. I discuss the significance of a "realist" rhetoric (Aune, 2001) in engendering a mode of journalistic identification with neoliberal logics that disavows its political and ideological commitments.

Chapter 6 examines the so-called "climategate" scandal of 2009, exploring how neoliberal and rational choice logics textured blogosphere and mainstream media representation of climate change scientists in the UK and US. I explore the analogies between media representations of scientists and politicians as self-interested actors, showing how both are made possible by the normalization of a culture that hates politics (Hay, 2007). Chapter 7 uses the 2011–2012 Leveson Inquiry into the UK press to explore the political resonances between the rhetoric of press freedom and the account of freedom articulated in the work of Hayek and Milton Friedman. I examine the place of neoliberal logics and antagonisms in journalistic criticisms of Leveson's (2012) proposal that a "statutory underpinning" should support any new press regulator.

Chapter 8 – the longest and most descriptive chapter in the book – examines the role of "media rituals" (Couldry, 2003b) in the construction of a particular neoliberal formation, tracking the interplay between national and international logics in the mediation of the "Irish Celtic Tiger". I examine a particular conjunctural representation of Ireland from the early 1990s onwards, moving between different empirical contexts and illustrations to show the ideological continuity between discourses circulating at home and abroad. The book ends by briefly reflecting on questions of strategic intervention largely implicit in the rest of the book. I ask how we might understand the contours of a radical democratic critique[7] of neoliberalism, especially in light of the concept's seeming increasing visibility as a signifier for everything that is wrong with the existing social order.

Some caveats

A book with the grand title of *Neoliberalism, Media and the Political* necessitates some caveats. The book's problematic is, in one sense, impossibly broad. The complex, multidimensional relationship between our three categories cannot be captured in a single text. This is *a* book about neoliberalism, media and the political, not *the* book. My account is a necessarily partial and fragmentary one, privileging my own intuitions, experiences and preoccupations. I cannot but explore particular aspects of a more general problematic.

One of the most obvious empirical limitations of the book – and it's a familiar caveat in media and communication scholarship – is the focus on "Anglo-American" and "liberal democratic" media systems (Hallin & Mancini, 2004). Chapters 2, 6 and 7 primarily reference the UK and US. Less predictably, Chapters 4, 5 and 8 examine two other countries aligned with Hallin and Mancini's liberal democratic model: Ireland and Aotearoa New Zealand. I analyse them partly for the simple reason that they are the two national contexts I know best. But there are also sound argumentative reasons for examining both countries, because at different historical moments neoliberals have cited them as "model" economies for other countries to follow. Both offer more than what might be patronizingly called "local" case studies: supplements to the real debates taking place in the metropolitan centre. On the contrary, both countries are exemplars of a more general "post-political" and "post-ideological" condition that normalizes, while also officially disavowing, a normative commitment to neoliberal policies. The globalization of Anglo-American media models (Hallin & Mancini, 2004; Thussu, 2007) suggests the argument might have resonances elsewhere, even if these are not explored here.

A second empirical limitation of the book is its primary focus on mainstream news media and journalism: what Couldry (2003b) calls "centring" media (see Chapter 8). Much of the argument could be extended to other media forms. We live in media cultures where the distinctions between news and entertainment, politics and popular culture (Street, 2001), mainstream media and social media are increasingly porous. Moreover, the prominence of concepts like "mediation", "mediatization" and "mediality" (Grusin, 2010; Livingstone, 2009; Marchart, 2011; Strömbäck, 2008) underscores the increasing scholarly interest in the ontological condition and significance of media: the referent for the thing called "the media" is no longer so clear-cut (Couldry, 2009; Cubitt, 2011). The convergence of mediums is evident in different parts of the book, most obviously in Chapter 6's examination of the discursive affinities between a blog aligned to a traditional newspaper and a blog run by climate-change sceptics. However, I am mainly focused on what is sometimes cast as the "predictable Other" of mainstream media (Zelizer, 2004; see also Curran, 2002), a critical attitude that I interrogate in Chapter 5. In marginalizing analysis of how neoliberal regimes are resisted and opposed, I hardly mean to suggest that resistance and opposition do not take place, either outside or within mainstream media cultures.[8]

The scope of the book is interdisciplinary: it necessitates crossing the boundaries between different fields. In one sense, this is part of the general condition of – if I lump all the categories I might identify with together – media, communication, journalism and cultural studies (Deacon, Pickering, Golding & Murdock, 2007). But an interdisciplinary approach is particularly important when analysing neoliberalism, given the comparative richness of the work and debates in other fields. The literature on neoliberalism is vast. Productive insights can be found in fields such as political analysis, critical political theory, sociology, economic and human geography, anthropology, political economy and critical discourse analysis, to name but a few. Moreover, critical media and communication researchers invariably look to other fields in operationalizing the concept, as I discuss in Chapter 1. That said, any commitment to interdisciplinarity is necessarily selective, privileging particular sources and lines of thought over others. Although the argument is inflected differently across chapters, the concerns of a media researcher should be discernible throughout.

Finally, a word about my use of discourse theory, since discourse analysis in critical media and communication studies is primarily associated with linguistic approaches. This book does not privilege close linguistic analysis of media texts in the fashion of critical discourse analysis and other methodologies.[9] Instead, I work with Laclau's expansive conception of discourse analysis: discourse analysis becomes a study of how the social is politically constituted. I analyse particular media texts, but these are embedded in the argumentative concerns of the particular chapter rather than elaborate methodological protocols. The rationale behind the selection and analysis of objects, texts, practices and contexts is pragmatic, adapted to the primarily theoretical nature of my argument. My empirical analysis is illustrative but attentive to questions of empirical specificity. The empirical object can be theorized without being reduced to a *theoretical* object.

Enough caveats. Let us begin with a discussion of how neoliberalism is articulated in the existing literature before justifying why the concept should be privileged in the first place.

1

Articulating Neoliberalism in Critical Media and Communication Studies

Looked at broadly, we can identify two distinct discourses about neoliberalism in communication and media studies and elsewhere. The first deploys the term to enact a familiar critical narrative where neoliberalism signifies a social order dominated by the logic of the market. This narrative has been given different articulations[1] in communication and media research. Neoliberalism has functioned as a descriptive and explanatory category in analyses of topics such as infotainment (Thussu, 2007), media ownership (Herman & McChesney, 1997), multiculturalism (Lentin & Titley, 2011), reality television (Ouellette & Hay, 2008), political marketing (Savigny, 2008), political consultants (Sussman & Galizio, 2003), intellectual property rights (Hesmondhalgh, 2008) and the cultural politics of voice (Couldry, 2010). Others have examined the communicative dynamics of "free market" regimes without explicitly deploying the term "neoliberalism" (Aune, 2001). More generally, the role of media and communication practices in the ideological constitution of neoliberalism is taken for granted in the wider literature (see Birch & Mykhnenko, 2010; Harvey, 2005; Jessop, 2010).

Yet, the authority of neoliberalism as a critical signifier has been interrogated by a second discourse. This critique has sometimes been made by those distancing themselves from critical research traditions, in some cases defending their work against the charge of ideological complicity with neoliberalism. However, frustration with the open-ended scope of the term has also been articulated by those who retain a clear commitment to interrogating what might otherwise be named as neoliberal norms. For example, Grossberg argues that a fixation on neoliberalism and neoliberalization can impede critical analysis. As he observes in an interview with Cho (2008):

Too often, the context is just described in terms of the dialectic between the global and the local or in terms of the neoliberalization of just about everything, a particularly unhelpful phrase, whether it is understood economically or governmentally. These are too glib and too easy. We need to find better ways of talking about regional, transnational, or even global contexts. Perhaps we should be looking at all of them but surely we have to figure out how to map the interconnections, the articulations (p. 107).

This chapter has three key objectives. First, I examine our first discourse above, organized around a broad distinction between critical political economy, cultural studies and governmentality perspectives. Second, I discuss how different authors have questioned the value of the concept of neoliberalism. Third, I end the chapter by clarifying my own take on the concept. I affirm the importance of the critique of neoliberalism. However, I recognize that scepticism about how the term is used is in one respect justified. As in other fields, neoliberalism is too often invoked as a "summary label", a "metaphor for the ideological air we all (must) breathe" (Peck, 2010, p. xii). At the same time, I argue that it would be a mistake to discard the concept; rather, we need to interrogate its formulaic iteration, yet try to operationalize it in a more critically illuminating way. I conclude by briefly outlining a rationale for recuperating the concept, in anticipation of the theoretical discussion of Chapters 2 and 3.

The political economy of neoliberalism

Neoliberalism is commonly defined as an economic ideology and philosophy. Within the field of critical media and communication studies, the concept is most obviously associated with the political economy literature. Mosco's (2009) broad definition of the political economy of communication captures the critical orientation of a field strongly influenced by Marxist theory: "the study of the social relations, particularly the power relations, that mutually constitute the production, distribution, and consumption of resources, including communication resources" (p. 2). For critical political economists, the concept of neoliberalism signifies a regime of capitalism that broke from the Keynesian model that shaped Western political economy after World War II (see, for example, Birch & Mykhnenko, 2010; Fenton, 2006; Harvey, 2005; Hope, 2012; Wasko, Murdock & Sousa, 2011). The shift radically altered the relationship between state, capital and labour. The production base of the Keynesian economy was supplanted by a global regime of financial capital and service industries, shifting manufacturing to countries where labour was cheapest. The notion of the welfare state as a protective mechanism for workers was systematically challenged, the very idea of welfare stigmatized. Flexible regimes of production became the norm, eroding the worker protections gained through the post-war "pact" between capital and labour. And the traditionally demarcated roles of management and ownership were fused through stock incentivization policies, facilitating the emergence of an elite neoliberal class focused on maximizing share prices.

The Marxist geographer David Harvey has formulated the best-known political economy analysis of neoliberalism, one regularly cited by media and communication researchers (see, for example, Freedman, 2008; Pickard, 2007). Neoliberalism had already been firmly established as a critical concept when his book *A Brief History of Neoliberalism* was published in 2005. Yet, Harvey reinvigorated a Marxist analysis of neoliberalism, emphasizing the central importance of class dynamics. His shorthand description of neoliberalism as a theory of political economy gave definitional clarity to a term Pickard (2007) suggests is often "ill-defined and broadly misunderstood" (p. 118):

> Neoliberalism is in the first instance a theory of political economic practices that proposes that human well-being can best be advanced by liberating individual entrepreneurial freedoms and skills within an institutional framework characterized by strong private property rights, free market, and free trade. The role of the state is to create and preserve an institutional framework appropriate to such practices (Harvey, 2005, p. 2).

Harvey's definition highlights how free-market regimes need the state's institutional support and protection, challenging one-dimensional perceptions of neoliberalism as a libertarian philosophy hostile to the state. Yet, the notion of a singular neoliberal "theory" is also an analytical convenience. The "liberal resurgence" (Beaud & Dostaler, 1997, p. 112) of the 1970s and 1980s drew on different theories of liberal political economy, including monetarism, supply-side economics, neoclassical, Chicago School, Austrian School, and rational choice/public choice theory (Beaud & Dostaler, 1997; Cockett, 1995). These theories were sometimes the site of intra-familial philosophical and methodological tensions (Mirowski, 2013). Yet, Gray (1986) suggests their "differences [were] in the end disagreements about transitional strategy rather than about the liberal goal" (p. 79). They coalesced to form a unified political economic vision grounded in a "reaffirmation of the virtues of the market and competition" (Beaud & Dostaler, 1997, p. 118) and strong rhetorical opposition to the idea of state intervention in the economy. The unity between different liberal theories was partly enabled by their identification of a shared antagonist in Keynesianism (see Chapter 2) and their common diagnosis of the capitalist and state crises of the 1970s. Neoliberals saw two features of the Keynesian paradigm as particularly untenable: the direct intervention of the state in the management of consumer demand and the development of a strong welfare state as a bulwark against the vagaries of capitalism (Lacher, 1999, p. 243).

Harvey (2005) describes neoliberalism as the ideology of global capitalism: the legitimizing front for "a project to achieve the restoration of class power" (p. 16) on a transnational scale. This project sometimes assumes a clear authoritarian and imperialist hue (see also Brown, 2003). Yet, it is packaged in ways that can secure popular consent, strategically exploiting the inherent human appeal of the language of freedom and individual rights. The rhetoric of free markets and free trade acts as the ideological cover for the establishment of a transnational regime of capitalist accumulation liberated from the comparative restraints on capital mobility during the Keynesian era. This global ideology is subject to national, regional and party-political variations, and articulated in contradictory ways that belie the notion of a singular neoliberalism. Yet, in Harvey's (2005) assessment, what is consistent across different formations is the valorization of two principles: the need to create "a good business and investment climate" attractive to global capital and the safeguarding of the financial system, especially in times of political crisis (p. 70). Conflict between these political priorities and upholding the official neoliberal doctrine should be anticipated, he suggests. However, in the last resort, doctrinal purity will be sacrificed to uphold a particular configuration of class-based power.

Harvey (2005) emphasizes the "systematic divergences from the template of neoliberal theory" (p. 70) within the universe of "actually existing neoliberalism" (Brenner & Theodore, 2002). These paradoxes are most obvious in the neoliberal account of the state. On the one hand, the state is the official enemy of the free-market project: the primary impediment to human freedom (see Chapter 7). Yet, on the other hand, it is central to institutionalizing the political and legal framework desired by neoliberals and, as we know, its life-support in times of crisis. Harvey's attentiveness to the neoliberal state's capacity to depart from ideological orthodoxy explains his scepticism about proclamations of the "end of neoliberalism" in 2008 and 2009 (Harvey, 2009), the popular assumption at the time being that the unprecedented state intervention in the financial system constituted an unpardonable breach of free-market doctrine. His account essentially predicted the political response to the crisis. The bank bailouts in different countries were but an extreme manifestation of the logic of the neoliberal state, which will do whatever it takes to sustain the operation of the "free market" because its own fate has become so intertwined with upholding the integrity of "the financial system and the solvency of institutions" (Harvey, 2005, p. 71). And this work of ideological repair is partly enabled by an infrastructure of "capitalist media": their default construction of a narrative that, as Harvey says of the recent crisis, all "too easily forgives and forgets the transgressions of a capitalist class" (Harvey, 2010, p. 291; see also Andersson, 2012) or fixates on the excesses of individual bankers, displacing a systemic understanding of the causes of capitalist crises (Dyer-Witheford & Compton, 2011; Fisher, 2009).

Neoliberalism and the political economy of media

Like Harvey, critical political economy of communication researchers take the capitalist system as their primary object of study. Analyses of the effects of neoliberalism on the organization of media, communication and information systems are situated within the logic and trajectory of the wider capitalist economy. Neoliberalism is conceptualized as a capitalist formation increasingly dependent on communicative processes and information flows (Dean, 2009; Hope, 2012). And the labour theory of value is extended to understanding the work done by audiences in the digital and social media ecology (Cohen, 2008). References to neoliberalism typically cue a normative critique of how media and communication systems in liberal democratic capitalist societies have become increasingly market-driven since the 1970s and 1980s (Garnham, 2011).

As in other fields, the term "neoliberalism" is often invoked cursorily in the political economy of communication literature: more of a useful storytelling device than a formally explicated concept.[2] The dominant narrative is derived from a long-standing Marxist diagnostic of the relationship between media and capitalism. Scholars examine the role of media institutions in ideologically legitimizing the capitalist system and their structural integration in the capitalist mode of production. Most emphasize how the capitalist character of public communication has been amplified in the neoliberal era. Concepts like "marketization", "commodification", "privatization", "deregulation" and "globalization" are synonymous with critical discussions of the pernicious effects of neoliberalism on media and the public sphere. These concepts have a wider currency in media and communication studies, articulated in research labelled neither Marxist nor political economy. Herman and McChesney (1997) examine how neoliberal policies justified in the name of the "free market" have facilitated the emergence of a media landscape dominated by transnational corporations, constituting a "political and cultural system" that McChesney (1998) elsewhere describes as oppressive of "non-market forces" (p. 9). Miller (2003) underlines "the decline in democracy under neoliberal conditions" (p. 5), embodied in a media system that primarily serves the interests of corporations and media owners. Freedman (2008) describes neoliberalism as a project committed to "inscrib[ing] market dynamics in *all* areas of media activity" (p. 53), normalizing policies that misconstrue the market as an instrument of democracy. And Dean (2009) argues the very idea of democracy has been debased by a "technological infrastructure of neoliberalism", a regime of "communicative capitalism" (p. 23) where all public communication is subsumed into the informational circuitry of capitalist networks.

Three broad themes are prominent in discussions of neoliberalism: media ownership and regulation, media production and media representations. First, studies of media ownership and regulation show how corporate media elites – the media wing of Harvey's neoliberal "ruling class" – have been facilitated by state regulatory regimes that privilege the interests of transnational capital (Ampuja, 2012; Hope, 2012). Critiques of a "state-capital nexus" are extended to transnational governmental bodies like the European Union and World Trade Organization, which increasingly assume the legal and political authority to determine how media and communications policies are formulated at a national level (Hesmondhalgh, 2008). Pickard (2007) identifies four key dimensions in the neoliberalization of media systems: "the privatization, deregulation, liberalization, and globalization of markets" (p. 121). Bundled together, they make for a familiar narrative of how the character of media systems has changed during the neoliberal era. Media and telecommunication resources previously owned by the state were systematically privatized, and media that nominally remained in public ownership were, to varying degrees, reconstituted as market and commercial enterprises. Legislation imposing restrictions on cross-media ownership and foreign ownership was removed or modified in the name of "deregulation" and "light touch regulation" (Mansell, 2011, p. 22). Competitive mechanisms were established in television and radio markets, liberalizing the terms of entry to what, in many countries, had been monopolistic media controlled by the state. And nominally "national" media systems were progressively globalized, structurally integrated into ownership regimes and distribution systems increasingly transnational in character (Hope, 2012). These policies have been widely critiqued, though it would be simplistic to suggest that everything attributable to the category of neoliberalism has been regarded in a uniformly pessimistic way. Mansell (2011) suggests "policy informed by the neoliberal agenda in the case of telecommunications arguably was helpful in dislodging the power of monopolies – public and private" (p. 21). And, in the case of the European Union, regulatory mechanisms that privileged neoliberal policies also helped safeguard public service objectives when the principle of universal access was threatened by the commercial bargaining power of media corporations (Flynn, 2009). However, like Harvey, political economy of communication researchers emphasize the gap between official neoliberal doctrine and the actuality of neoliberal media regimes. Policies scripted in the name of competition, diversity and pluralism have spawned media systems dominated by corporate interests, producing oligopolistic market structures in some of the countries that most enthusiastically embraced the neoliberal agenda (Hope, 2012; Thompson, 2012).

A second thematic strand of political economy research explores how neoliberalism has altered the institutional conditions governing the production of different kinds of media content. Those with managerial responsibility for the production of media and journalism have internalized the assumption that, whatever else they might do, they must maximize profits and audience ratings. Tensions between journalistic and profit-oriented objectives are nothing new. However, the relative importance of economic concerns has progressively increased in the neoliberal era, nurtured in production regimes that demand more of media workers and devalue other normative concerns (Cushion, 2012; McChesney, 2012). Fenton's (2011) analysis of the condition of journalism in the UK is indicative (see also Fenton, 2010). The production of a "public interest" news ecology has been undermined by various cost-cutting measures, commodifying journalism "at the expense of ideal democratic objectives" (Fenton, 2011, p. 64); competitive pressures have resulted in a homogenization of media attention where everyone chases the same story; and journalists have been forced to adapt to a commercial environment where they are increasingly reliant on public relations source material, a regime of "news production more akin to creative cannibalization than the craft of journalism" (p. 64). These developments become symptomatic of a neoliberalized news culture. Journalists and others are structurally forced to operate in conditions dominated by "the ruthless logic of an economic system that demands ever-increasing profit margins" (p. 65). And these trends assume a more brutal form in the digital ecology, as quantitative measures of audience attention become key surveillance mechanisms for determining news value and the value of journalistic labour.

Third, researchers have examined the effects of neoliberal production regimes on the nature and quality of media content. Soft-focus media and journalistic formats have become a kind of generative grammar of the neoliberal age, with news and current affairs reconceived as another potential source of profits (Louw, 2005). Thussu (2007) attributes the creation of a "global marketplace for infotainment" to the establishment of a "neoliberal global [media] policy regime" (p. 48). The result has been the globalization of "a US-style ratings-driven television journalism which privileges privatized soft news – about celebrities, crime, corruption and violence – and presents it as a form of spectacle, at the expense of news about political, civic and public affairs" (p. 8). The logic of television formats has been generalized across the news ecology, incorporated in news values schemas that universalize a tabloid and market-oriented sensibility (Harcup & O'Neill, 2001). Working-class narratives become increasingly invisible within a capitalist media universe that privileges the concerns of the most affluent publics and demographics (Chakravartty & Schiller, 2010). And a culture of media spectacle facilitates a more politically partisan journalism steered by the political priorities of media owners.

Neoliberalism and cultural studies

The standard political economy argument about neoliberalism, media and journalism will be evaluated more critically in Chapter 5. For now, let us consider what cultural studies perspectives on neoliberalism – and later governmentality studies – offer as a point of difference. Demarcating cultural studies analyses of neoliberalism from political economy accounts is, in one sense, counterproductive. It reinscribes a theoretical dichotomy often premised on questionable philosophical assumptions and simplistic readings of the "Other" position (Peck, 2006). It sidelines work aligned to both approaches (Berglez, 2006; Fenton, 2006; Hearn, 2008; Miller, 2010). And, irrespective of the different conceptual vocabularies, it obscures critical researchers' shared focus on neoliberalism as an interchangeable name for the dominant political economic system, dominant ideology and the dominant mode of governmentality. Critical political economy scholars are unlikely to disagree with much in Giroux's (2010) analysis of how popular culture textures the character of US neoliberalism. Critical cultural studies scholars would not question the drift of McChesney's (2012) analysis of the effects of market mechanisms on US journalism. And our exemplary Marxist, Harvey, is hardly indifferent to the role of discourse, culture and ideas in the constitution of neoliberalism.

Nonetheless, the theoretical differences between political economy and cultural studies are socially real, part of the sedimented history of the field of critical media and communication research. They are institutionalized in the journals academics publish in, the conferences they attend and the books they read. And they are internalized in different theoretical assumptions, analytical priorities and political dispositions – in short, the habitus (see Chapter 5) that emerges from a particular scholarly trajectory. The historical tensions between political economy and cultural studies can also be mapped onto a historiography of neoliberalism. The Birmingham School's effort to make sense of the UK crisis of the 1970s signified the emergence of a prototypical cultural studies identity. That crisis spawned Thatcherism. And it generated a theoretical disagreement internal to Marxist theory about the new political formation, in which the Birmingham School's best-known figure, Stuart Hall, played a crucial role.

Hall (1988) highlighted Thatcherism's importance as an ideological and political formation fusing "neoliberal doctrine within conservative philosophy" (p. 46). Ideology has been given different articulations within Marxist theory (Eagleton, 2001). Yet, in its dominant political appropriation, ideology was typically equated with a relatively superficial domain of "ideas", masking the "real" material workings of capitalism. This view was encapsulated in Marxists' traditional appeal to a base-superstructure model of capitalist societies. Ideas, politics, culture and language are positioned as the regional domains of a capitalist social "superstructure" which is determined, "in the last instance", by the mechanics and materiality of the economic "base" (Hall, 1988, p. 3). Hall's analysis of Thatcherism directly challenged this view. He did so from within the universe of Marxist theory, drawing on Gramsci's concept of hegemony, Althusser's concept of articulation and, later, the poststructuralist reworking of both concepts by Laclau and Mouffe (Morley & Chen, 1996).[3] His principal target was a Marxist theoretical dogma that explained the emergence of the Thatcherism "superstructure" as an epiphenomena of capitalist processes, attributing little significance to its specific ideological, political and cultural underpinnings. Hall (1988) regarded that analytical short-circuiting as indicative of a general weakness in Marxist political strategies – embodied in a tendency to treat ideology as a domain of *mere* ideology, as "just a set of…con-tricks whose cover will be blown as soon as they are put to the stern test of material circumstances" (p. 49).

Hall insisted Thatcher's "authoritarian populism" (p. 7) merited a serious political and ideological analysis from the left that "rigorously avoids the temptations of economism, reductionism or teleological forms of argument" (p. 3). Thatcherism signified "a profound reshaping" (p. 5) of the class configuration of UK society. It could not be accounted for in doctrinaire assumptions of fixed class interests that failed to satisfactorily account for the politically constituted nature of class formations. Thatcherism's "translation of a theoretical *ideology* into a populist *idiom* was a major political achievement", and its articulation of neoliberal economic prescriptions into a "language of compulsive *moralism* was, in many ways, the centrepiece of this transformation" (p. 47). Thatcher spoke directly to "real and manifestly contradictory experiences" (p. 5) of a social democratic formation where the state had become an oppressive presence in people's lives. Thatcherism's capacity to secure political consent was no mere "rhetorical trick or device"; rather, it had a "rational and material core…that works on the ground of already constituted social practices and lived ideologies" (p. 5). And at the heart of that hegemonic labour were media institutions, which Hall recognized played an important role in defining "the common sense of the times" (p. 48).

Hall's sensitivity to the ideological, political and cultural dynamics of Thatcherism was one of the formative influences on the emergence of a general cultural studies identity that questioned the adequacy of traditional Marxist analysis. Ideas, culture and language were repositioned as constitutive factors in the making of sociopolitical formations, generating a new emphasis on the importance of media and popular culture "representations", "discourses" and "texts" in creating political and ideological subjectivities. The work pioneered by Hall and others has spawned different trajectories. Critical cultural studies researchers retain Hall's emphasis on analysing the overall social conjuncture, transposing the spirit of his analysis of Thatcherism to contemporary neoliberal formations (Bowman, 2007; J. Gilbert, 2008, 2011). Hall (2011 & 2013) reaffirmed the urgency of critiquing neoliberalism in 2011, writing a strong indictment of the Tory/Liberal Democrats coalition government in the UK. Other strands of cultural studies focus on relatively narrow readings of popular culture texts and practices, often loosely connected to an analysis of the wider social conjuncture. Hall's (1980) semiotics-based analysis of media texts also became one of the precursors to the emergence of a critical discourse analysis identity, which, most obviously in the work of Norman Fairclough (2002), takes the heavily mediated language of neoliberal capitalism as one of its central objects of analysis.

Neoliberalism and governmentality studies

Hall's interrogation of Marxist theory anticipated the emergence of Foucauldian governmentality studies as the main programmatic rival to a Marxist analysis of neoliberalism in different fields (For an overview of Hall's engagement with Foucault, see Hall [2001]). Rose's (1993) application of Foucault's insights to the analysis of contemporary social imaginaries was especially influential in marking out the "analytical machinery" (p. 283) of governmentality studies as a departure from Marxist social analysis, for reasons broadly aligned with Hall's critique of Marxism (Rose, O'Malley & Valverde, 2006). Foucault (2007) asserted a critical distance from a Marxist analytic in his 1977–1978 lecture series, "Security, Territory and Population", which he conceded would have been more accurately called a "history of 'governmentality'" (p. 108). He advanced a conception of liberal "political economy" (pp. 106–108) that broke from the "hyper-Marxization" (p. 24) of post-1968 France, one less tied to the image of a centring power structure – capitalist "relations of production" – determining all other "mechanisms of power" (p. 2). He also distanced himself from the concept of ideology in accounting for subjects' identification with a particular social formation. The "physics of power" encapsulated in the concepts of bio-power and governmentality "is not exactly, fundamentally, or primarily an ideology. First of all and above all, it is a technology of power" (p. 49).

Foucault invoked governmentality to describe the ensemble of mechanisms, techniques, tactics and procedures for exercising power over populations that emerged in tandem with the historical development of "laissez-faire" liberalism in 18th century France. This liberal social order did not represent an absolute historical break with disciplinary forms of power. Yet, in its "dominant characteristic", it facilitated a relatively permissive social formation that did not simply focus on subjecting people to "obligatory rules", but instead sought to *act on* an understanding of "how and why" they acted the way they did in the first place (p. 40). Foucault developed the concept of governmentality alongside the concept of bio-power: "the set of mechanisms through which the basic biological features of the human species become the object of a political strategy" (p. 1). Both were linked to a genealogical analysis of how the relationship between "nature" and "government" changed in a historical formation – the birth of liberalism – where the "absolutely modern" idea of "the population" (p. 11) became the primary object of political power. This formation was enabled by the development of territorial scales of government and systems of power (p. 66) that could operate at a distance and on "the population" as a whole, rather than simply particular individuals.

Foucault linked this new regime of power to the emergence of "economy" (see further discussion in Chapter 8) as an "essential issue of Government" and political practice (p. 95). The "establishment of an economy, at the level of the state as a whole" (p. 95) became crucial to the governmentality mechanisms of the laissez-faire state and its cultivation of a preferred mode of conduct that linked the original domain of economy – the management of home and family – to the logic of elite administration. The result was a fundamental reconception of the state: a governmental regime "both external and internal to the state" (p. 109), diffused in regimes of power and control that presupposed direct analogies between the comportment of the self and the "good government of the state" (p. 95). Foucault challenged the notion of an all-powerful functional state with the capacity to "takeover" society (p. 109): the vision embodied in the figure of "the police state" (Foucault, 2008, p. 17). Liberal modernity was reconceptualized through the "'govermentalization' of the state" (Foucault, 2007, p. 107): the rationality of a decentred power structure is, in a sense, built into the centring logic of the state, the latter recast as a facilitator of liberal political and economic freedoms (Foucault, 2008, p. 63).

In his lecture series a year later, Foucault (2008) explored how the governmentality strategies of early liberalism were reconfigured in neoliberal regimes, interrogating those who saw nothing more than a reinvigoration of older "free market" doctrines. On the contrary, he argued that neoliberalism represented a fundamental break with the "laissez-faire" (p. 20) assumptions of classic liberalism. Both liberal formations envisioned a regime of market-based freedoms and individual property rights. Yet, neoliberal theorists offer a fundamentally different political account of the relationship between market and state. For classic liberals, the state was represented as an impediment to the natural order of the marketplace. Notions of human and social progress were aligned with the doctrine of a non- or minimally-interventionist state. Governmentality strategies sought to supervise a given human nature, anchored in an ideological confidence in "the market" as the best institutional guarantor of natural human impulses.

Foucault recognized how the classic liberal's suspicion of the state was, if anything, intensified in the "state phobia" (p. 187) of neoliberal thought (see Chapter 7). However, he stressed (Foucault, 2008) how the anti-statist rhetoric is counterposed by a positive neoliberal vision of the state that constructs it as central to the project of politically enabling neoliberal regimes. Neoliberalism represents an "intervening liberalism" (p. 133), from its first concrete articulation in the ordoliberalism of postwar Western Germany – a context defined by the particular challenges of establishing a regime of state legitimacy in a political atmosphere where the state was "mistrusted" by everyone. Ordoliberals inverted the liberal vision of a "space of economic freedom" relatively unencumbered by the state by "adopting the free market as organizing and regulating principle of the state, from the start of its existence up to the last form of its intervention" (p. 116). They rejected the "naïve naturalism" of laissez-faire liberalism because it assumed that the social and cultural underpinnings of the market economy existed "as a sort of given of nature, something produced spontaneously which the state must respect (p. 120). Instead, neoliberals realized that the "human nature" envisioned by neoliberal theory needs to be politically produced: constructed through a strategy of bio-political governmentality mediated by the state and, as in an earlier liberal regime, dispersed in a variety of institutional settings and assemblages. This vision enables a mode of state intervention very different from a policy of systematic intervention in the "mechanisms of the market economy" (p. 138), the dystopian vision that Hayek and others attributed to the socialist ideal of a "planned" and "controlled market" (see Chapter 7). Rather, it exalts state "regulating actions" that act on the "conditions of the market", enabling the very conditions of possibility of a neoliberal social order (Connolly, 2013; Oksala, 2010).

Neoliberal governmentality, subjectivity and media cultures

Foucault had little to say about the specific place of media and journalism practices in constituting neoliberal regimes. And his account of governmentality has been relatively underexplored in the journalism studies literature (for exceptions see Andrejevic, 2008; Higgins, 2008; Nolan, 2006). Nonetheless, the concept has been one of the key concepts informing the analysis of neoliberalism in critical communication and cultural studies (Grossberg, 2010). Studies of neoliberalism as a dispersed "formula" and "rationality of rule" (Rose, 1993, p. 284) have gained particular traction in the reality television literature, indicative of how neoliberal subjectivity is conceptualized in a wider body of cultural studies work. Ouellette and Hay (2008) characterize reality television makeover programmes as everyday sites of a "highly dispersed" (p. 473) neoliberal governmentality, disseminating techniques and prescriptions for how individuals and populations should conduct themselves and take responsibility for their lives. The makeover or "life intervention" (p. 475) programme functions as a constitutive part of a bigger neoliberal project of privatizing notions of citizenship and welfare, inculcating the assumption that the entrepreneurial self is responsible for determining his or her own prosperity within the competitive rationality of neoliberal societies. Sender (2006) explores a similar line of argument in her study of the programme *Queer Eye for the Straight Guy*, drawing on Rose's analysis of neoliberalism as a technology of self-governance. The programme's focus on mentoring the fashion and consumerist sensibilities of dowdy heterosexual men enacts the wider neoliberal objective of promoting a culture of male consumption. And it normalizes neoliberal explanations of individuals' failure to self-actualize: their failure to do all they must do to ensure their flourishing as productive bearers of "human capital" (Foucault, 2008).

McCarthy's (2007) description of reality television as "a neoliberal theatre of suffering" emphasizes the genre's political significance, its dramatization of the affective sensibilities of neoliberal regimes (see also J. Gilbert, 2011). Combining the concept of governmentality with Berlant's analysis of affect, McCarthy (2007) discerns a cruelty in the makeover genre's enthusiasm for individual stories that take spectacular "failure[s] of self-government" (p. 21) as its base working material: spectacles routinely staged as class antagonisms (Wood & Skeggs, 2011). Couldry's (2010) discussion of the links between reality television formats and the affective labour of the contemporary workplace extends McCarthy's dramaturgical metaphor, describing both as "place[s] of compulsory self-staging, required teamwork, and regulation by unchallengeable external authority" (p. 78). Reality television becomes a "suitable performance space" (p. 82) for enacting the "oxymoron of neoliberal democracy" (51), naturalizing the rationality of an aggressive individualism and a "self-improvement culture that does not necessarily rate caring for others as a high priority" (p. 80).

Hearn (2008) examines how practices of self-branding have become strategic imperatives of neoliberal regimes, compelling subjects to fashion identities that have internalized the telos of a neoliberal individualism. The production of subjectivity is subsumed into capitalist value chains, collapsing any "meaningful distinction between notions of the self and capitalist processes of production and consumption" (p. 212). Goodwin, Lyons, Griffin and McCreanor (2014) extend Hearn's analysis of different mediated forms to social networking sites, arguing that the online visibility of youth drinking cultures is symptomatic of a general structural need to brand the self under neoliberal governmentality. "Young people's online self displays become a rational response" (p. 65) to hegemonic rituals that compel subjectivity to be publicly performed and celebrated, generating a regime of "identity work" and "free labour" (p. 69) exploited by the online marketing practices of the drinks industry.

Critiquing the critique of neoliberalism

The range of theoretical sources, and the breadth of media and cultural practices, articulated in the analysis of neoliberalism is vast and has only been covered in a fragmentary way here; I have not sought to offer a comprehensive literature review. Nonetheless, a broad-stroke distinction between critical political economy, cultural studies and governmentality approaches helps construct a general picture of how the term "neoliberalism" is put to work in critical media and communication studies and elsewhere. We now need to consider a quite different articulation of the concept, one that has emerged in response to its perceived ubiquity in critical rhetoric. This discourse questions the coherence and analytical value of appealing to neoliberalism, suggesting the concept's privileged status can impede the work of critical social analysis. Versions of this critique have been articulated from within the critical political economy and governmentality literatures. Garland and Harper (2012) suggest critical theorists should be critiquing and interrogating "capitalism" not the politically obfuscating term "neoliberalism". And Nickolas Rose, one of the foundational figures of governmentality studies, has distanced himself from the term. Rose et al. (2006) recognize that governmentality researchers have rendered "neoliberalism visible in new ways". Yet "in certain respects" the ubiquity of the concept as a "master category" has become a "handicap" (p. 97):

> ...it readily lends itself to a kind of cookie-cutter typification or explanation, a tendency to identify any program with neoliberal elements as essentially neoliberal, and to proceed as if this subsumption of the particular under a more general category provides a sufficient account of its nature or explanation of its existence (pp. 97–98).

Scepticism about the critique of neoliberalism is contextualized by a more general turn in social and political theory interrogating the condition of critique. Much that is performed in the name of critique has simply "run out steam", Latour (2004) suggests, "like those mechanical toys that endlessly make the same gesture when everything else has changed around them" (p. 225). He blames a popularization of critique and "quick readings" of critical social theory for normalizing a post–9/11 conspiracy theory culture: an "absurd deformation" of the weapons of social critique that – in a reproach of his own earlier work – "are our weapons nonetheless" (p. 230). Ranciere (2009) offers his own "critique of critique", though he retains a much sharper focus on the political constitution of the social order (p. 25). Interrogating the condescending nature of a critical posture that "demystifies" on behalf of the apparently mystified, he argues much critique betrays an authentic critical tradition because it assumes a depoliticized and ironized form "entirely disconnected from [a] horizon of emancipation" (p. 32). Billig (2003) discusses the paradoxes resulting from the institutional success of critical identities in the academy. A default critical hostility towards marketized discourses can obscure how "the critical" has become something of a brand label in its own right – a marketing strategy blind to its own participation in the cultures it interrogates.

This book affirms the importance of critique and – since it's headlined in my title! – the specific value of critiquing something called "neoliberalism". However, instead of dismissing those who question the value of the term or, worse, denouncing them as neoliberal collaborators, I want to ask: what is justified, and what is problematic, about the claim that appeals to neoliberalism often produce little more than a formulaic mode of critique? To that end, let us briefly consider three examples of how the concept of neoliberalism has been critiqued in communication, media and cultural analysis (for a more detailed critical discussion, see Phelan, 2014) before considering the general implications in the final section of the chapter.

Terry Flew questions the value of the concept of neoliberalism in a number of articles, including one co-authored with Stuart Cunningham (Flew, 2008, 2009; Flew & Cunningham, 2010). Both are members of the creative industries faculty at Queensland University of Technology, which has sometimes been the target of scathing critiques for its perceived capitulation to neoliberalized norms and renunciation of a critical scholarly ethos (see McGuigan, 2006). In a review of Freedman's (2008) book, *The Politics of Media Policy*, Flew questions Freedman's reliance on neoliberalism as an "omnibus term": a "single organizing prism" for mapping the relationship between media policy regimes in the "two quite different countries" of the United Kingdom and United States (p. 128). "All roads...seem to point towards the implementation of some or other form of neoliberal policy", Flew concludes, so that "even when policies would appear to be quite different, they are in fact quite the same, all explicable under the rubric of variants of neoliberalism" (p. 128).[4]

Flew (2009) refines his critique of the concept in an essay reflecting on the rise of the concept of "cultural economy", maintaining that "the development of neoliberalism as a meta-concept in critical theory constitutes a substantive barrier to more sustained engagement between cultural studies and economics" (p. 1). He interrogates a neo-Marxist analysis of neoliberalism that frames the popularization of Chicago School economics, the rise of Thatcher and Reagan and the articulation of a third way political identity as linear developments in the emergence of neoliberalism as a ruling-class ideology. Flew and Cunningham (2010) develop these arguments in a more comprehensive defence of creative industries against the charge of neoliberal collusion. Their critique of the concept of neoliberalism is aligned with a sharper indictment of critical scholarly identities. They cite Nonini's sarcastic observations about the utility and malleability of the term for "progressive scholars" who can at least "agree that whatever neoliberalism is, they don't like it" (cited in Flew & Cunningham, 2010, p. 119).

Although most clearly situated within the field of human geography, Clive Barnett's work explores the politics of culture and the role of media infrastructures in the constitution of public space (Barnett, 2003). His widely cited polemic (Barnett, 2005) against the critique of neoliberalism echoes Flew and Cunningham in a number of respects. He laments its use as a convenient catch-all term for a bundle of distinct processes; he questions the tendency to define neoliberalism through simplistic oppositions between state and market, individual and collective; and, most provocatively, he wonders if it functions as a consolation term for leftist academics engaging in revelatory interventions that are not half as revealing as they think. Nonetheless, Barnett's (2003) work affirms a critical sensibility, alert to the political conditions of public life. His scepticism about the reliance on neoliberalism as a "descriptive concept" and neoliberalization as an "explanatory concept" (Barnett, 2005, p. 8) is motivated by a concern that the possibility of radicalizing a liberal democratic inheritance can be obscured by critical discourses that disparage values like individualism and freedom as neoliberal proxies.

"There is no such thing as neoliberalism", Barnett (2005) insists; indeed, he assumes an ironic distance from the term by persistently citing it in scare quotes, performatively illustrating how the reified object called "neoliberalism" is partly made by critics themselves (p. 9). Contra Flew, he interrogates a trend (see Larner, 2003; Miller, 2010; Springer, 2012) towards reconciling a Marxist political economy analysis of neoliberalism with "post-structuralist ideas of discourse and governmentality derived from Foucault" (p. 7). Barnett argues Marxist and Foucauldian accounts of neoliberalism have been articulated together in a way that remains lodged in Marxist functionalist assumptions, but in a fashion that now communicates a reassuring sensitivity to difference and the openness of neoliberalism to diverse articulations (p. 7). Maintaining that the different ontological, epistemological and normative assumptions of both theoretical traditions should not be elided, he claims Foucault's account of governmentality has been mainly "instrumentalized for the purposes of shoring up the holes in the Marxist narrative" (p. 8).

Our final author, Lawrence Grossberg, articulates more of a broad-stroke and impressionistic critique of how neoliberalism is used (Cho, 2008; Grossberg, 2010), voiced as part of a general interrogation of the condition of cultural studies and the pre-programmed nature of some of its dominant concepts and terminologies. He is concerned that "lazy" (p. 2) appeals to neoliberalism can foster a heavy-handed mode of critique, rather than alertness to contextual specificity, emerging social phenomena and a politics of becoming. Cultural studies needs to formulate more nuanced and persuasive stories of contemporary conjunctures, he argues, rather than recycle a universal neoliberal story in essentialized ways from context to context. Like Barnett, his target is the condition of critique itself, and the adequacy of the critical vocabulary of neoliberalism in illuminating the challenges of the present. Both wonder if the term should be abandoned because "it might actually compound rather than aid in the task of figuring out how the world works and how it changes" (Barnett, 2005, p. 10). Appealing to neoliberalism "lets us off the hook", Grossberg suggests, and "we would be better off without it unless its meaning is always specified and contextually located" (p. 141).

Grossberg follows Barnett in criticizing Marxist and governmentality articulations of the term (and the work of Clarke [2008, 2010] is an important reference for both authors). Both theoretical traditions invoke neoliberalism and neoliberalization in totalizing ways that reduce the particular and the novel to the terms of the already known (Grossberg, 2010, p. 141). Different discourses and practices are constructed as "equivalent and identical" (p. 132), all merely symptomatic of an a priori neoliberal logic rather than different contextual articulations whose relationships to each other necessitate open-ended analysis and exposition. Nonetheless, Grossberg balks at declaring neoliberalism an entirely redundant term; rather, it can still enable useful conjunctural analysis so long as it is responsive to the particular empirical context. "Whatever it [neoliberalism] is", the focus has to be on the "question [of] how is it dis- and re-articulated to existing practices, projects and discourses, or onto specific – old and new configurations" rather than prefabricated explanations and discourses (p. 141).

Recuperating neoliberalism as an object of critique

The specific critiques are not without their blind spots and simplifications (for further discussion, see Phelan, 2014). However, all three are, in some respects, perfectly justified. Flew is right to suggest neoliberalism often functions as an "omnibus term". Barnett is right to maintain that appeals to a reified neoliberalism can simplify the analysis of social change. And Grossberg is right to argue that the category can "let us off the hook", cultivating a formulaic reliance on a generic neoliberal story that recycles stock-in-trade arguments.

Yet, the most obvious comeback is that similar arguments have been made by others who continue to privilege neoliberalism as an object of critique. Peck (2010) recognizes the inadequacy of a sweeping grand narrative in understanding the variegated trajectories of neoliberal reason. Wacquant (2012) notes the reductive tendencies in both Marxist and governmentality accounts, suggesting both offer an inadequate account of the state. And Crouch (2011) critiques the limits of a commonplace state–free market binary for defining neoliberalism, because it obscures the corporatized and anticompetitive tendencies of neoliberal regimes and the state's internalization of neoliberal logics.

In response to critiques of the concept, we might therefore suggest the problem with the concept of neoliberalism is not with the category as such; rather, as with all categories, the problem lies with how it is articulated and operationalized. The category is too often articulated in a way that does too much analytic work on its own, obscures the specificity and paradoxes of different social formations or remains lodged in a denunciatory mode of critique that, as Clarke (2010) observes, becomes so "fascinated [with] tracing the dominant" it ends up simply "confirm[ing] its dominance" (p. 340).

The critique of the critique of neoliberalism does not offer a convincing case for discarding the category from our critical vocabulary (as if categories are easily discarded). If we purge it on the grounds that it signifies a unitary object that is not really a unitary object, well, then, we might have to discard a whole lot of other categories too: society, economy, culture, media, capitalism and so on.

At the same time, the critique should not be dismissed because it highlights problems with how the term is articulated as a loose signifier for everything and nothing. Ahead of the purposeful theoretical discussion of Chapters 2 and 3, let me end this chapter by quickly describing how this book attempts to forge a critical sensibility that productively responds to our critics.

Arguments for and against using the category of neoliberalism ultimately come down to the question of *what*'s in a name? What theoretical and analytical assumptions underpin our decision about naming, and how do we understand the relationship between the name and "the thing" it represents? The concept of neoliberalism offers a particular way of critically naming the social, more likely to be invoked by critics of neoliberalism than any putative neoliberals themselves. The name gives analytical and narrative shape to myriad social changes and processes that, whatever our theoretical approach, cannot be pinned down to a single empirical horizon or referent. Barnett is therefore right: "There is no such thing as neoliberalism", if by that we mean a unitary object with an unambiguous real-world referent or constitutive status (see also Castree, 2006). We might describe it instead as an "impossible object" that "only exists...as an effort to construct that impossible object" (Laclau & Mouffe, 2001, p. 112).[5] The name takes on the analytically necessary, yet also "impossible", task of describing and explaining social changes that are irreducible to discrete empirical objects or subjects, or abstract doctrinal prescriptions. Questions like what is neoliberalism, where is it located and how is it articulated are inherently contestable (Collier, 2012). In recognizing problems with the term, my argument is not to suggest there is a "correct" way of using it somehow missed by others. Nor, as I illustrate throughout the book, is it to deny the many productive insights and intuitions in the existing literature.

Constructing neoliberalism as if it were a unitary object has an obvious polemical and political value. It helps us identify ideological, political and cultural features of particular social formations and highlight similarities between one formation and another. Moreover, if we want to talk about neoliberalism at all (write articles and books about it), we cannot but sometimes speak of it in simplifying and abstract ways. However attentive we are to particular contextual articulations, analysing neoliberalism necessarily entails a labour of conceptual abstraction.

Nonetheless, as critical analysts of neoliberalism, we should be wary of over-relying on abstract discourses or, as Grossberg (2010) suggests, letting our political commitments override our empirical analysis. The pressure to either stridently affirm or stridently dismiss the concept of neoliberalism can be strong, since how we speak of it, or whether we speak of it at all, is a marker of political-intellectual convictions. Identifying social objects and practices as neoliberal can engender a form of "aspect blindness" (Wittgenstein, 1973, p. 213), where other ways of naming the social are obscured. Empirical phenomena labelled "neoliberal" are too often cursorily disparaged rather than deemed worthy of additional analysis and explication. One defensive response to those critical of how the term is used would be to suggest that no one has argued neoliberalism exists in a monolithic form, and that the critical target is therefore a strawman. Yet, while few would explicitly argue that there is a singular neoliberalism, the category is routinely rendered as such in banal rhetorical formulations that represent the "impossible" object as a fully present structure or agent with the totalizing power to cause, make, determine and act on a variety of social objects and practices. Reified discourses of this kind often leave us with little more than a new telling of a familiar neoliberal story rather than productively illuminating the immanent political and strategic logics of neoliberalized formations.

Against an excessive use of the reified category of neoliberalism, I argue in Chapter 3 that it might be more productive to speak of neoliberal and neoliberalized logics that are always contextually articulated with other political, social and fantasmatic logics. Glynos and Howarth (2007) describe "the logic of a practice [as] the rules or grammar of the practice, as well as the conditions which make the practice both possible and vulnerable" (p. 136). To conceptualize neoliberalism as a series of constitutive logics, dialectically articulated with other logics, underscores the limits of reducing our analysis of social life to the convenient nominalization "neoliberalism". It might also heighten our alertness to how the logic of "things" could be articulated as other than neoliberal, as a counter to the kind of fatalism that often permeates critical discourses (Clarke, 2008).

Yet, we also need to go beyond a still relatively abstract analysis of neoliberal "logics". We need to formulate an analysis of neoliberalism that "keeps agents and agency in sight" (Peck, 2010, p. xi) and, as Barnett suggests, encourages productive forms of midlevel theorizing to bridge the gap between the two dominant accounts of neoliberalism. This point is particularly important in a communication and media studies context given the role of the media in mythically connecting quotidian social worlds to a macro-level infrastructure of power (Couldry, 2003b). Bringing the concept of neoliberalism "to earth" (Peck, 2010, p. xi) might enable us to better understand how neoliberalized logics are produced by social institutions and agents that do not see themselves as neoliberal. And it might help us develop a critical sensibility that does more than condemn a sedimented social infrastructure for being neoliberal, perhaps enabling a mode of critical analysis that can both oppose and reckon with the given (see Barnett, 2006). How those intuitions might inform my theoretical understanding of neoliberalism will now be explored in Chapters 2 and 3.

2
Neoliberal Discourse: Theory, History and Trajectories

Neoliberalism has often been conceptualized as a discourse (Holborow, 2012b). Bourdieu and Wacquant (2001) describe it as a "double" discourse that "although founded on belief, mimics science by superimposing the appearance of reason" (p. 4). Fairclough (2002) cites "neoliberal political discourse" as one of the constituent elements of a new capitalist formation where value is accrued through signification and branding practices (Hearn, 2008). And rejecting the "false dichotomy" (p. 133) between Marxist and governmentality perspectives, Springer (2012) commends a discourse-based account of neoliberalism which conceptualizes it as a "mutable, inconsistent, and variegated process that circulates through the discourses it constructs, justifies, and defends" (p. 135).

Situating neoliberalism as a discursive phenomenon has spawned productive insights in different fields, gaining most purchase in the governmentality and critical discourse analysis literatures. However, references to neoliberal discourse can be problematic for two reasons linked to the concept of discourse more generally. First, discourse is sometimes defined in a conceptually loose way as a synonym for language or, in a more careful rendering, is defined from a theoretical perspective that presupposes an ontological distinction between discursive practices and social practices (Chouliaraki & Fairclough, 2001). The concept of discourse, both its everyday and theoretical signification, may be inherently linked to language. Yet, as conceptualized here, discourse is not simply *interchangeable* with language. For my main theoretical source, Laclau and Mouffe (2001), discourse is the conceptual name for the "structured totality" (p. 105) that emerges from the relatively stable articulation of linguistic *and* extra-linguistic practices. In other words, the distinction between discursive and social practices is collapsed into the theoretical assumption that *all* social practices are discursive practices.

The second problem overlaps with the first; indeed, it is animated by statements like the one I just made – all social practices are discursive practices – as if to suggest that nothing else "matters" but discourse. Describing neoliberalism as a "discourse" immediately anticipates the objection: "but it is *not* just a discourse: it is also a *material* phenomenon, inscribed in material objects and practices". The configuration of critical media and communication studies may have changed considerably since Stuart Hall interrogated the Marxist orthodoxy of the 1970s and 1980s (see Chapter 1). And, as a stand-alone proposition, Best (2014) suggests "no one today would dispute the materiality of discourse" (p. 272).[1] Yet, the old theoretical debates are still discernible in analytical frameworks that, often with little pause, separate discourse from materiality, representation from action, and rhetoric from reality – as if these distinctions are entirely straightforward and obvious.

Contrary to some strong critiques of their work (Cloud, 1994; Geras, 1987; Rustin, 1988), Laclau and Mouffe (1990) do not collapse the distinction between discourse and materiality. They recognize the existence of a sphere of "mere referential materiality" – a domain of physical objects imagined independently of their human and social circulation (p. 100). However, like Hall, they interrogate how the distinction between discourse and materiality has traditionally operated in Marxist theory, to position discursive, ideational and linguistic phenomena as qualitatively different from – and ultimately of secondary importance to – material phenomena. For them, the discursivity of a social practice cannot be ontologically distinguished from its materiality, because discourse itself is material. If discourses are to operate as "structured totalities", they *must* be materialized in different social objects and practices, otherwise the social world would exist as an amorphous "field of discursivity" (p. 111) without clear material shape or definition. Laclau and Mouffe's discourse theory is not without its limitations in accounting for the materiality of the social world. As I suggest in Chapter 3, our discussion of neoliberalism, media and the political needs Bourdieu's field theory as a theoretical supplement. Yet, the simple point I want to underline here is that privileging the concept of discourse should not imply an indifference to neoliberalism's materiality. On the contrary, to analyse neoliberalism as a discursive phenomenon means critically understanding its material composition in different objects, institutional regimes, practices, subjectivities and dispositions.

This chapter moves between a theoretical and empirical register. I discuss how my conception of neoliberalism is indebted to Laclau/ Laclau and Mouffe's discourse theory. And the theoretical discussion is interspersed with a summary overview of the historical emergence and political trajectory of neoliberalism. I draw on discourse theory concepts to examine two ideal type articulations of a neoliberal identity (there are, of course, more than two neoliberalisms), highlighting neoliberals' emphasis on winning the "war of ideas" in media channels and elsewhere. I reflect on the political-intellectual underpinnings of neoliberalism, from its heterodox origins in intellectual and policy debates of the 1930s and 1940s, to its political capture of governance structures in the 1970s and 1980s, to the emergence of the third way neoliberalism of the 1990s and 2000s. The chapter ultimately lays the groundwork for the discussion of the concept of neoliberal logics in Chapter 3.

Discourse theory and the political

Ernesto Laclau's work, both his individual writings and collaborative work with Chantal Mouffe, offers a sustained reflection on the concept of "the political" (Laclau, 1990, 1996, 2000, 2004, 2005, 2006; Laclau & Mouffe, 2001).[2] Laclau and Mouffe (2001) depart from everyday discourses that bind the political to the institutional architecture of representative democracies. Rather, they treat the political as the ontological horizon of *all* social practice, meaning that everything signified under the category of "social objectivity" is ultimately founded on the logic of the political (pp. x–xii). Laclau (1990) conceptualizes the political as a signifier of the inherently contestable and dislocatable nature of any social formation, simply meaning that a given formation could always be constituted differently. For example, to talk of the family or the university as sites of the political is to suggest that how we socially organize the family or university is politically contestable and open to the possibility of different configurations.

For Laclau and Mouffe (2001), "the central category of political analysis" (p. x) is hegemony. The logic of the political is, in effect, the logic of hegemony. The concept of hegemony has been a staple part of critical media studies vocabulary since the 1970s. Conceptualized differently by different disciplinary traditions, it is perhaps most widely articulated as a synonym for how elites determine the political organization of society. Within the cultural studies tradition popularized by Stuart Hall and others, the concept signifies how *consent* is politically and ideologically secured for a particular social formation, drawing on the account of hegemony developed by the Italian Marxist theorist Antonio Gramsci. Laclau and Mouffe's conception of hegemony broadly overlaps with cultural studies approaches (Bowman, 2007). They credit Gramsci with "producing an arsenal of concepts...which are the starting point of our reflections in *Hegemony and Socialist Strategy*" (Laclau & Mouffe, 2001, p. ix). Yet, they also broke from some of the Marxist underpinnings of Gramsci's work. Laclau and Mouffe's declaration of a "post-Marxist" identity signalled a desire to formulate an analysis of politics that went beyond the essentialist Marxist assumption that "the economy" and "class" ultimately determined the structural constitution of the social order (p. 69). The problem for Laclau and Mouffe was not the relevance of either economy or class, but rather how, in their assessment, both were conceptualized as naturalized "objects" beyond the logic of political articulation (p. 69).

The concept of hegemony has been given different theoretical iterations by Laclau (Howarth, 2004), intersecting with his development of a number of other concepts, including discourse, empty signifier, affect and universality. In more recent work, Laclau conceptualizes hegemony as the signifying "operation" where a particular identity assumes a "totality or universality" that is, strictly speaking, impossible (Laclau, 2005, pp. 70–1). For instance, imagine a mundane journalistic claim about what "the public wants". The statement signifies a referential object that does not exist: a universal public that speaks with one voice. It is, in a strict sense, an "impossible" claim, yet it is also clearly "possible" because it is the kind of statement we hear all the time. When a particular signification of "the public" assumes a certain contextual stability and coherence so that it seems universal and objective (for example, "the public wants tax cuts"; "the public hates politics"), we can speak of an effective hegemonic operation.

Discourse theory has, alongside a wider poststructuralist literature, sometimes been criticized for its thematic privileging of particularity and difference over universality. The universal register and scope of Marxist class analysis, it is argued, is displaced by a narrower horizon of "identity politics" preoccupied with analysing the structuring effects of gender, ethnicity and sexuality, or exalting the politics of social movements. However, this post-modernist stereotype does not sit easily with Laclau: on the contrary, his account of the political is all about negotiating a space between a strong universalism and strong particularism. He speaks of a "failed" universalism where universality is reconceptualized as a "tendentially empty" horizon (Thomassen, 2005, p. 293): constituted through hegemonic struggles between different political identities and – in a reworking of Gramsci's idea of the "collective will" (Laclau & Mouffe, 2001) – different coalitions of political identities. For Laclau, all relatively stable identities are hegemonically constituted because of the simple assumption that any identity could be articulated differently. He recognizes how certain articulations of identity are more likely than others because of the sedimented nature of identity: the doctrinaire Marxist might be reconfigured as a card-carrying member of the third way, but continue to subscribe to the objectivist view of history embodied in his or her former identity (Finlayson, 2003). The logic of identity is, in effect, structurally incomplete – hence the paradoxical emphasis on its impossibility – because no matter how complete or total a particular identity might be, it is never invulnerable to failure or dissolution. Transposed to a wider social scale, the concept of hegemony signifies a process where different political formations try and incarnate a regime of social objectivity that assumes the status of a universal horizon. To speak of neoliberal hegemony, then, is to signify a universe where neoliberal logics, assumptions and priorities have been institutionalized in the objective organization and intersubjective comportment of the social order.

Let's consider an illustrative example that anticipates the concerns of Chapter 7. Freedom is one of the key signifiers of neoliberal identity; the appeal to freedom, especially economic and individual freedom, has been a central part of the political and ideological vision articulated by different neoliberal theorists and politicians (see Hayek, 1960; Friedman, 1962). However, neoliberals construct a particular conception of freedom: a negative view of freedom in contrast to the positive view of liberty and freedom associated with left-wing developmental philosophies (see Connolly, 2013; Gray, 1980, 1986; Sen, 1999). Within the neoliberal universe, freedom is defined primarily as freedom from coercion, especially the coercive actions of the state. To describe the neoliberal view of freedom as socially hegemonic would be to suggest that freedom is primarily articulated in neoliberal ways, implying that when most people think and speak of freedom they understand it as freedom from state interference. When this view of freedom becomes common-sensical, it is effectively universalized and materially embedded in a variety of institutional, social, interpersonal and individual practices. Yet, this universalization of a neoliberal logic of freedom is ultimately impossible, because it only ever represents a particular conception of freedom that can never signify everything freedom could signify. Put simply, there are other ways of articulating freedom that cannot be accounted for within neoliberal discourse (Couldry, 2010; Sen, 1999). However, when the neoliberal view of freedom becomes taken for granted, its contestability can be obscured and other articulations of freedom are marginalized or rendered incoherent in light of the hegemonic conception.

How people signify freedom will, of course, depend on the other signifiers it keeps company with: in other words, how they are articulated together in the structured totalities called discourses. These totalities are constituted through the relatively stable, if also structurally precarious, combination of different signifiers: what Laclau and Mouffe (2001) conceptualize as the dialectical interplay of a logic of difference and logic of equivalence. The logic of difference signifies the differential elements within the structural organization of a discourse, while the logic of equivalence signifies their commonality in relation to antagonistic elements outside the discourse. This commonality is captured in the form of an "empty signifier" (Laclau, 1996, 2005), tendentially empty because of its generative capacity to bring different elements together in opposition to a particular social formation. Let's take difference first. Imagined as a simple ideal type, neoliberal discourse is the structured totality that emerges from the relatively fixed articulation of the differential elements "freedom", "economic freedom", "market" and "individual". The "market" is posited as an institutional guarantor of human freedom. Freedom is understood primarily as economic freedom and freedom from state coercion. And the agency of the individual is privileged over the agency of the collective, because, within the neoliberal universe, the latter is code for a socialist state, the coercive power of trade unions and an incoherent epistemology (Hayek, 1991). Cementing the structural associations between these different signifiers necessitates much more than the patterned interplay of linguistic elements (as if a discursive totality was nothing more than repetitive "talk"). They need to be institutionalized in different sedimented forms and practices: in trade agreements, monetary policies, savings and investment strategies, state development plans, housing policies, public policy programmes, regulatory architectures, corporate strategies, property rights, journalistic and media conventions, human resource policies, auditing regimes and so on. And they need to be inscribed in people's subjectivities and affective sensibilities – in the dispositional tendencies that make neoliberal regimes possible (Connolly, 2013). These subjective investments may take an obviously ideological form, evident, for instance, in the evangelical and abrasive register of the Tea Party. However, they may also manifest themselves in much more prosaic ways, arguably more emblematic of a fatalism about the possibility of political alternatives as strong ideological convictions. Jeremy Gilbert speaks of an atmosphere of "disaffected consent" in contemporary UK (cited in Clarke & Newman, 2012, p. 11), where consent is begrudgingly given to austerity policies.

The logic of difference therefore references, at its simplest, the different constitutive elements of a discourse. Following Saussure and others, it signifies how the meaning of each element is determined by its relational differences from the other elements within the discursive system (Howarth, 2000). But how might we then understand the relationship between the elements within a discourse and the elements *outside* it? As we will see later in the chapter, Laclau answers this question by exploring the relationship between two key concepts: antagonism and heterogeneity. Let's focus simply on the concept of antagonism here. Like the different elements within a discourse, discursive totalities are not just defined positively by what they are; they are also defined negatively by what they are *not*. To be a neoliberal is to not be a socialist, to not be a Marxist, to not be a Keynesian – to not be something or someone else, however that "Other" might be contextually articulated. The concept of antagonism captures how this dual logic of identity formation is explicitly represented. It describes discursive elements that are, strictly speaking, outside a particular discourse or identity, excluded from its internal "system of differences" (Laclau & Mouffe, 2001, p. 111). However, these outside elements are, at the same time, central to the structural constitution of a discourse, because they construct a clear political boundary between those who identify with a discourse and those who do not. For example, socialism is an explicit "constitutive outside" (Thomassen, 2005, p. 307) to neoliberalism because it signifies a philosophy, identity and politics that should be rejected by the committed neoliberal. Yet, socialism is simultaneously central to the project of neoliberal self-representation. It enables the construction of an antagonistic frontier demarcating "us" from "them"; the neoliberal paradoxically needs "the socialist" otherwise the structural coherence of the neoliberal's own identity dissolves. A utopian impulse to see beyond the neoliberal present is potentially negated by a politics of disidentification, dramatizing the perceived unworkability and totalitarian logic of the socialist alternative (see Chapter 7). This is where the logic of equivalence is crucial. The act of disidentifying with an antagonist becomes crucial to the strategic construction of a discursive totality that brings different identities and elements together. It enables a shared political identity that would not be possible otherwise: the different elements are, in effect, rendered "equivalent" because of their identification of a shared antagonist. Laclau (2005) emphasizes how new hegemonic frontiers are brought into being through the construction of political antagonisms, prototypically staged as a populist front against an established social order. The antagonist gives psychic and affective energy to a radical political demand, becoming a signifier of everything that should be excluded from the desired social imaginary.

The historical emergence of neoliberalism[3]

Discourse theory helps us understand how neoliberalism is constituted as a discourse. However, let's break from the theoretical register of the previous section to offer a brief overview of how the concept of an antagonistic identity maps on to the historical emergence of neoliberalism. The political arrival of neoliberalism is typically traced to the 1970s and 1980s. However, its emergence had a much longer gestation period, anchored in the work of an intellectual vanguard from the 1930s and 1940s onwards (see Cockett, 1995; Mirowski, 2013). It was a textbook example of an antagonistic discourse, constructed in explicit opposition to the existing social order.

The "neoliberal thought collective" (Mirowski, 2013) subscribed to a common market-orientated philosophy and politics. Yet, as the concept of logic of difference would suggest, its different constituent parts were marked by theoretical and methodological differences (see Connolly, 2013) that never dissolved. Mirowski (2013) suggests the Mont Pelerin society, a key incubator of neoliberal thought (see further discussion below), contained "at least three distinguishable sects or subguilds: the Austrian-inflected Hayekian legal theory, the Chicago School of neoclassical economics, and the German ordoliberals" (p. 43). They existed in a "productive tension": indeed, Hayek admitted in the 1980s that there was "the constant danger that the Mont Pelerin Society might split into a Friedmanite and Hayekian wing" (cited in Mirowski, 2013, p. 42). What tamed these differences – in other words, what rendered them equivalent – was everyone's clear identification of a shared antagonist: a social order variously named as Keynesian, collectivist, welfarist, socialist or social democratic. The articulation of a positive neoliberal vision was, from the outset, intertwined with an explicit critique of collectivism, both in its extreme totalitarian form and in the guise of a Keynesian and social democratic consensus. The Keynesian crisis of the 1970s was therefore an event that neoliberals had been anticipating for a very long time (see Chapter 1). They came to it with a ready-made theoretical diagnosis of the crisis and with clear political prescriptions for its remedy (Hay, 2004).

Cockett (1995) traces the embryonic emergence of an Anglo-American neoliberal identity after World War II. One key figure was Frederick Hayek, the Austrian-born economist, social theorist and political philosopher who was based at the London School of Economics (LSE) in the 1930s and early 1940s. Hayek and others had made initial attempts to revive enthusiasm for a market-based order in the 1930s (Cockett, 1995, p. 9). These commitments were enacted in a famous methodological debate between Hayek and Keynes in the 1930s over the possibility of a planned economy: Keynes's confidence in the state's capacity to manage economic processes pitted against Hayek's epistemological trust in the market's ability to self-coordinate. The efforts to renew a liberal economic programme were thwarted by the war and did not regain momentum until the 1944 publication of Hayek's *The Road to Serfdom* (p. 56). The book demurred from a blanket condemnation of state intervention in the market: indeed, even Keynes had favourable things to say about it (Cockett, 1995, p. 890). Nonetheless, it articulated a clear antagonism against socialist conceptions of economy and society, representing the period's enthusiasm for state planning as a form of enslavement that undermined individual and economic freedom in the name of the dubious principles of political and collective freedom. For Hayek (1944), the telos of "collectivism" was inherently totalitarian, because of its impulse "to organise the whole of society and all its resources for [a] unitary end" (p. 42).

The book was no detached academic treatise. It was, in Cockett's view, a calculated attempt to influence British public opinion and shape the post-war trajectory of British political economy. The argument was not particularly original: much of it had already been made by Hayek's Austrian School mentor, Ludwig Von Mises (p. 77–78). What distinguished Hayek's book, however, was its forceful and accessible register and the clarity of its political and intellectual antagonist: "The originality of *The Road to Serfdom* lay in its polemical political style transferring the more abstruse academic debate on planning of the 1930s to the centre of political discussion" (p. 79). The book had an immediate political impact. Cockett maintains its central thesis – that "there was no 'middle way' between totalitarianism and a liberal, competitive economic system" (p. 79) – was "the central focus of the 1945 general election" (p. 92) campaign in Britain. To liberally minded Conservatives, opposed to the welfare state commitments articulated in the Beveridge Report and elsewhere,[4] the publication of the book "appeared as manna from Heaven" for it gave them "at one blow, the intellectual apparatus to assail the gathering political enthusiasm for the post-war planning which they had, up to then, only managed to postpone" (p. 91). The direct influence of Hayek's intervention should not be exaggerated: Cockett suggests some key Tories, most notably Churchill (p. 93), probably had not read Hayek's book. Yet, the spirit of its argument was clearly discernible in the Tories' campaign rhetoric: as Churchill put it in one speech, "liberty, in all its form, is challenged by the fundamental conceptions of socialism" (p. 94). And the Tories even directly intervened to ensure the book's ongoing publication despite war-time paper rations (pp. 93–94).

The Conservatives' appeal to liberal values ultimately failed, and the Labour Party secured electoral endorsement for the post-war settlement between capital and labour. Yet, for Hayek, the experience illustrated what was to become a dominant theme in his future work: the central importance of winning the "war of ideas" (Hames & Feasey, 1994, p. 233) as a precursor to formal political success. That war was imagined on an international scale and, in the immediate aftermath of the 1945 publication of an American edition by the University of Chicago Press, *The Road to Serfdom* "created the same sort of intellectual ferment in the USA as it had in Britain" (Cockett, 1995, p. 100). Despite the immediate failure to secure popular support for a neoliberal programme in either country, the book's positive reception signified a wider international interest in reviving liberal ideas. These energies crystallized in the formation of the famed Mont Pelerin society in 1947 – what Mirowski (2013) dubs the Mount Sinai of neoliberalism, such is its mythical and sacred status within the neoliberal imaginary (p. 41).

Mont Pelerin was the brainchild of Hayek. Made up "largely of economists" (Cockett, 1995, p. 109), its 39 founding members included such intellectual luminaries as Milton Friedman, Karl Popper, Ludwig Von Mises and Michael Polanyi (pp. 107–114). Named after the Swiss Alps resort where its first meeting was held, the international liberal society and discussion group (it never actually published anything under the Mont Pelerin banner) "became the focal point of international efforts" (p. 108) to defeat the new collectivist orthodoxy. It focused on the long-term revival of liberal prescriptions, though Peck (2010) suggests it had its first "policy victory" in the "radical monetary makeover" of West Germany after World War II, spearheaded by the Mont Pelerin member, and subsequent German Chancellor, Ludwig Erhard (p. 5).[5] The role of the Mont Pelerin society can certainly be exaggerated: "a one way diffusion model of neoliberalism will not do" (p. 6), Peck argues, if we want to understand the variegated trajectories of neoliberal thought. At the same time, it was undoubtedly an important actor in the development of a neoliberal project and discourse. Mirowski (2013) even suggests it represented a pioneering institutional form in the "sociology of knowledge", evolving "into an exceptionally successful structure for the incubation of integrated political theory and political action outside of the more conventional structures of academic disciplines and political parties in the second half of the twentieth century" (p. 43).

Through its formation alone, Mont Pelerin became a key "nodal point" (Laclau & Mouffe, 2001) in the hegemonic construction of a "new liberalism" (Friedman cited in Mirowski, 2013, p. 38), at a time when the idea of the "free market" was regarded as suspect. Many of its most prominent members wrote books later canonized in conservative and libertarian circles.[6] And, through its cultivation of a wider political-intellectual formation, Mont Pelerin facilitated the emergence of different Anglo-American neoliberal think-tanks in the 1960s and 1970s (see also Miller, 2010). The establishment of the Institute of Economic Affairs (IEA), the Centre for Policy Studies (CPS) and the Adam Smith Institute in the UK were important institutional antecedents to Thatcher; Milton Friedman described Anthony Fisher, the founder of the IEA, and a regular Mont Pelerin attendee, as the "single most important person in the development of Thatcherism" (Cockett, 1995, p. 122). Fisher's influence extended to other countries. He worked with the Fraser Institute in Canada, the Centre for Independent Studies in Australia, and established the Atlas Foundation in New York in 1981, which facilitated the development of an international think-tank infrastructure in the 1980s and 1990s (p. 307). Mont Pelerin was also aligned to a wider network of US think-tanks like the American Enterprise Institute (AEI), the Hoover Institution, Heritage Foundation and the CATO Institute, all of which helped prepare the ground for the political emergence of Reaganism (Hames & Feasey, 1994; Rodgers, 2011) and the hybrid of neoliberal, conservative and evangelical identities specific to the US (Connolly, 2008; Birch & Tickell, 2010).

Hayek's conviction about winning the "war of ideas" was clearly shared by others; the phrase was "a particularly prominent slogan" (Rodgers, 2011, p. 1) among US conservative intellectuals and propagandists during the 1970s and 1980s. Indeed, Susan George (1997) speaks ironically of a "Gramscian Right" (p. 1) (see also Birch & Tickell, 2010), who realized – better than most on the left – that "for ideas to become part of the daily life of people and society they must be packaged, conveyed, and propagated through books, magazines, journals, conferences, symposia, professional associations, student organisations, university chairs, mass media and so on" (George, 1997, p. 3). Neoliberals knew that political success necessitated infiltrating and politicizing social and cultural terrains beyond the world of formal institutional politics. And that necessitated a particular focus on the symbolic power and authority of media institutions, at a historical moment when "media logic" was encroaching on other social domains (Altheide & Snow, 1979).

Milton Friedman was a particularly important figure in the mediation of US neoliberalism, skilfully packaging neoliberal prescriptions and antagonisms in accessible and folksy ways. He wrote regularly for the *Wall Street Journal* (Birch & Tickell, 2010, p. 50), a key media centre in the dissemination of neoliberal discourse (Rodgers, 2011, p. 69). His 1980 book with his wife, Rose Friedman, *Free To Choose: A Personal Statement* (Friedman & Friedman, 1990), was not only a national bestseller, it was also accompanied by a television series broadcast in America and Britain in 1980 and later shown in, among other countries, Australia, Holland, Japan, Singapore and Canada. The novelist and philosopher Ayn Rand was another important figure in cultivating popular identification with neoliberal ideas, relentlessly juxtaposing a heroic individualism against a loathed collectivism. Although disparaged by literary critics for their ideological dogmatism, her novels *The Fountainhead* and *Atlas Shrugged* "went on to become enormous best-sellers, and to this day sell tens of thousands of copies annually" (S. McGrath, 2007).[7]

George's notion of a Gramscian right is worth explicating, because it captures the self-consciously antagonistic nature of the neoliberal project – its desire to disrupt popular identification with socialist ideas. Neoliberals' self-image as the "intellectual shock troops" (Rodgers, 2011, p. 1) of a free-market revolution bore much affinity with Gramsci's figure of the "organic intellectual". Eagleton (1991) attributes the organic intellectual with the role of creating a "two-way passage between political analysis and popular experience" (p. 120) that disrupts the rationality of the existing social order and creates the grounds for – in Laclau-speak – a new "hegemonic universal". Neoliberals understood that political success depended on "combating much that is negative in the existing empirical consciousness of the people" (Eagleton, 1991, p. 119). Abstract philosophical propositions and debates needed to be packaged into forms that could percolate the political mainstream and capture people's subjectivities, but, at the same time, embedded in the unthreatening image of "a nation of regular individuals" (Connolly, 2013, p. 59). Hayek insisted the prescriptions of the "abstract thinker" needed to infiltrate the political subjectivity of "second hand dealers in ideas" (cited in Cockett, 1995, p. 123) before they could become the "common property" (Hayek, 1960, p. 113) of the people. Friedman invoked similar metaphors to emphasize the importance of giving a political-intellectual project a material and institutional base:

> It takes many kinds of people to make a movement. And one of the most important things are publications. In any activity you have manufacturers, wholesalers and retailers; and all three are essential and necessary. There are only a relatively small number of manufacturers of ideas. But there can be a very large number of wholesalers and retailers (cited in Doherty, 1995).

The think-tanks were particularly important neoliberal "wholesalers" in proactively targeting media organizations as sites of an everyday cultural politics (they wouldn't have needed Laclau to tell them that the constitution of "the social" is political). Hames and Feasey (1994) advise caution in assessing think-tank influence on Anglo-American policy developments of the 1970s and 1980s, if "influence" is taken to mean "specific examples of public policy that can solely or even predominantly be shown as the responsibility of the think-tanks" (p. 227). Where think-tanks did have a clear visibility and influence, however, was on the media, exercised through the deployment of aggressive marketing and public relations techniques that worked on journalistic and audience subjectivities (p. 233). This ideological labour played a crucial role in regulating the political mood in Britain and elsewhere in the 1970s, naturalizing a mediated "crisis" narrative that prefigured a neoliberal reconstitution of the state (Hay, 1996; Hall, Critcher, Jefferson, Clarke & Roberts, 2013).

Another factor that reconfigured the mediated political environment of the 1970s and 1980s was the new public visibility of – if I can broadly interchange – "neoliberal", "conservative" and "new right" intellectuals (Birch & Tickell, 2010). From a context where the "conservative movement had virtually no presence in the media and appeared intellectually feeble" (Hames & Feasey, 1994, p. 304), where even the phrase "conservative intellectual" was regarded as "virtually a contradiction in terms" (p. 234), figures like Friedman and William F. Buckley Junior become the harbingers of a televisual habitus now institutionalized, in a hyper-aggressive form, in the house style of broadcasters like Fox News. They helped boost the profile and credibility of neoliberal policy prescriptions in everyday lifeworlds. But, perhaps most importantly, they normalized a culture of interrogating the disposition of socialist and left-liberal intellectuals: playfully mocking them as the real "elitists", the true ideological antagonists to the interest of "regular people" (see Chapter 7). This new class of media intellectuals cultivated a rhetoric and sensibility that was antagonistic towards the state and politicians: adept at illustrating the folly and "unintended consequences" (Hirschman, 1991) of policies articulated in the interests of the collective and society. And they anticipated the "conviction politics" style of Thatcher and Reagan, both of whom were equally skilful at staging neoliberal antagonisms within the performative constraints of media spaces.

Antagonism, heterogeneity and ideology

The concept of antagonism clearly captures some of the defining features of neoliberalism's historical emergence. Different iterations of a free-market identity were united through their shared antagonism to a collectivist orthodoxy that constructed the state as an agent of societal welfare: a necessary counter to the destructive effects of the market. Neoliberalism has, consequently, been routinely defined through the idea of a perennial antagonism between state and market – as if the logic of state intervention is, by definition, anti-neoliberal. Yet, as I already suggested in Chapter 1, this shorthand is reductive and limiting. It misses neoliberals' articulation of a positive vision of the state: their desire to reconstitute the state as an agent of market order (Crouch, 2011; Foucault, 2008; Wacquant, 2012). A one-dimensional emphasis on neoliberal antagonisms also limits our capacity to understand the trajectory of post-1980s neoliberalism: namely, the widespread embedding of neoliberal policies within governmental regimes that officially disavowed the politics of ideological antagonisms – and, in some instances, repudiated neoliberalism (Giddens, 2000).

Here Laclau's development of the concept of heterogeneity as a supplement to the concept of antagonism is useful. Laclau and Mouffe (2001) originally described antagonism as "constitutive" of identity, implying that identity is always constructed through the differences between self and other. These antagonisms, as we saw in the last section, often take explicitly confrontational forms, where one political identity asserts its opposition to another. However, the ontological scope of Laclau's concept of antagonism goes beyond the everyday signification of the term as a synonym for hostility and enmity. Antagonisms also extend to situations where the relationship between self and Other may be friendly and intimate (a romantic relationship, for instance), if obviously still potentially conflictual. As an ontological category, antagonism does not imply a full-on conflict or "war" with "the Other", even if that impression is suggested by the word's everyday connotation (and even if Laclau himself typically relates the concept to moments of visible social conflict).

However, in later work Laclau suggests that the "outside" or "limit" to a discourse or identity cannot be understood simply through the concept of antagonism. He also recognizes the importance of an "outside" and "excess" that escapes representation: a radical field of discursive differences that are not explicitly named as antagonistic differences (Laclau, 2004; Stäheli, 2004; Thomassen, 2005). Laclau captures this radical outside through the concept of heterogeneity: a horizon of being that is "ineliminable" or "constitutive" of identity. The "constitutive outside" to a discourse is, accordingly, reconceived as consisting of two distinct analytical levels: an antagonistic dimension, where one identity is represented in opposition to an Other, and a heterogeneous dimension, which denotes elements not represented by the antagonism (Laclau, 2005; Thomassen, 2005).[8]

How might this analytical distinction between an antagonistic outside and a heterogeneous outside be useful to us here?[9] Well, let's start by imagining a prototypical neoliberal discourse that constructs socialism as the antagonistic Other, juxtaposing the magic of the capitalist market against the oppressive collectivism of state planning. Heterogeneity describes discursive differences not captured within the logic of that antagonistic representation. For example, let's imagine a political subjectivity that champions "free trade" alongside a proposal to radically redistribute surplus value, or a political subjectivity that denounces corporate capitalism while also affirming the organizing capacity of markets. Laclau's technical description of heterogeneous elements as "non-representable" is clearly not meant in a strict literal sense: I have just identified potential examples, as he does in his own work (Laclau, 2005). Instead, heterogeneity describes discursive differences that will seem incoherent in a particular hegemonic universe, because they do not cohere with the antagonistic logic that normally structures the field of political struggle. They signify discursive differences that could be articulated, but which struggle to gain traction and credibility because of the assumption of a fundamental antagonism between socialism and capitalism.

Laclau transposes the distinction between antagonism and heterogeneity on to two different conceptions of ideology, understood in a general sense as particular discourse or identity that presents itself as universal (Laclau, 1990; Laclau, 2006). All discursive structures are, as I noted earlier, constituted through the dialectical interplay of a logic of difference and logic of equivalence. The relative privileging of either logic produces a qualitatively different kind of hegemonic formation that maps on to two different conceptions of ideology. The first kind of ideological regime takes an overtly antagonistic form, organized around the explicit construction of a discursive frontier demarcating "us" from "them". It privileges a logic of equivalence that simplifies the division of social space, forcing different identities to accommodate themselves to a boundary-marking antagonism. For example, consider how the neoliberal discourse discussed in the last section sought to construct the space of political differences around the stark choice of either supporting a regime of market freedom or supporting a coercive regime of state planning and which was largely successful in establishing this regime of truth in the 1970s and 1980s. Or consider how the post-9/11 declaration of a "war on terror" likewise simplified the division of social space into a political subjectivity that was either "with us or against us". Now, it is not as if we cannot imagine alternatives to these discursive antagonisms. And it's not as if critiques of these binaries were not articulated by someone at the time. However, once sedimented in institutional practices and political subjectivities, these discursive antagonisms have real material effects on how the social and political world is organized, forcing different political identities to accommodate themselves to certain political realities (Laclau, 2005). They are, in effect, naturalized: no longer treated as politically contingent divisions, but accepted as "inevitable" configurations of social space – signifiers of a discursive logic that must be internalized by anyone hoping to have his or her social demands "heard" within a particular conjunctural context.

However, Laclau suggests ideology also takes a second form that paradoxically disavows the politics of ideological antagonisms and privileges a logic of difference over a logic of equivalence. The figure of an explicit antagonist is obscured or downplayed, displaced by a countervailing emphasis on the universal harmony between different social identities. For example, let's imagine a government's response to a national economic crisis articulated through the image of a unified political community "who are all in this together". And let's imagine this community is not structured around the identification of a clear antagonist who is blamed for the crisis (a foreign state, for example); instead, it is articulated as a "real" reconciliation of different interests – government, business, labour, civil society, public service and so on – that is "beyond" political ideology. Laclau would conceptualize this as an ideological regime for two reasons. First, even in cases where political antagonisms are downplayed, social formations still need an antagonistic outside to be rendered coherent. The notion of a "unified community" is ultimately impossible, because the community will still need to constitute itself in opposition to antagonistic elements that threaten or reject its identity. For example, the antagonistic element might be a politically marginal left-wing identity that criticizes the economic telos and rationality of the community, or it might be criminal elements that try to exploit the economic crisis for their own advantage. Unlike cases where there is a clear political division of social space, Mouffe (2005) suggests antagonistic representations in "post-ideological" or "post-political" communities typically assume a moral, rather than political, register (see Chapter 5). The antagonist is constructed in opposition to the "entire community", beyond the pale of reasonable identities.

The second reason why Laclau (2005) would see these regimes as ideological brings us back to the concept of a "heterogeneous" outside

(p. 98). Even in situations where different elements are represented in the name of "the community", those different elements still retain an "ineliminable particularity" that cannot be discursively captured. For example, even if trade unions acting in the interests of "labour" became an institutionalized part of the community, it is still only a particular articulation of "labour" that does not exhaust the political potential of the category. The logic of difference structuring the "unified community" is, in other words, only a particular discursive logic that does not preclude the combination of the same elements in different ways. For example, even if "the community" claims to have reconciled the differential elements "capital" and "labour", their power relation could potentially be reconfigured – either through micro-political contestation within a given discursive structure or, more radically, through the articulation of a new discourse that constructs a clear antagonism between the precarious condition of labour and the imperatives of capital. The key point: the different constitutive elements of a discourse are never exhausted by their particular articulation because of the radically heterogeneous character of signification (simply meaning: any element in a discourse could potentially be articulated differently).

Third way neoliberalism

Laclau's analytical distinction between two different types of ideological regime offers a useful perspective for understanding how neoliberalism has been constituted in ways that deviate from a neat Mont Pelerin script. The problem with universalizing the latter is that it privileges an ideal-type consistent with the prescriptions of the most doctrinaire neoliberals. This limitation is inscribed in much of the academic literature, especially in quick appeals to neoliberalism. The image is sometimes of clear-cut ideological antagonisms that pitch the market against the state, the individual against the collective, and economic freedom against political freedom. These binaries have, to be fair, hardly been created out of nothing: there is much in the work of Hayek, Friedman and others that give them life and sustenance, not to mind the secondhand "free market" rhetoric of neoliberal politicians and media cheerleaders. However, in trying to grasp the condition of actually existing neoliberalism, we will not get very far if we over-rely on simplistic shorthands or universalize a particular discourse as the blueprint for what neoliberalism really is. Against the idea of a "fixed" neoliberalism, Peck (2010) emphasizes its "contradictory" and "polymorphic" articulations: "perhaps...the closest one can get to understanding the nature of neoliberalism is to follow its *movements*, and to triangulate between its ideological, ideational, and institutional currents, between philosophy, politics, and practice" (p. 8).

For those prototypical neoliberal formations, Thatcherism and Reaganism, the articulation of a coherent free-market identity necessitated a strong antagonism towards the naturalized authority of Keynesian and welfare-state discourses. The latter were the antagonists that needed to be politically defeated to enable a proper functioning of the capitalist system. Peck (2010) speaks of the "roll-back" (p. 22) face of neoliberalism that attacked the existing social order and advanced a "total critique of Keynesian rationality and welfare-state governments" (p. 5). Qualifying the simple ideological clarity of that antagonistic representation risked undermining the clarity of the hegemonic intervention. However, different heterogeneous elements were evident in the policies of both formations that could not be easily reconciled with free-market rhetoric. Public spending increased during the Thatcher administrations, despite the official ideological commitment to fiscal prudence and "scaling back" the state (Eaton, 2013), and bureaucratic power was extended in a new enthusiasm for auditing mechanisms (Power, 1997). Likewise, the "military Keynesianism" of the Reagan years belied the neat ideological narrative, enabling a regime of extravagant defence and security spending that would re-emerge after 9/11 (Ungar, 2012).

However, heterogeneous elements problematizing the logic of a stark ideological antagonism between market and state did find articulation in the third way (Giddens, 2000) version of neoliberalism that emerged in different Western democracies in the 1990s. The notion of an inherent ideological antagonism was supplanted by a post-ideological or post-political imaginary, which read the end of the Cold War as signifying a rupture with the ideological antagonisms of the 20th century (Fukuyama, 1989). This enabled a more affirmative and rounded representation of the state than was possible within the discourse of antagonistic neoliberalism (Finlayson, 2003). The market and state should now work together, it was assumed, in a new entrepreneurial spirit to guarantee better economic *and* social outcomes. As Finlayson (2003) describes New Labour in the UK, "a kind of social democratic critique of Thatcherism" was articulated as a supplement to "the Thatcherite critique of social democracy" (p. 63). The state could therefore be represented as a proactive facilitator of market regimes and practices, belying the mythical impression that the "free market" precluded the possibility of state intervention. And the impression of an all-out war on the welfare state was softened by the image of a "workfare state" attuned to the rationality of

the market (MacLeavy, 2010). At the same time, the state was rearticulated as a bulwark against the detrimental effects of market forces, and
a certain ideological distance was assumed from the notion that "the
market", on its own, offers a solution to each and every social problem. All up, the official third way imaginary signalled a political project
no longer fixated on abstract and metaphysical ideologies, grounded
instead in a practical ethos that reconciled the principles of economic
efficiency and productivity with the spirit of social democracy. Politics
and government were, accordingly, reconceived as technocratic and
managerial domains (Hay, 2004): focused on the practical question of
what mix of policies works best in different contexts ("a little bit of free-
market liberalism here, a little bit of social democracy there"), rather
than illustrating the global correctness of a particular ideology.

On its *own* terms, therefore, the third way was construed as less ideological than the strident neoliberalism of the 1980s. The point of the
metaphor, after all, was to suggest a reasonable in-between horizon to
the ideological extremes of pure free-market capitalism and an uncom-
promising socialism. Its supporters might concede that it could be
described as an ideology in its own right. But its modality was that of "an
anti-ideology ideology", wilfully contaminating and mixing different
ideological identities and political discourses (Fairclough, 2001; McLennan, 2004). One illustrative case was Celtic Tiger Ireland (see further
discussion in Chapters 5 and 8), a third way imaginary in everything
but name. Within the self-interpretations of Irish political and media
elites, the Celtic Tiger was widely celebrated for its political pragmatism
as opposed to its ideological commitments. The discourse was made possible because the Irish case was articulated through neo-corporatist institutions that marked a clear departure from the confrontational politics
of Thatcher (Irish elites' most obvious referent for a free-market identity). Within this imaginary, one could simply cite the spirit of "social
partnership" (Allen, 2003) between the state, transnational capital, trade
unions and civil society to communicate the impression that ideological
differences no longer really mattered. And, even if its neoliberal pedigree was conceded, Irish elites might have plausibly claimed that it still
showed how the hegemonic embedding of market-friendly regimes
did not need to assume the antagonistic form evident elsewhere. If
this was neoliberalism, it was officially constructed as a pragmatic and
ideologically hybrid neoliberalism: a practical venture in bringing different constituencies and interests together to serve the "national
interest", rather than a product of some rigid ideological prescription
or antagonism.

The problems with the third way's official imaginary are, of course, well known (Fairclough, 2000; Finlayson, 2003; McLennan, 2004; Mouffe, 2005). Indeed, one of the strategic issues currently facing political parties that explicitly marketed themselves under the banner is how much ideological distance they should now assume from an identity that, to its critics on the left, amounted to little more than a cosmetic rebranding of neoliberalism. Here I want to underline the incoherence of the third way's claim to be beyond ideology. Indeed, if we align it with Laclau's discussion of ideological regimes that obscure the antagonistic logic of the political, third way neoliberalism is arguably even more effective and potent as an ideological formation than the confrontational neoliberalism of the 1980s because it is embedded in the (post-political) fantasy of a holistic reconciliation of state and market, the economic and the social, the individual and the collective. What's more, if we follow Foucault's (2008) analysis, it represents simply a different species of neoliberalism to the neoliberalism of Thatcher and Reagan. In fact, Foucault (2008) reminds us that the metaphor of a "middle way" was first articulated by the German ordoliberals: embodied in the figure of a "social market" that constructed the state as an "economic state" and which treated "economic growth" as the "only true and fundamental social policy" (p. 144). The reconciliation of ideological differences within contemporary third way formations took an analogous form, naturalizing logics of economic efficiency and productivity in policy domains previously shielded from market forces (Hay, 2004; Peck, 2010; Wacquant, 2012). Market and state were "reconciled", but in a fashion that privileged the former and neoliberalized the latter. The theoretical fantasy of a free market acting in the name of social justice and the public good obscured a regime of political economy subordinate to corporate power, where the state increasingly asserted its agency by internalizing the interests and rationality of monopolistic corporations (Crouch, 2011). And citizens followed suit, adapting their own agency to the forms of value and capital consecrated in neoliberal regimes (Couldry, 2010; Hearn, 2008).

The third way had its own mediated dimensions. It, too, had a think-tank infrastructure to help cultivate the desired policy orientation and political subjectivity in the media and elsewhere: organizations like Demos in the UK and the Progressive Policy Institute in the US. Perhaps its defining incarnation, Blair's New Labour project in the UK, became synonymous with an increasingly professionalized model of political communication, fixated with public relations "spin", political branding and media visibility (Couldry, 2010; Fairclough, 2000; Finlayson, 2003;

McNair, 2004). The heightened consciousness about political branding was in part a response to the structural changes effected by neoliberal political economy in the 1980s. The normalization of marketing and polling techniques inculcated a consumerist mode of identification with politics (Savigny, 2008), resulting in an overprivileging of the concerns of the "floating voter" (Stanyer, 2007). The conception of the political audience was progressively narrowed: as Hall (2011) puts it, "the middle ground – the pin-head on which all mainstream parties now compete to dance – became the privileged political destination" (p. 714). Identification with political ideology was supplanted by a third way fidelity to the ideology of political marketing. Politics was reconceived as another "product" and "commodity", increasingly subordinate to the "mood" of the market (see Chapter 4).

My focus on two ideal type neoliberalisms is not intended as an exhaustive historical chronology. Rather, it offers a theoretical heuristic for thinking about some of the most obvious differences within a spectrum of neoliberal and neoliberalized identities. Our discussion could be extended to other neoliberal formations: the authoritarian alliance of neoliberal and neoconservative identities in the post-9/11 Bush administrations (Brown, 2003; Harvey, 2005); the "post-ideological pragmatism" of Obama, who Peck (2010) suggests "can sound almost Hayekian in his embrace of market idealism" (p. 237); or the "revolutionary" project of the Conservative/Liberal Democrat coalition in the UK, which Hall (2011) suggests has "arguably [been] the best prepared, most wide-ranging, radical and ambitious of the three regimes which, since the 1970s, have been maturing the neoliberal project" (p. 719). The latter case has seen an intensification of political and class antagonisms, already encoded in New Labour's enthusiasm for workfare programmes and the discourse of individual responsibility. Tyler (2013) documents how public support for punitive welfare regimes has been energized by a "heightened stigmatization" of "the underclass" (p. 90; see also Wacquant, 2007), all dramatized on a media stage and justified in the name of "austerity" (Clarke & Newman, 2012).

However, one of the arguments at the core of this book is to suggest that the importance of third way neoliberalism goes well beyond those political formations that explicitly marketed themselves under the banner. Indeed, of our two stylized neoliberal formations, I argue it offers the best template for diagnosing the (disfigured) condition of "actually existing neoliberalism" because its modality of a post-ideological neoliberalism has become generalized; and, most importantly, this modality has a clear homology in how journalists and others comport themselves as ideologically and politically disinterested in media spaces (see Chapter 5). It does not follow, of course, that evangelical neoliberal identities which relentlessly praise the market and relentlessly attack the state are of no interest to us (see Chapter 6): indeed, one of the ironies of our investigation is that this Punch and Judy version of neo-liberalism is often presupposed as the very definition of neoliberalism when the term is explicitly cited in mainstream media (see Chapter 4). Instead, we need to explore the relational dynamic between different kinds of neoliberal and neoliberalized identities if we want to properly grasp the problematic of neoliberalism, media and the political. Let us now consider how such an approach might be formulated through the concept of neoliberal logics.

3
Neoliberal Logics and Field Theory

Chapter 2 introduced our principal discourse theoretical categories and related them to a discussion of two distinct types of neoliberal formation. We now need to clarify the general implications for the rest of the book. Integral to all the discourse theory concepts we have considered so far has been the concept of logics (in the plural). When Laclau (2004) speaks of a hegemonic, discursive, antagonistic or heterogeneous logic, he is "not referring in the least to formal logic in the usual sense" (p. 305). Rather, like Lacan, Deleuze and others, he subsumes the three branches of the medieval university curriculum – grammar, rhetoric and logic – under the category of logic. Laclau emphasizes the "context-dependent" nature of logics, dismissing "the very idea of a general logic" (p. 305): the image of structures and systems with absolute logical foundations. "A logic is nothing else than a rarefied system of objects governed by a cluster of rules which makes some combinations and substitutions possible, and excludes others" (p. 305).

Glynos and Howarth (2007) position the concept of logics as the "basic unit of explanation" (p. 8) of discourse theoretical social analysis. They organize their logics-based approach around an analytical distinction between social, political and fantasmatic logics. Social logics describe naturalized social practices whose "rules and grammar" (p. 34) are internalized in the objectivity of the social order. They signify a horizon of social sedimentation, a concept Laclau (1990) appropriates from Husserl to describe the taken-for-granted dimensions of everyday life – the routinized practices that "forget" and "conceal" the conditions of their own emergence (Glynos & Howarth, 2007, p. 34). Political logics signify, in contrast, the conditions of possibility of those practices, their radical contingency and their structural vulnerability to dislocation.[1] They signify, in other words, the logic of hegemony: how institutionalizing "society" is ultimately a terrain of hegemonic struggle and political contestation. Fantasmatic logics describe the psychic and affective dimensions of signifying practices: the fantasies that sustain a subject's attachment to a particular discourse. They help explain subjects' identification with sedimented social routines and practices (social logics). And they energize the discursive construction of political antagonisms (political logics), where different identities find commonality through their shared opposition to an identifiable Other(s).[2]

Neoliberal and neoliberalized logics

Glynos and Howarth's methodological schema is not applied programmatically in this book. Nor do I theoretically explore how their three master logics might potentially be supplemented by a specific conception of media and journalistic logics, though I invoke the latter categories at different points in the book.[3]

However, their privileging of the concept of logics shapes my theoretical account of neoliberalism. The basic intuition of my approach can be simply stated: instead of over-relying on appeals to a reified "neoliberalism", it is more analytically productive to conceptualize neoliberalism as a series of discursive "logics" that are always hegemonically articulated with other discursive logics. A neoliberal logic is a logic that neoliberalizes the social, either in the form of reproducing an already sedimented social logic or in the form of a political logic that extends and intensifies the process of neoliberalization. Put in simplified definitional form, I define neoliberalization as:

> The process where market-based logics and practices, especially logics of market determinism, commodification, individualization, competitive ritual and self-interest, are dialectically internalized and generated in particular social regimes.

This simple shift in orientation has, I argue, important implications for how we might think and write about neoliberalism and how we articulate it in relation to other social phenomena. It engenders caution about representing the concept as a causal or deterministic force in its own right, as if "neoliberalism" existed in some pure ontological or ideological form that entirely colonizes the practices and subjectivity of social actors. And it focuses our attention on variegated processes of neoliberalization, rather than the image of a monolithic neoliberalism (Peck, 2010). Neoliberalism is, as we saw in Chapter 1, a useful term for identifying political, ideological and cultural continuities between different social domains and practices. As an object of political antagonism, it energizes the demand for a different kind of social order that breaks from the repressive instrumentality of the present. Yet, as a concept, it can encourage a "subsumptive" form of analysis (Glynos & Howarth, 2007), where appealing to neoliberalism can sometimes explain too much too easily. It can become the end point of analysis, as if it's enough to be told once again that we live in a time of neoliberal hegemony (Ferguson, 2009). The term potentially becomes an analytical fetish, insufficiently mediated through the immanent rationality of the social universe it purports to describe or explain.

Clarifying the differential features of their approach, Glynos and Howarth (2007) reflect on what they call the "problem of subsumption"[4] (p. 166): forms of social analysis that are over-reliant on theoretical or empirical generalizations. They see the problem as consisting of four overlapping elements. First, "specific cases" of an empirical phenomenon are "subsumed under over-arching universal laws, causal mechanisms, or law-like causal generalizations". Second, the appeal to a concept is "seen to exhaust completely" the object it purports to explain. Third, the application of "abstract concepts to concrete phenomena leaves the former untouched by the practice of application itself". Or, fourth, in a "pure inversion" of a subsumptive operation, researchers commit to a "kind of 'empiricism' or 'pure descriptivism'" that treats the exhaustive analysis of specific cases as a sufficient explanation in itself (p. 166).

The problem of subsumption embodies a classic concern of social science research "which maps historically on to the opposition between explanation and understanding" (p. 188): do we privilege the "universal" scope and ambition of the subsumptive explanation, or do we privilege explanations of "particular" cases? The problematic can be transposed to the debates explored in Chapter 1: do we subsume our explanations of the social world under the master category of "neoliberalism", or do we discard it completely because it might hinder our capacity to understand the particular?

Glynos and Howarth reject this dichotomous logic: "the opposition between universal or general subsumption on the one hand, and thick-descriptive particularity on the other, is not necessary" (p. 188). Instead, drawing on Laclau's concept of hegemonic universality, they reformulate the opposition between the universal and the particular as a relational and discursive one. In place of the figure of a "subsumptive" relation, they privilege the concept of an articulatory relation, counterbalancing a focus on the "conditions of possibility" of social practices (their universalizing and political dimensions) with an alertness to their empirical specificity – the irreducible differences between one empirical case and another. Translated into the concerns of this book, this research strategy endeavours to avoid an overly subsumptive analysis of neoliberalism, where, as Grossberg (2010) and others fear, a universal story is imposed on different empirical cases and contexts. Instead, we need to capture how neoliberal logics are always articulated with other social logics, often in messy and paradoxical ways that do not neatly cohere with the idea of a *neoliberal* totality (Peck, 2010).

Media articulations

So how might this logics approach inform a specific analysis of neoliberalization and media? Let's begin by quickly noting three general implications for the analytical approach formulated in this book. First, discourse theorists focus on the "onto-political" (Connolly, 2008, p. 69) conditions of social practice. Attention is paid to the hegemonic logics that make particular objects and practices possible, rather than simply assuming a world of taken-for-granted objects. This raises the question of how we might understand the naturalized object called "the media". The object of a media or mediated analysis cannot be regarded as obvious, especially in a world where "everything is mediated" (Livingstone, 2009). For instance, Cubitt (2011) argues "spreadsheets, databases and geographic information systems" are "the dominant media of the 21st century" (p. 7). Understood in these broader terms, mediation can be conceptualized as a general ontological condition, broadly synonymous with the logic of discursive articulation (see Laclau & Bhaskar, 1998). This philosophical problematic is not explored purposefully in the book (Marchart, 2011), though it briefly resurfaces in my discussion of Timothy Mitchell's work in Chapter 8. My object of media analysis is, in one sense, a common-sensical one. Yet, at the same time, my focus on the political condition of media and journalism practices rejects any naturalized tendency to treat "politics", "the media" and "society" as separate domains and objects. On the contrary, the assumption that media and journalism practices are deeply political, in Laclau's sense, is at the heart of my argument.

Second, Glynos and Howarth commend a research strategy that paradoxically assumes and denies a horizon of "social objectivity". Simply put, we need to describe the social logics that structure a particular media practice. Yet, we also need to keep in view how the practice could be articulated differently. This inculcates an analytical disposition located in-between an ideal type distinction between explanatory/objectivist research and hermeneutical/subjectivist research. Explanatory approaches focused on abstract structures or mechanisms are problematic because they risk speaking over agents' own self-interpretations of their practices. And hermeneutical approaches are limited because they can end up simply collating agents' interpretations and descriptions, downplaying the structural context of action. Glynos and Howarth (2007) describe the "passage through self-interpretations...[as] a necessary starting point for any social science investigation" (p. 157), in keeping with hermeneutical and interpretivist methodologies. However, they insist our "understanding and explanations cannot rest on [self-interpretations] alone" (p. 157). We also need to illuminate the onto-political conditions that enable such interpretations to "be" in the first place (p. 157).

What implications might this have for critical media analysis? Let's imagine a study that depicts a particular media representation as "ideological". And let's imagine the mode of analysis is cursory and denunciatory: the ideological character of the representation is taken to be obvious, subsumed into the researcher's a priori assumption that it serves an elite class interest or is a structural expression of neoliberal hegemony. The journalist's representation is disparaged – reduced to an instrument of ideology. Glynos and Howarth suggest a different approach, a conception of critique closer in spirit to Foucault.[5] The journalistic representation needs to be taken seriously analytically, though it does not follow that we are then left with nothing but the journalist's interpretation of the phenomena. Rather, we shift to an ontological-level analysis that attempts to explain how the ideological commitments internalized in the journalist's interpretation have been made possible. The description of a social practice from a discourse theory perspective becomes an act of critical redescription, illuminating the different compositional elements regulating the practice, and helping us see how it might be constituted otherwise.

Third, Glynos and Howarth note how their approach can "deploy theoretical concepts and empirical generalizations derived from other traditions, so long as their use is accompanied by suitable acts of reactivation, deconstruction, commensuration and articulation" (p. 188). This means in principle that my analysis of neoliberalism, media and the political can draw on conceptual and empirical insights from other literatures: political economy, governmentality and so on, and that the development of the argument in later chapters can deploy a wider set of theoretical resources. Glynos and Howarth qualify the methodological principle because of their concerns about the dangers of a theoretical eclecticism where discourse theory concepts are combined with other theoretical concepts with no reflection on their ontological or episte-mological compatibility (Laclau, 2004). For example, let's imagine a discourse theoretical analysis of class that simultaneously presupposes the primacy of class in a traditional Marxist mode, barely recognizing the contradiction. Basic narrative concerns preclude me from engaging in detailed operations of "commensuration" every time I appropriate concepts and insights from other theoretical traditions. However, I end this chapter by briefly reflecting on how I reconcile my use of discourse theory with Bourdieu's field theory, my other key theoretical source.

Neoliberal logics and media regimes

We now need to consider how a discursive logics approach might inform our understanding of mediated political cultures. Conceptual-ized abstractly, we can identify at least five neoliberal logics as important in the neoliberalization of media regimes,[6] partly drawing on insights established in the existing media literature (see Chapter 1). First, a logic of market determinism, which describes how social agents internalize the assumption that institutional practices, including media practices, must be justified in market terms. This logic can be inflected in media spaces in different ways. It might be articulated as a triumphant ideo-logical faith in the free market, in the spectacular fashion exemplified by some business television pundits and analysts. Or it might be articu-lated in a common-sense manner, consistent with journalists' "realist" sensibilities (see Chapter 5) and their own institutional embeddedness in market structures. Journalistic identification with the market is some-times dialectically tied to a suspicion of the state, enabling a homology between neoliberal and journalistic subjectivities that is most obvious in the rhetoric of the "free press" (see Chapter 7).

Second, a logic of commodification, which describes the increasing commodification of media and social identities. This is evident in the increasingly hyperbolic marketing of journalistic identities and, more furtively, in the network of surveillance and data-gathering practices that govern contemporary media and political communication systems (Stanyer, 2007). And it is exemplified in the self-commodification and self-branding (Hearn, 2008) strategies of media intellectuals and pun-dits, who fine-tune the kind of performative dispositions that confer competency, authority and prestige in particular media spaces and for-mats (Bourdieu, 1998b).

Third, a logic of individualization, which denotes a media privileging of individual, rather than collective, identities, and the normalization of self-expressive modes of public discourse (Corner, 2003; Stanyer, 2007). This logic is evident, for example, in the increasing presidentialization of election campaigns and the strategic importance of personal life narratives as forms of political capital. It is exemplified by a discourse of individual responsibility and the pressures to perform the self in mediated spaces (Goodwin et al., 2014; Hearn, 2008). And it is discernible in a variety of journalistic field practices: in the increasing economic and symbolic profits that can be reaped from personality-driven forms of journalism; in the inflexion of "objective" news reportage through an opinionated register; in the enthusiasm for self-expressive, cheap contributions from "you, the audience"; in the preference for personalized forms of storytelling; in the journalistic performance of affect; in the fetishization of news vox-pops with "ordinary" (Couldry, 2003b) individuals; and in a fourth-estate posture of holding individuals to account (see Chapter 6). This logic is often articulated with a fourth logic, a logic of competitive ritual, which captures the increasing normalization of competitive idioms and rationalities in public communication (the exemplary form being reality television; see Chapter 1).

Fifth, a logic of self-interest, which describes the tendency to explain publicly visible behaviour and action in narrow self-interested terms. Hay (2007) argues that rational choice assumptions have become naturalized in common-sense discourses about politics (see Chapter 6). His argument applies, a fortiori, to journalist dispositions, though I am not suggesting that journalists, as a rule, consciously adhere to a neoliberal or rational choice picture of the world. However, it is worth noting how some of the key constitutive elements of a generalized rational choice disposition – its logic of methodological individualism, its focus on the immediate and the synchronic rather than the historically constituted and its default attribution of self-interested motives to social and political actors – have close homologies in a news values disposition that is specifically journalistic and also the basis of a more general performative competency in media spaces.

These logics are introduced here as ideal type conceptions, ahead of the specific empirical analyses of later chapters. They represent some of the key constitutive features of neoliberal media imaginaries, embodying a particular regime of publicness and subjectivity. I do not mean to imply that these logics are, by definition, always regressive, or that they are not open to being articulated differently. Neoliberal logics are not essentially neoliberal logics, because even exemplary logics, such as the logic of individualization, are never monopolized by their neoliberal signification (see Conclusion). The discursive effect always depends on the contextual articulation and what other social, political and fantasmatic logics are in play. Some progressively articulated media identities might just as conceivably be structured by logics of individualization as Fox News anchors. Projections of self-interested motivation are hardly bound to neoliberal discourse. And it would be wrongheaded to blanketly condemn media regimes that, in some respects at least, have democratized the relationship between journalists and audiences. Rather, my argument is that when articulated as a typically messy, yet nonetheless coherent totality – we could even say its messiness is its discursive strength – these logics help enculturate and normalize a neoliberalized imaginary in media spaces.

The antagonistic dimension underpinning this neoliberalized imaginary is, as I suggested in Chapter 2, crucial. The most important antagonistic dimension from within a neoliberalized media imaginary is basically anti-intellectual, anti-elitist and anti-ideological (see Chapter 2), the performative assumption being that proponents of a neoliberal identity somehow share none of these Othered attributes. "Intellectuals", "elites" and "ideologues" become code for socialists, statists and left-wing do-gooders who are repressive of neoliberal freedoms (see Chapter 7). And these antagonists are cast as the intellectual sponsors of a wider set of scapegoats and antagonists: "dole spongers", "welfare mothers", "immigrants", "the underclass" and so on (Lentin & Titley, 2011; Tyler, 2013; Wacquant, 2007). The affective power of this antagonistic discourse is considerable, because of its capacity to infuse a raft of wounded subjectivities and amplify a general culture of existential resentment (Connolly, 2008) and political cynicism (see Chapter 6). My argument is not intended as a sweeping empirical claim about the anti-intellectual character of mass media spaces. Nor should it be seen as an echo of Bourdieu's (1998b) tendency to disparage the sphere of journalistic common sense (Ekström, 2003). However, it is to suggest that when challenges to neoliberal regimes are articulated, they are often met with a market populist discourse (see also Blumler & Kavanagh, 1999; Frank, 2000) that is articulated as democratic and egalitarian (Aune, 2008), and often scathing of political dispositions that look to the state rather than the market. This antagonistic dynamic assumed a very theatrical form in the Tea Party's representation of Obama, mystifying the latter's own affinity with the discourse of third way neoliberalism (Jutel, 2013; Peck, 2010). This antagonistic discourse is not impenetrable and, in an increasingly porous journalistic field, there is hardly an absence of media and popular culture spaces to critique its more fantasmatic enactments. However, it is a crucial part of our neoliberal inheritance, perhaps most potently internalized in a subjective disposition that is neoliberalized, rather than evangelically neoliberal: regulated by what Layton (2010) calls "dominant individualistic norms...that unlink the social from the individual" and see dependency, on others or the state, as shameful (p. 312).

A field theory supplement

Conceptualizing neoliberalism as a series of discursive logics, always hegemonically articulated with other social logics, helps us dereify the concept. In place of a unitary and fully formed neoliberalism, it sensitizes us to differential logics within social regimes that cannot be reduced to the category of neoliberal (see Skeggs, 2014). In redescribing the world through the social ontology of discourse theory, it brings attention to points of potential rupture in the social order: what could be the discursive materials of a new hegemonic universal. Yet, if our intention is to present a less abstract analysis of neoliberalism, the adequacy of the concept of logics raises its own questions. Isn't the concept of a logic itself an abstraction? Doesn't it risk producing its own kind of subsumptive analysis where everything is incorporated into a new master category? If discourse analysis constitutes a form of radical materialist analysis, can the materiality of the sedimented social world be adequately captured by the concept of logics?

I address these objections by using Bourdieu's field theory as a sociological supplement to discourse theory (Bourdieu, 1977, 1990, 1991, 1998a, 1998b, 2005a, 2005b; for a more detailed discussion, see Phelan, 2011a). The justification for doing so develops some of the theoretical affinities between Bourdieu and Laclau's work (see Lane, 2006). Both emphasize the relational logic of the social. And both underscore the political nature of "social objectivity". Like Laclau's concept of discourse, Bourdieu's concept of the field assumes "the real is relational" (Benson & Neveu, 2005, p. 3), emphasizing how subjectivities are formed in how agents are "acting and reacting in relation to one another" (p. 11). Bourdieu's concept of the "political field" does not have the expanse of Laclau's concept of the political, essentially correlating with a world of formal institutional politics (Swartz, 1997). Yet, his concept of a "meta-field" of power (cited in Swartz, 1997, p. 136) resonates with Laclau's concept of a hegemonized social objectivity, because it grasps how the relations between different social fields are politically constituted. Instead of a stand-alone political field, the entire spectrum of social fields – economic field, journalistic field, cultural field and so on – are reconceived as sites of "the political". The argument for articulating Bourdieu with Laclau also builds on Glynos and Howarth's schematic distinction between political logics and social logics. If the category of political logics highlights the radically contingent nature of the social order, concepts like field, habitus, symbolic capital and doxa facilitate a richer sociological account of how social logics are reproduced in different sedimented forms: in institutions, bodies, language, affective sensibilities, measures of value, forms of prestige and capital.

Even if already well known, let us briefly outline some of Bourdieu's key concepts. Habitus captures how social logics are inscribed in agents' subjectivities: internalized in a set of "durable and transposable" (Bourdieu, 1977, p. 72) dispositions that regulate people's cognitive perceptions and bodily comportment. These dispositions are the sedimented embodiment of an agent's individual history. But they are never simply individual dispositions, for they are always structured by the different social universes – familial, educational, class, gender and so on – traversed and negotiated by the agent (Bourdieu, 2000, p. 138). Bourdieu describes these social universes as fields. "To think in terms of field is to think relationally" (Bourdieu & Wacquant, 1992, p. 97), to presuppose that agents' habitus are marked by the "objective relations" of the social fields they operate in. The dialectic between field and habitus is supplemented by the category of doxa: Bourdieu's name for the prereflexive categorical schemes that are taken for granted within a particular field. They constitute a "set of fundamental beliefs which d[o] not even need to be asserted in the form of an explicit, self-conscious dogma" (Bourdieu, 2000, p. 15). Taken together, an agent's habitus signifies an individuated subjectivity that is also a social subjectivity because it has internalized the objective structures and doxa of a particular social field. However, this does not mean a mechanically determined subjectivity that precludes no individual variations. Nor does it imply that the "objective" organization of a field cannot be politicized and contested. Instead, habitus operates as a generative "system of dispositions" (Hilgers, 2013) that facilitates creative invention and dynamic variations, rather than slavish subordination to a rigid, prescriptive code.[7]

Bourdieu gives us conceptual resources for understanding the complex dynamics of social reproduction that cannot be adequately grasped by Laclau's abstract appeal to social sedimentation. The practices of specific institutions do not interest Laclau (2004) much: indeed, he "pleads happily guilty" to the charge that there is an empirical deficit in his work because it is "concentrated on the ontological dimension of social theory rather than on ontical [i.e., empirical level] research" (p. 321). He is interested in how particular social regimes are politically institutionalized, ruptured and transformed; how they operate within the horizon of a sedimented social (see Wodak, 2009) is less his concern.

In contrast, Bourdieu's conception of society as a composite of different fields enables a more nuanced mezzo-level analysis of how the social order is constituted and reproduced. Aligned to the concerns of this book, it focuses empirical attention on how neoliberal logics are institutionally distributed and organized: materially embedded in the power relations between different fields, in the power structures within particular fields, in the dispositional tendencies of different social agents and in the affinities of habitus between agents in different social fields.

By highlighting the "affective transaction" (p. 141) between field and habitus, Bourdieu (2000) captures how agents' social dispositions are embedded in particular institutional and cultural spaces, factors not clearly grasped by Laclau's reliance on an abstract psychoanalytical model of subjectivity. Bourdieu brings attention to "embodied beliefs, passions, and pulsions" that work below the level of conscious identifications: "social injunctions...addressed not to the intellect but to the body" (p. 141). He would likely question the adequacy of the concept of identificatory logics in explaining agents' submission to and complicity with particular social regimes, because of its discursive affinity with a historical privileging of consciousness as the primary object of political interventions (Bourdieu, 2000, p. 181; Bourdieu & Eagleton, 1994).

In one sense, then, the case for using Bourdieu as a sociological supplement to Laclau rests on a familiar reading of Bourdieu as a theorist of social reproduction. However, it would be a mistake to reduce Bourdieu's corpus to the motif of reproduction – as if a given set of field conditions are fixed and preclude the possibility of political and social change. Instead, reading Bourdieu as a political theorist, Wacquant (2004) suggests:

> For genuine and lasting progressive change to occur, a politics of fields aimed at structured power relations must of necessity be supplemented by a politics of habitus, paying close attention to the social production and modalities of expression of political proclivities (p. 10).

The argument will be taken up purposefully in Chapter 5. But Wacquant captures the key point: in addressing the problematic of neoliberalism, media and the political, we need to think in terms of a politics of the journalistic field and habitus, otherwise we risk falling into the trap of simply seeing sedimented media regimes, and the mundane performative dispositions they inculcate and naturalize, as neutral transmission mechanisms of political practice. Instead, they exemplify what Bourdieu (2000), with a nod to Foucault, calls "the ordinary order of things": a locus of social domination that is "continuous and often unnoticed" (p. 10) but which structures "the material conditions of existence" (141). They embody, in short, the logic of symbolic violence, a violence that is typically hidden and unrecognized and which the dominated party is complicit in "because they help to construct it as such" (p. 171). It amounts to the "inscription of a relation of domination into the body", where the "efficacy of external necessities depends upon the efficacy of an internal necessity" (p. 169). This violence might take the form of ded-icated and serious journalists being forced to work with news genres and formulas governed by economic field logics; political field agents feeling structurally obligated to "play the media game" and comply with often-trivializing media scripts; or citizens internalizing prefabricated media conventions so as to appear "competent" in media spaces.

Treating Bourdieu as a theorist of social change also enables produc-tive resonances with Laclau's account of the political. Instead of nat-uralizing the given condition of a field, fields are conceptualized as hegemonic terrains: politicized when challenges are asserted against the power structures governing how different species of symbolic capital – economic capital, cultural capital and social capital (Bourdieu & Wacquant, 1992, p. 119) – are determined, distributed and internalized. Analyses of the inter-field tensions between different social fields might be enriched by the concept of social antagonism (see Bernanke, 2013). And discourse analyses of media and journalistic cultures might be more clearly linked to ethico-political critiques of the kind of performative dispositions consecrated in media spaces, politicizing the conditions of possibility of journalistic field practices.

Conclusion

This chapter examined the concept of neoliberal logics, following on from the discussion of discourse theory in Chapter 2. I identified five ideal type discursive logics in the neoliberalization of media regimes. However, I suggested we should not expect to find these logics at work as some neat totality, for neoliberal logics are always articulated with other social, political and fantasmatic logics. I then discussed my use of Bourdieu's field theory as a theoretical supplement to Laclau's discourse theory. I argued Bourdieu gives us conceptual resources for talking about and politicizing the social that are not satisfactorily grasped by simply appealing to the abstract concept of logics.

A word about how different concepts, including the concept of logics, are deployed in later chapters. I am wary of dutifully translating every substantive discussion into discourse theory or field theory concepts. Nor do I outline a formal typology of logics in each empirical instance. Instead, discourse theory and field theory provide the theoretical scaffolding for the analysis presented in the rest of the book. Chapter 5 offers the most explicit discussion of field theory, examining the relationship between neoliberalism and the journalistic habitus. However, before that, let us first consider how the concepts of neoliberalization and neoliberal logics might illuminate the empirical analysis of a 2011 media-political event in Aotearoa New Zealand.

4

Neoliberalism and Media Democracy: A Representative Anecdote from Post-Rogernomics New Zealand

If the story of neoliberalism is typically narrated as an Anglo-American-centric 1980s story focused on the political victories of Thatcher and Reagan, for dramatic effect, the story sometimes turns to Aotearoa New Zealand. New Zealand underwent one of the most extreme neoliberal experiments of the 1980s (Gray, 1998a), radically altering the character of a society historically defined by the values of the welfare state and "the social democratic ideal of [a] harmonious classless society" (Kelsey, 1997, p. 20). The country became a "laboratory" for the deployment of neoliberal theories, its small-scale, weak parliamentary structures and relative economic vulnerability providing "almost perfect political, economic and intellectual conditions in which to experiment" (p. 19). The New Zealand neoliberal story was, in its local vernacular, the story of "Rogernomics", named after Roger Douglas, the Minister of Finance of the Labour Party government that came to power in 1984 and which was re-elected in 1987.

Douglas was the public front of a neoliberal vanguardist project that "*chose* to take" Williamson's "Washington Consensus" prescription "to its neoliberal extreme" (Kelsey, 1997, p. 19; Williamson, 2003), subjecting the country to a "structural adjustment programme" that made "Thatcher look timid" (Menz, 2005, p. 49). Previously controlled markets were liberalized, much of the infrastructure of the social democratic state was deregulated and "any state activity with a potentially commercial function was corporatized" (Kelsey, 1997, p. 23). The "New Zealand model" was heralded in elite financial media like *The Economist*, the implementation of a free-market programme by a nominally socialist government giving the story an additional news hook (p. 8). However, it was 1993 before the country started recording significant economic growth and, as Menz (2005) suggests, "the immediate results of neoliberal adjustment were nearly 10 years of stagnation in terms of real GDP growth and rapidly increasing unemployment" (p. 51).

The media were, of course, an important part of the story. The national media system was reconfigured according to the same neoliberal script (Herman & McChesney, 1997; Hope, 1999, 2012; Thompson, 2012). Different media markets were liberalized and integrated to an unprecedented degree in international circuits of capital. The state removed legislation imposing limits on foreign and cross-media ownership, regulating the media system in the interests of corporations. And the nominally "public service" television broadcaster became a full-on commercial network, normalizing a culture of personality-driven and emotive programming.

Like others in the society, the relatively weak national media and journalism culture was overwhelmed by the "blitzkrieg" (Easton cited in Kelsey, 1997, p. 33) tactics of the new regime – its textbook decree that "there is no alternative". "Market newspeak" (p. 335) became the new common-sense vocabulary in media spaces and elsewhere. Terms like "freedom", "devolution", "partnership", "accountability", "liberation" and "empowerment" were disseminated as the code words for the project of rolling back the state. As with Thatcherism, they appealed to people's contradictory experiences of the state, personified in New Zealand by the authoritarianism of the previous Prime Minister, Robert Muldoon. "Pejorative terms such as *regulated, interventionist, vested interests, featherbedding, inefficiency,* [and] *dinosaur unions*" become staple elements of news discourses "vilifying past economic arrangements" (Hope, 1999, p. 101), naturalizing the impression that the post-1984 programme represented a necessary break from the past. The new order was not without challenge in the media and elsewhere, even if political contestation increasingly assumed a culturalist register that Gilbert (2012) suggests mystified the class dynamics of the new formation. The emergence of a popular anti-neoliberal antagonism gained sharper definition when the local Tories, and traditional enemy of the left, The National Party, came to power in 1990, ratcheting up the project of economic reform with "cuts to government spending and [a] radical labour market programme" (Kelsey, 1997, p. 6).

This chapter is focused on the New Zealand of the near present, grounded in a critical examination of a political news story from April 2011. However, our discussion needs to begin in the New Zealand of the 1980s, for Rogernomics, subsequently reincarnated as the "Ruthanesia" policies of the National government (named after Minister of Finance, and Mont Pelerin member, Ruth Richardson) remain absolutely central to making sense of the contemporary conjuncture. The New Zealand story of the last 30 years has essentially been a post-Rogernomics story marked by political continuity, but also ambivalence. The Labour Party that returned to government in 1999 did so under a "third way" banner, seeking to recuperate the party's social democratic heritage after its capture by free-market ideology. And, after the three-term Labour-led government left office in 2008, the new National-led coalition offered its own, more business-friendly version of a third way identity, equally keen to distance itself from the hard-line governments of the past. Accordingly, the impression sometimes cultivated in the worlds of political marketing and media punditry is that "neoliberalism" is something that happened in New Zealand's past, perpetually bound to the shock-tactic politics of earlier regimes. Indeed, an antagonism to the Rogernomics era has even seeped into commercial branding strategies: one bank launched a television advert in 2013 boasting how it held on to its independence against a predatory alliance of state and corporate capital in the 1980s, symbolized by old archive footage of Douglas (TSB Bank, 2013).

I use the event of Don Brash's "extraordinary coup" of the ACT (Association of Consumers and Taxpayers) Party in April 2011 to explore how neoliberal logics are contextually articulated in the New Zealand of the present. Brash and ACT offer an interesting case study for different reasons. ACT has been the country's most committed free-market party of the last 20 years, co-established by Roger Douglas after his continued membership in the Labour Party became untenable. Brash has been aligned to the neoliberal vanguard since the 1980s, serving as the country's reserve bank governor from 1988 to 2002. He was elected to Parliament in 2002, rising to the position of National Party leader a year later. His leadership of the National Party was controversial. It marked a return to the abrasive political style and strong pro-business agenda of the Rogernomics and Ruthanesia eras. National's initial success in public opinion polls was driven by the construction of different political antagonists, most demagogically the country's indigenous Maori population (Hager, 2006). The party was marginally defeated at the 2005 election, and Brash resigned as National leader in 2006 and from Parliament a year later. His "coup" of ACT in April 2011 therefore had the aura of a dramatic political return (the metaphor of neoliberalism as "zombie" [Fine, 2010] comes to mind), once again in the name of an unreconstructed 1980s-style "reform" agenda. Our case study allows us to see how a doctrinaire neoliberal identity is relationally con-structed in the New Zealand of the present, both within the logic of the journalistic field and political field. I highlight messy and paradoxical dimensions of the press coverage that are obscured by the notion of a monolithic neoliberalism. Nonetheless, I show how the mediated con-struction of the coup was inscribed in social logics institutionalized in the Rogernomics era, against the simplistic assumption that we are now post-neoliberal.

Constructing neoliberalism: Media blind spots

Let's begin six months on from Brash's coup – on the night of the November 2011 election that one political journalist called "an unmiti-gated disaster" (Espiner cited in TVNZ, 2011) for the ACT Party and its leader, Brash. The outcome had been widely anticipated during the elec-tion campaign (ACT returned a single seat won by John Banks, down from its previous five). Indeed, by that stage, the man Brian Edwards (2011) dubbed "the political embarrassment called Don Brash" had become easy comic material: the subject of several fake Twitter accounts and, when he was not being denounced as a "racist" for Maori bashing, lampooned as a "dinosaur stuck in the oppressive past" (Small, 2011).

Two media commentaries on the political death of Brash, both articu-lated by figures affiliated with the mainstream political left, are espe-cially interesting because they explicitly referred to neoliberalism. The first was a pre-emptive political obituary published a week out from election day by Chris Trotter (2011b), one of the country's best-known left-wing commentators. It considered Brash's place – or more like his lack of place – in the so-called "teapot tapes" meeting between serv-ing Prime Minister John Key and ACT MP John Banks (an event that became the defining media spectacle of the 2011 election campaign because of the inadvertent audio recording of a "private" meeting staged for the cameras).

Trotter (2011b) read the meeting as evidence of an "electoral alliance" designed to oust Brash as leader of ACT and reflected on the strategic parallels with the Brash "coup" earlier in 2011. Brash's desire to "reha-bilitate ACT" was attributed to his "ideological" conviction that "when it came to keeping the National-led Government on the *straight-and-narrow neoliberal path* [italics added] he was the only man for the job". Conversely, the identity of National Party leader and Prime Minister John Key was distanced from neoliberalism. The policy prescription that emerged from Brash's earlier leadership of a "taskforce dedicated to closing the wages-gap with Australia" was described as a "hard-line neoliberal prescription" that did not "impress the Prime Minister, who more or less dismissed Dr Brash's recommendations out-of-hand". Trotter therefore concluded that the "electoral alliance being forged [at the teapot tape meeting] was not between conservatives and neoliberals, it was between the Centre-Right and the Far-Right", as represented by "the genial and urbane Mr Key and the aggressive...provincial" and "outrageous right wing populist" Mr Banks.

The second media commentary was the reported comments of Otago University politics lecturer Bryce Edwards in an Anthony Hubbard (2011) article published a week after the November 2011 election. Framed by the assumption that the election results illustrated a "battle for the political middle ground [that] left those on the edges out in the cold", Hubbard wondered why "the left-wing Mana party and the right-wing ACT party did badly in the election". Edwards was cited to support the claim that the election illustrated a "new centrist consensus" in politics, leaving little room for those outside it. "We have an incredibly centre-oriented political sphere at the moment", Edwards said. "There is just not the ideological mood for more diverse politics". The point is reinforced when Edwards invokes neoliberalism: "Edwards suggests that ACT's economic stance – its neo-liberal or Rogernomics-style model – is now out of date. 'The tide's gone out on neoliberalism, just as the tide's gone out on the [left] ideologies that sought to counter neoliberalism'".

Trotter's and Edwards's conceptualization of neoliberalism is marked by similar blind spots and limitations. For Trotter, neoliberalism is defined through the metaphor of a "straight and narrow path" that is distinguished from the identity of the current National-led government. The characterization of Brash as a "hard-line neoliberal" implies there are different ways of being neoliberal. However, by representing Key as contemptuous of Brash's policy prescriptions, Trotter situates Key and National as something other than neoliberal, a perception that, as we will see later, also informed Trotter's (2011a) assessment of Brash's return earlier in the year. Edwards's double use of the "tide" metaphor articulates a similar logic even more forcefully: "The tide's gone out on neoliberalism, just as the tide's gone out on the [left] ideologies that sought to counter neoliberalism". The comment exemplifies a wider discourse that constructs the present as a post-ideological and post-political age (Dean, 2009; Mouffe, 2005), a logic routinely projected onto Key's political persona (see Bryce Edwards, 2011).

Trotter and Edwards rearticulate a popular discourse that gained traction at the high point of the global financial crisis in 2008, which anticipated the "death" or "end of neoliberalism" (for a critical discussion, see Harvey, 2009; Stiglitz, 2008). The supposition is that the term "neoliberalism" implies an ideological coherence and faith in the free market that can no longer be attributed to politicians like Key. The implication is that the contemporary political landscape needs to be understood as a "post-neoliberal" one (see, for example, Rustin, 2011), in recognition of how political and governmental actors are now more amenable to policy measures that break from rigid neoliberal prescriptions.

From the vantage point of 2014, this post-neoliberal discourse already seems dated because of the emergence of a "hyper-neoliberal" (Fuchs, 2012) austerity programme as the primary political response to the crisis (see Crouch, 2011). Yet, interpreted on its own terms, this post-neoliberal discourse makes at least two problematic assumptions from the perspective of how neoliberalism is conceptualized in this book. First, it typically defines neoliberalism as a specifically economic ideology: a clearly delineated set of technical policy measures that privilege market mechanisms in the ideological construction of the social order (see Stiglitz, 2008). Economic and economistic concerns are clearly pivotal to the constitution of neoliberal identities and formations. However, the shorthand privileging of the economic, as a distinct social sphere, deemphasizes the extent to which neoliberalism can be understood as a political, social and cultural phenomenon (see, for example, Brown, 2003; Couldry, 2010; and Dean, 2009). Conceptualizing neoliberalism in a more expansive way therefore underlines the need for caution in declaring the "end" of neoliberalism, as some were inclined to do when different national governments bailed out their banking systems in 2008.[1] Narrowly focusing on particular policy developments in determining whether neoliberalism has ended or not also ignores the cumulative structuring effects of earlier political decisions in naturalizing and embedding neoliberal logics and dispositions that do not simply disappear as a consequence of particular policy changes.

The second and more fundamental problem with the post-neoliberal discourse is that it obscures how the political institutionalization of a neoliberalized social order has been marked by a messy and contradictory relationship with neoliberal doctrine (see Chapter 2). Contrary to Trotter's metaphor, there has never been a "straight and narrow neoliberal path", but a messy and variegated political trajectory that cannot be reduced to a singular ideological blueprint or a simplistic antagonism between market and state (Birch & Mykhnenko, 2010; Peck, 2010). These paradoxes were originally noted in Polanyi's (1944) analysis of how the nominally free-market programmes of the 19th century relied on a strong state that contradicted the doctrinal hostility to state intervention. And, as we saw in Chapter 1, they have been explored more recently in, for example, Hall's (1988) study of Thatcherism, Harvey's (2005) analysis of different national articulations of neoliberalism and Foucault's discussion of the neoliberal state. We cannot, therefore, adequately comprehend the phenomenon of "actually existing neoliberalism" (Brenner & Theodore, 2002) if we restrict our understanding to self-constructions of political identity, or over-identify with neat typologies of the political field that represent different identities as discrete. We could even suggest there has never been a "pure" neoliberalism (Peck, 2010), and to presuppose such a thing is to construct a convenient strawman that allows other neoliberalized identities to present themselves as comparatively reasonable, pragmatic and non-ideological.

Yet, the desire to transcend the concept of neoliberalism – to render it "post" – should not simply be dismissed, for, as I suggested in Chapter 1, scepticism about how the concept is deployed as a descriptive and explanatory category is justified. The concept is too often articulated in a monolithic and one-dimensional way in media and communication studies and elsewhere: as a straightforward name for the social totality that assumes a doctrinal and ideological coherence that is at least partly an idealist projection of the critical gaze itself (Bowman, 2007). Commenting in a specific media studies context, Hallin (2008) suggests that building "the story of recent social change...in terms of the shift to neoliberalism" often "rests content with vague and simplistic formulations, which...are far from adequate to understand the changes that have taken place in media and social systems over this period" (p. 43).

Developing on the Chapter 3 discussion of neoliberalization and neoliberal logics, I position Brash's April 2011 coup of ACT as an empirical event that illuminates the "socially reproduced form" (Peck, 2010, p. xii) that neoliberalization takes in the "mediated publicness" (Thompson, 1995) of contemporary New Zealand. I draw summarily on Meyer's (2002) concept of "media democracy", which describes the repressive structuring effects that mainstream "media communication has on the substance of the political itself" in liberal capitalist democracies (p. xi). He argues that media logics have now "colonized" the formal political process: that "media-led processes" and "their peculiar logic of communication" (pp. xi–xiii) have become key factors in determining the political and material condition of modern liberal democracies.[2] Meyer's argument focuses attention on the *political* implications of mainstream news media practices (hence my use of the hyphenated term *media-political*), as opposed to naturalized media discourses that construct politics as a discrete phenomenon that journalists simply cover. However, let us start by examining how the political return of Brash was represented in a naturalized media register before asking how the particular discursive regime was made possible.

The return of Brash as an empirical event

The series of events that culminated in Brash's appointment as ACT leader in April 2011 was widely framed as an "extraordinary coup" ("Brash Too Extreme", 2011) in media reportage.[3] What was most extraordinary about the story was that Brash was not even a member of Parliament or ACT when he announced his intention to challenge the incumbent leader Rodney Hide. Brash justified his intervention in the interests of a "reform" agenda in New Zealand, in a context where it was widely suggested that – led by what Brash called the "toxic" brand Hide (Watkins, 2011a) – ACT might lose all its seats in the November 2011 election. The fate of the political right had been the focal point of media speculation earlier in 2011, with rumours that well-financed representatives of the New Zealand "business community" had asked Brash to lead a new political party. Fearing a split in the libertarian right-wing vote, Brash balked at the prospect of a new party, though the threat that he might establish one gave a brutal authority to his leadership challenge: either Hide would do the right thing and resign from his untenable position as ACT leader, or else Brash would establish a new political party that would annihilate ACT in the next election (Watkins & Small, 2011).

The story bore implications for the stability of the de facto coalition government then in power and possible future coalition arrangements. Since 2008, New Zealand had been governed by a novel alliance of National – by far the dominant party with 44.93 per cent of the electoral vote – and the minority parties: ACT (3.65 per cent), the Maori Party (2.39 per cent) and United Future (0.87 per cent) (Electoral Commission, 2008). The self-avowed "centre right" National did not actually need the support of all three parties. Yet, the arrangement had the strategic advantage of enabling National to position itself as the government's "sensible centre" (Louw, 2005, p. 76): the comparatively moderate identity in-between the putative extremes of the right-wing ACT and the culturally distinct Maori Party. This strategic logic was evident in John Key's refusal to assign any ministerial portfolio to Roger Douglas (itself indicative of a residual antagonism to the Rogernomics era), who, after a ten-year gap, returned to Parliament as one of the ACT Party's list MPs in 2008. In popularity terms at least, National's strategy proved very effective, with polls showing consistently high levels of support for National and Key, whose affable persona was widely represented as the embodiment of a pragmatic "anti-political and anti-ideological" style and identity (see Bryce Edwards, 2011).

Brash's April 2011 intervention to take over ACT was partly motivated by his perception that National under Key had tamed its instinct for fundamental economic reform. This necessitated a reinvigoration of ACT's original mission, he argued, which had been sidetracked by Hide's "celebrity politics" (Street, 2012) persona. Brash's dissatisfaction with National was central to his publicly expressed rationale for leaving a party that he – alongside his then finance spokesperson Key – had brought to within 1 per cent of being the leading political party in the 2005 election. In an open letter to Key published as an advert in several papers on May 12, 2011, Brash reproached Key on several fronts, while also inducing him to assert a shared antagonism against "our opponents". He accused Key of resiling from commitments they had both affirmed in opposition and of governing in a manner that – because of the government's perceived tentativeness about dismantling some of the policies of the previous Labour-led government[4] – was preoccupied with assuaging the concerns of Maori Party voters and those of "Labour and Green voters who crossed over to you in 2008" (Brash, 2011). "Why are you [Key] running New Zealand for our opponents", Brash implored, especially when "you have spent the last three years building up probably the greatest reserves of prime ministerial popularity in New Zealand history".

Key's response to Brash's ACT leadership bid in April 2011 was consistent with his strategic interest in affirming the pragmatic nature of the National political brand. He did not rule out the possibility of either a future coalition arrangement with a Brash-led ACT or a future ministerial portfolio for Brash. But he was quick to characterize Brash as a political "extremist" opposed to his own moderate identity. "From National's perspective we are in a different space. We very much see ourselves as a Centre-Right party. We are not a political party that follows an extreme Right-wing doctrine" (cited in Small, Watkins & Mccammon, 2011).

The Labour Party predictably sought to make political capital from Key's attempt to distance himself from Brash, emphasizing the historical links between "the Key/Brash extreme team" and speculating on the possible backroom involvement of National strategists in Brash's coup (Labour Party, 2011). However, Key's preferred framing of the relationship with Brash was reproduced in different newspaper reports, with headlines and leads either emphasizing Key's desire to distance himself from Brash ("Brash Too Extreme", 2011) or his reluctance to entirely rule out a future coalition relationship ("PM Not Dispelling", 2011). The omissions in Key's self-serving characterization of Brash as an extremist was noted by some, with John Armstrong (2011) in the *New Zealand Herald* suggesting that Brash could conceivably retort that "he is only campaigning on much the same manifesto he did with National in 2005". A similar point was made more forcefully in a *Dominion Post* article by Luke Malpass, a policy analyst with the Centre for Independent Studies – a key Australian node in the international neoliberal think-tank infrastructure (see Chapter 2). Suggesting that Brash was merely articulating a policy prescription that "has much in common" with the agenda of the Labour-led coalition in Australia, Malpass argued that the knee-jerk labelling of Brash as an "extreme right-winger" showed how "left-wing New Zealand had become" and "how far New Zealand has drifted down a path of fuzzy, socialist sentiment, with little hard analysis of policy" (Malpass, 2011).

Malpass's framing of Brash's intervention as a realist antidote to the dominant political consensus was echoed elsewhere. A *Dominion Post* editorial (Editorial, 2011) suggested that, "with Brash at the helm of ACT", National's desire for a "credible party to its right on the political spectrum" had now materialized, "but it could be more credible than National wants". The editorial reinforced the theme of Brash's credibility, describing him as a "serious politician", in contrast to the frivolous Hide, "as evidenced by his seizure of the leadership of a party of which he wasn't even a member" and his desire "to lead ACT not to safety or even respectability but to a position of influence in the next government". The paper expressed admiration for what it saw as Brash's clarity of purpose in seeking to finish "the business [he] left unfinished when he stepped aside as National Party leader in 2006 – setting New Zealand on a course to close the economic gap with Australia", an objective which Key and his Finance Minister, Bill English, now merely cite as a vague "'aspirational' goal". The editorial conceded "few, if any" of Brash's policy prescriptions "enjoy popular support". However, it suggested that "a return by ACT to the economic agenda it was formed to promote will be a welcome addition to a political landscape presently dominated by soundbites, photo opportunities and blather". "The country cannot indefinitely continue to borrow to maintain a standard of living it cannot afford", warned the paper. "A debate is needed about choices and the consequences of choices", which Brash has the credibility to promote.

The notion that Brash's intervention represented a forthright, potentially "revolutionary" challenge to the New Zealand political establishment was given unlikely credence in a May 13 *Dominion Post* column by Chris Trotter (2011a). Trotter surmised that "Dr Brash's revolutionary project on behalf of the Right" is to dismantle the "'cradle to grave' welfare state" that "came under sustained political assault from Sir Roger Douglas and Ruth Richardson between 1984 and 1993". "Dr Brash's mission – 27 years on – is to finish the job", suggests Trotter, echoing – like the *Dominion Post* editorial – the "unfinished business" trope of a book published by Douglas in 1993 (Douglas, 1993). Trotter positioned Brash as someone outside the elite and political establishment, who, if he is to be successful, "must lead an uprising *against* [italics added] the political elites". Despite his aversion to Brash's ideological project, Trotter's analysis rearticulated some of the central assumptions of the wider media discourse by positioning the neoliberal Brash as anomalous with the current political consensus (assumptions that, as we saw earlier, were reinforced by Trotter's analysis of Brash later in the year).

Neoliberalized media democracy: A representative anecdote

So why construct a wider theoretical argument about the relationship between neoliberalism, media and the political with an overview of an empirical event centred on the fate of a marginal neoliberal party in New Zealand? The mediation of the Brash coup might be partly explained through a standard critical political economy lens (see Chapter 5). The changes initiated in the Rogernomics era are now deeply sedimented in the ecology of a corporatized media system (Hope, 2012), symbolized in the particular case by the recycling of news content across newspaper titles.[5] However, I want to take a different approach by working through the discursive logic of the media representations themselves. The return of Brash is an interesting empirical case because it offers a good representative anecdote of how New Zealand's media democracy has been neoliberalized in ways that are typically not talked about (Billig, 1999) in the everyday register of "centring" media-political spaces (Couldry, 2003b). Instead of presupposing neoliberalism as a descriptive or explanatory category, I want to critically redescribe *how* precisely the media politics of the empirical event was neoliberalized and how that discursive regime was made possible (Glynos & Howarth, 2007).

The Brash case illustrates how New Zealand's media democracy is regulated by a hegemonic formation that needs to be situated in terms of the neoliberalization – and the often paradoxical, fragmented and messy neoliberalization – of a wider set of social practices and identities. Five dialectically[6] linked features are highlighted here that also illuminate the more general "conditions of possibility" (Glynos & Howarth, 2007; Laclau & Mouffe, 2001) of neoliberalized media regimes.

First, the construction of the Brash story shows how, despite the commonplace critical naming of the present as "the age of neoliberalism" (Hallin, 2008, p. 43), *overt* neoliberal identities like Brash and ACT are often widely regarded with disfavour and cast as fringe identities both within the internal discursive configuration of the institutional political field and the wider field of mass media discourse. It may seem like an obvious, even trivial point. After all, we know ideological formations are often most successful when they conceal their explicitly ideological pedigree; or, in the ideological move par excellence, position themselves – in the way Key's identity is constructed by himself and others – as opposed to ideology. Nonetheless, if it is an obvious point, it is one that has not been adequately recognized in critical discourses about neoliberalism, which are often too quick to name the dominant ideological formation as "neoliberal" without satisfactorily exploring these paradoxes. The question of how political and social identifications (Burke, 1969) are articulated as part of a shared, intersubjective lifeworld (Coole, 2005) is important in a critical media studies context, particularly given the widespread assumption that the media is part of an ideological infrastructure that reproduces neoliberalism. If the social logics of journalists and others with symbolic authority in, over and through the media do reproduce neoliberalism, well, then, more recognition needs to be given to how they often do this by paradoxically distancing themselves from neoliberal logics – indeed, *ideology* in general.

Second, in a social and political context dominated by mass media representations and images, journalism's tendency to disavow ideology is dialectically reproduced in the tendency to treat the given social order as non-ideological, as exemplified by the widespread representation of Brash as *the* ideological one. Key can, in a manner deemed credible to some at least, conceivably construct his identity as non-ideological simply because he is *not* Brash. Thus, the more Brash reproaches him, the more the truth of Key's anti-ideological identity is affirmed. The orthodox left-right mapping and differentiation of political identities still takes place; politics is not without some explicit ideological content. Yet, political distinctions are reproduced in a social context that is often profoundly ahistorical and guided more by product placement and marketing logics than substantive or broad-ranging political differences. Hence Key can affirm his non-ideological identity by simply avoiding an abrupt overhaul of Labour policy initiatives, or by repackaging default neoliberal policies like privatization in the softer qualified language of "mixed ownership models" (Small, 2011). This strategically desired identity is implicitly affirmed by Brash and Malpass's hyperbolic construction of Key's identity as "left wing", even if the left-wing identity he has allegedly been contaminated by resembles nothing more daring than a New Zealand inflection of third way discourses (Duncan, 2007).

The charge of left-wing hegemony can, in one sense, be dismissed as nonsense. Yet, I propose that the Brash case attests to a more general discursive and phenomenological feature of today's media democracies that had perhaps its most theatrical incarnation in the political stand-offs between the Obama administration and the Tea Party: that ideology functions most commonly and effectively in hegemonic media discourses as a pejorative epithet to censure either modest attempts to tame sedimented neoliberalized norms, which are immediately represented as "socialist" *or*, paradoxically, to condemn zealous identification with "free market" doctrine. What is rendered invisible in these hegemonic media representations is recognition of the extent to which the existing social order *is* structured by neoliberal logics. This enables, whatever about its implausibility, an enduring self-construal of neoliberalism as a minority and threatened identity (see Hayek, 1960; Friedman, 1962; Phelan, 2007a) which struggles to be heard in mainstream media cultures allegedly dominated by "socialist" and "left-liberal" doxa. This is illustrated in our empirical example by the casual presupposition at the start of Malpass's (2011) article: "IF ANYONE doubts how Left-wing New Zealand has become, one need look no further than the recent pronouncements of Australian Prime Minister Julia Gillard". It is also echoed in *The Dominion Post's* hope that Brash's return may see a potential subversion of the current "political landscape" and Trotter's idiosyncratic positioning of Brash as an anti-establishment figure, both of which situate the arch neoliberal as someone at odds with the present.

Third, Key may enact an identity consistent with a familiar "end of ideology" and "post-political" logic and style (Brown, 2003; Dean, 2009). Yet, through his embrace of what Savigny (2008) characterizes as the ruling ideology of political marketing, he is, in another sense, governed just as rigidly as Brash by a neoliberal logic that upholds "the primacy of the market in all aspects of political life" (p. 64). Distinguishing between politics as ideology and marketing as ideology, Savigny argues that the latter "serves to legitimate the activity of marketing per se" (p. 66), so that "politics becomes about markets and market competition. Prescription for political action is focused on marketing values and beliefs, rather than political ones" (p. 75). This is to say that Key's strategic desire to distance himself from Brash is less because of his aversion to the latter's political agenda, but governed more by his internalization of a marketing-based conception of politics that – based on his own party's internal research data and publicly available opinion polls – shows how the all-important centrist electoral market does not like Brash or the kind of sharp political identity he represents. Assuming an antagonistic disposition towards Brash, at least on a media stage, is a potential source of political capital for Key, for to do otherwise, and wholeheartedly align himself with Brash's preferred antagonism against "our opponents", would sully the coherence of Key's "post-ideological" brand. In that sense, Key has mastered political marketing and public relations techniques that became emblematic of the neoliberalization of the New Zealand public sphere in the 1980s and 1990s (Hope, 1999) – practices that Brash embraced, but routinely bungled, when he was leader of National (see Hager, 2006). However, by casting Hide's "brand" as "toxic", Brash's takeover of ACT shows how his own actions are structured by political marketing logics that allow him to more easily reconcile his "conviction politics" style with the pursuit of a niche target market. Therefore, both political identities exemplify a now hegemonic view that politics can be satisfactorily understood according to a political marketing universe of competing political "brands", where, as Finlayson (2003) argues, the "ideological content of political marketing is not contained in the message...but in the very fact that politics has to go to the market in the first place, that it has to submit to that logic and cannot develop its own" (p. 48; see also Savigny, 2008, p. 75). The "ideology of market relations is secured" by normalizing the idea that "a policy can only be a good policy if it can be sold, because nothing has any worth if it cannot obtain value at market" (Finlayson, 2003, p. 49).

Fourth, Brash's aggressive, corporate-style takeover of a political party he was not even a member of shows how the niceties of the democratic process constitute no great impediment to the doctrinaire neoliberal. The anti-democratic character of Brash's intervention recalls the blitzkrieg regimes of the past, given that much of the post-1984 Rogernomics programme was justified in the language of perpetual crisis that dominated New Zealand politics at the time (Kelsey, 1997). Amplified by these collective memories, as well as more recent memories of the manipulative tactics when Brash led National from 2003 to 2006 (Hager, 2006), this historical backdrop helps us better understand the aversion to Brash, and an *explicitly* ideological politics, that comes through in much of the reporting. In that respect, what I described earlier as the ahistorical construction of the space of political differences is ahistorical in a qualified sense only, since Key's political strategy and posture, as well as the marketing data that structures the public articulation of that identity, is heavily mediated by these collective memories.

At the same time, much like the casting of Brash as the uniquely ideological one, these collective memories are strongly individualized, so that asserting a political distance from the earlier historical period is often enacted by simply distancing the relevant political personality from ideological bogeymen like Brash and Roger Douglas. In other words, the focus on *the individual* as the locus of political agency and responsibility, itself a key constitutive element in both the neoliberalization *and* mediatization of political and social practices (see Blumler & Kavanagh, 1999), deflects attention from a more structurally orientated analysis of the ideological continuities between past and present.

Journalism's anti-ideology ideology

The final, multi-dimensional feature of the Brash case I want to highlight is the one of most relevance to this book: the specific role of media and journalistic logics in the enactment of neoliberalized discursive norms. These logics work as a subset of Glynos and Howarth's (2007) social logics, enabling the reproduction of a neoliberalized media democracy. The dialectical dimension of the analysis is particularly important here. I contend that we cannot understand the dynamic articulation of neoliberalized regimes and practices without analysing the specific role of media and journalistic logics in their constitution and naturalization. Two aspects of our empirical example are particularly salient. First, it is hard to see how we can understand the normalization of an "anti-ideological" and "post-ideological" politics, as personified by Key, without considering the homologies with mainstream journalism's own tendency to cultivate an anti-ideological disposition. This is to say that, despite the extensive critiques of the notion of journalistic objectivity, the journalism culture in Aotearoa New Zealand remains embodied in an ongoing identification with atheoretical and hand-me-down notions of objectivity, neutrality, balance and media pluralism. This journalistic disposition is articulated as an anti-ideological ideology and style, performed as "an interest in disinterestedness" (Bourdieu, 2000, p. 125). However, much like Key's anti-ideological posture, the journalistic tendency to disavow ideology and politics cannot be accepted on its own terms. Instead, we need to explore – as I will do in Chapter 5 – how certain tendential features of the journalistic habitus (Bourdieu, 1998b), particularly its "no-nonsense" focus on the empirically given and the concrete, resonate with what Aune (2001) describes as the rhetoric of "market realism".

This realist posture and disposition is illustrated in the particular case by *The Dominion Post* editorial's valorization of Brash's seriousness and the presupposition that he is willing to confront economic and political realities that others are in denial about. The paper may refrain from explicitly endorsing Brash's agenda, yet it suggests his return should be welcomed because, unlike others, he at least faces up to the condition of the world as it *is*, rather than wishing it might be otherwise. The key point to underline here is the role of media discourses of this kind in reproducing and regulating the "is-ness" and precarious positivity of the social world (Laclau, 1990) – a form of material-discursive power that plays a crucial role in determining the strategic context in which a wider set of social and political identities are articulated. Banal discourses of this kind deemphasize the contingency and contestability of the social order, while simultaneously displacing this ideological commitment behind a realist posture that "doesn't do ideology".

Second, it is also difficult to see how the normalization of a political marketing paradigm grounded in an eternalization of liberal democratic norms can be satisfactorily understood without reflecting on its capacity to resonate with journalistic logics and sensibilities. By this I mean journalists', especially political journalists', shared identification with sedimented discourses about the nature of democracy (as *liberal* democracy) and the increasing internalization of the assumption that journalistic field identities need to justify their own existence in market terms. This convergence of identities is not without paradox. On the one hand, the incessant polling of public opinion is now a central element in journalism's production and marketing strategies (Stanyer, 2007). Yet, on the other, *The Dominion Post*'s lament about a "political landscape presently dominated by soundbites, photo opportunities and blather" ("Editorial: National may find ACT very different") shows how journalistic field identities communicate an archetypal aversion to marketing and PR practices. The journalistic convergence with political marketing discourses resonates more deeply in the homologous identification with the normative assumption that politics must be "accountable" to the market, which, if rearticulated in a more exalted rhetoric, bears a strong "family resemblance" to the classic watchdog journalism principle that political elites must be accountable to the public. This fourth-estate discourse, in which the journalistic field assumes the role of holding others to account on behalf of a pre-constituted public, is not without value as a democratic vision (see Curran, 2002). However, as with political marketing's normative submission of politics to "market realities", journalistic appeals to accountability can repress the logic of "the political"

(Laclau & Mouffe, 2001). This is because of centring media's privileged role, even in the digital age (Couldry, 2009), in determining how the very category of "the public" – its needs, demands and affective mood – is constituted.

Conclusion

This chapter examined the media politics of Don Brash's takeover of the neoliberal ACT Party in April 2011. I suggested it offered a representative anecdote of the (anti)political condition of post-Rogernomics New Zealand. On the one hand, the coverage suggested a popular antagonism to Brash's overt neoliberal identity, as exemplified by John Key's depiction of his former party leader as a political "extremist". This anti-neoliberal logic is partly made possible by a naturalized discourse that aligns "neoliberalism" with the radical Rogernomics and Ruthanesia experiments of the late 1980s and early 1990s, the truth effects of which are reinforced by the marginal standing of ACT in recent elections. Yet, on the other hand, the personalized antagonism to Brash obscures the extent to which different neoliberal logics, most obviously a logic of political marketing and a logic of individualization, structure the media-political representation of the coup. The coverage illustrated the naturalized authority of a third way, post-political discourse (see Chapter 2) that constructs the present as something other than neoliberal, reinforced by the hope of some that the doctrinaire Brash might shake up the political environment. I argued this post-political regime is partly made possible by journalists' own identification with a post-ideological style, personified by the strategic political identity of John Key. But Key's mediated political identity is also regulated by the latent political energy of an anti-Rogernomics collective memory that must be strategically managed in the New Zealand of the present. We might describe it as a political mood without a sufficiently coherent antagonist, other than the pantomimic figure Brash.[7]

Let me end by briefly citing another journalistic commentary in the aftermath of the 2011 New Zealand election, equally emblematic of a post-political universe. Reflecting on the fallout of Key's victory at the election, the political journalist Tracy Watkins (2011b) lauded the merits of David Shearer's candidacy for the then open position of Labour leader, after previous leader Phil Goff resigned after the election. The article offers a near-perfect reiteration of some of the sedimented logics structuring the representation of the Brash case. Shearer is described as the "candidate from central casting", because, like John Key, "he's the *anti-politician, which means the public instantly warm to him* [italics added], and he has a back story that only a Hollywood script writer could dream up". He is also celebrated as a "political newbie" who, unlike his rivals for the leadership contest, "carries no baggage from past administrations" and is "not hide bound by tradition or ideology".[8]

Could one cite a better example of how mundane media discourses, self-construed as politically and ideologically indifferent, naturalize the truth effects of neoliberal logics? These media representations and projections were crucial to Shearer's success in the leadership campaign. But, more importantly, they helped determine the *conditions of possibility* of his success on grounds that internalized an anti-politics sensibility (see Chapter 6). This is to say that the real political significance of the political journalist's discourse is not in its bog-standard speculative observations about who might be the next Labour leader or its vulnerability to the familiar charge of journalistic bias. Rather, it is in its reproduction of taken-for-granted presuppositions that project the anti-political disposition of John Key onto a homogenous and classless "public", that assume ideology is a political liability (because, of course, ideology is now passé) and that marketizes and commodifies politics by representing good "back stories" and "brand-freshness" as key determinants of political success. These presuppositions are effectively ontologized: posited as logics, truths and realities that prefabricate and structure the "objective" conjunctural condition of politics *and* political journalism. That they are presupposed, in New Zealand and elsewhere, underscores the need for a critique of neoliberalism that interrogates the journalistic dispositions that naturalize these social logics. Let us do just that in the next chapter by critically reflecting on the relationship between neoliberalism and the journalistic habitus.

5
The Journalistic Habitus and the Realist Style

The focus of this chapter can be distilled into one key question: how do journalists, and in particular mainstream political journalists, identify with the thing called neoliberalism? It's a deceptively simple question, because our answer depends on the ontological and epistemological assumptions we bring to it. We might come to the question with a deep epistemological scepticism about the very notion of "neoliberalism", as some journalists are inclined to do (see, for example, O'Brien, 2013b). Or we might bring different understandings of how political subjectivities are formed, and different assessments of the place of the political in the constitution of human subjectivity. The question generates myriad sub-questions. Does journalistic identification with neoliberalism emerge through active engagement with neoliberal thought? Is it socially engineered by neoliberal news sources and public relations agents? Or does identification with neoliberal logics work more through a kind of ideological and cultural osmosis, where journalists and others unconsciously internalize a set of common-sense assumptions that they would never describe as an "ism"?

Posing the question as a general question is, of course, an analytical convenience. Different journalists will identify, or disidentify, with neoliberal logics in different ways. As I suggested in Chapter 2, there are various ways of being neoliberal. The disposition of the financial journalist will differ from that of the political journalist. At the same time, it is never simply a matter of *individual* identification, because the subjectivity of individual journalists is relationally tied to the subjectivity of other journalists. In place of the myth of the journalist as a heroic individual, or indeed the inverse image of a journalism dominated by an all-determining structure, our question is best grasped by recognizing how journalistic dispositions are socially embedded in the structure and institutional practices of the journalistic field.

My argument brings together different elements. I begin by critically evaluating how the question of journalistic identification with neoliberalism is typically answered in critical media and journalism research. I then introduce the concept of post-ideological neoliberalism, signifying a form of neoliberalized identification that is articulated as pragmatic rather than ideological. I next discuss Bourdieu's concepts of the journalistic field, doxa and habitus. And I follow that with a more general discussion of the relationship between journalism, politics and ideology. I then introduce Aune's (2001) concept of "market realist" rhetoric, suggesting that, alongside the concept of post-ideological neoliberalism, it offers a productive framework for understanding how journalists identify with market logics. I then put my argument to work empirically, examining some of the discursive logics structuring how *The Irish Times*'s political editor, Stephen Collins, has represented the economic crisis and austerity. I end by clarifying how Collins's journalistic habitus is neoliberalized, though, drawing on Muhlmann's (2010) radical democratic account of journalism, I also show how it needs to be critically understood in a way that goes beyond the charge of neoliberal complicity.

Neoliberalism and journalism: The standard argument and its limitations

Let's start by briefly considering how the question of journalistic identification with neoliberalism is typically answered in critical communication, media and journalism research. We might call it the critical political economy answer, though, as I suggested in Chapter 1, the answer has currency in a wider body of media and communication literature. And it has increasing authority among media and political activists. The answer is often articulated cursorily or implicitly, advanced as part of the contextual framing of the researcher's analysis. Journalistic identification with neoliberalism is explained with reference to various structural factors that shape media systems, but which shape society more generally. Neoliberalism is articulated as the general name for the capitalist present – a force, logic and mode of rationality governing the entire social ecology.

The core argument can be simply stated: mainstream journalism is neoliberal because it is produced within a corporate media infrastructure governed by the ideology and priorities of neoliberal capitalism (see, for example, Andersson, 2012; Chakravartty & Schiller, 2010; Dyer-Witheford & Compton, 2011; Fenton, 2011; Grantham & Miller, 2010;

Hirst, 2012; Hope, 2012; Louw, 2005; McChesney, 2012; Thussu, 2007). Journalists may typically align themselves with left-liberal political views, even if political affiliations can change markedly further up the newsroom hierarchy (Hanusch, 2013). Yet, these views are effectively colonized by structural forces geared towards producing social representations aligned with the interests of capital. Neoliberalism signifies a profound intensification of a historical alignment of journalism and capitalism, accelerated by the corporatization and globalization of news media systems. Neoliberalism is (and has been) internalized in different ways: in the political reregulation of media policy regimes aligned to corporate priorities; in the political subjectivity of media owners, managerial and editorial elites; in the general decline of journalistic beats (labour reporters for instance) aligned to the social democratic state; in the increasing commodification and marketization of journalism and journalists; in the weakening of public service broadcasting and public interest news; in the normalization of a culture of infotainment and news spectacle; in the emergence of a journalism of neoliberal partisans; in the relative invisibility of working-class narratives in mainstream journalism; in the co-opted and promotional register of business journalism; in the mainstreaming of financial news; in the progressive undermining of journalists' work conditions; in the privileging of neoliberal news sources; in corporate public relations strategies; and in media representations that privilege neoliberal logics. In short, neoliberalism tells a story of how journalism's already limited autonomy within capitalist media systems has been progressively undermined since the 1980s, leaving journalism cultures increasingly subject to the instrumentalist rationality of the market.

How should we regard these familiar arguments? Well, as I recognize at different points in the book (see in particular Chapters 7 and 8), conventional political economy analysis is a crucial element of any comprehensive examination of the relationship between neoliberalism and media. Journalistic identification with neoliberalism is partly determined by journalists' structural positioning within a media system progressively corporatized and marketized since the 1980s. Idealistic journalistic objectives are increasingly colonized by profit-oriented concerns, a trend compounded as traditional media institutions struggle to establish viable business models in the digital news ecology. Political economy analysis (and not just in a Marxist mode) focuses critical attention on the structural and institutional forces governing a market-driven media system – factors often invisible in the front-stage comportment of journalistic and media identities.

However, this standard critical political economy argument, as styl-ized here, is inadequate for different reasons. The basic intuition of situ-ating the media system within the logic of the wider social-economic system is a sound one. However, as with any productive social theory, the things we "see" through the political economy lens can potentially become a form of "blindness", hindering our capacity to see other aspects of a phenomena (Burke cited in Foss, Foss & Trapp, 1990; Wittgenstein, 1973). In that vein, I identify at least three problematic tendencies in the standard political economy story that impede critical understanding of the problematic of neoliberalism and journalism: first, journalistic identities are rendered subordinate to the logic of capitalism; second, journalistic representations are seen as simply expressive of neoliberal interests; and, third, the mainstream media is disparaged as a politically hopeless space.

First, there is a residual tendency in political economy analysis to treat journalists' practices as epiphenomena of their structural location in the capitalist system. Journalists reproduce neoliberalism because they work within a neoliberal system, cast as relatively straightforward transmit-ters, reproducers or apologists of neoliberal ideology. Journalists' own perspectives on their practice are, accordingly, displaced or not taken seriously. Or claims of journalistic agency are dismissed as forms of ideological mystification, masking journalists' complicity with a wider infrastructure of power.[1] In its softer form, this argument recognizes the capacity of individual journalists to challenge neoliberal orthodoxies – there are cracks within the system. However, in its stronger form, the prototypical journalist is depicted as an automaton: an unthinking agent of the dominant ideology; a peddler of various myths – the myth of the "free press", the myth of the "watchdog"; the myth of "objectiv-ity", the myth of "investigative journalism" – that obscures journalism's embeddedness in a neoliberal social order.

Second, critical analyses of media often represent neoliberalism as a singular force or ideology: an essentially economic object *acting on* the world of journalism. These constructions can, as we suggested in Chapter 1, conceal the messiness and paradoxes of neoliberalized regimes. They foster the impression, even in analyses sympathetic to journalism, that neoliberalism is a unitary object imposed on jour-nalism and media cultures from "outside", which journalists then reproduce as part of their own structured submission to a top-down infrastructure of power. What is relatively displaced is a specific analysis of *journalistic* representations: those elements of journalists' representa-tional practice that cannot be reduced to the category of neoliberalism.

Journalistic representations are inscribed in something closer to a classic transmission model of communication, because of a default assumption that mainstream journalism is essentially expressive of neoliberal interests. In primarily focusing on how neoliberal logics are reproduced *through* the media, the question of how media and journalistic logics are themselves neoliberalized is comparatively neglected.

Third, if capitalist media are expressive of neoliberal interests, critical analyses of mainstream journalism can end up simply restaging what Garnham (2011) calls a "drearily familiar" story (p. 42), because what is there to know if we already know the media *is* neoliberal? Mainstream media is cast as a politically hopeless and ideologically contaminated space: absorbed in a fog of spectacle, illusion and triviality. Or when counter-hegemonic voices do get media coverage, critics predictably lament the capacity of the dominant neoliberal imaginary to co-opt critique and neutralize or distort radical political challenges. Radical political energies, some insist, must be directed instead into an infrastructure of alternative media – and entirely new political sites and spaces – because mainstream media have been captured by neoliberal reason (Andersson, 2012). The political project of strengthening a radical democratic and anti-capitalist media ecology can only be affirmed; the possibility of a different mainstream public sphere is surely dependent on the discursive practices taking place in counter-public spheres (Dahlberg, 2007). Yet, by demarcating alternative media spaces as the authentic site of "the political", the political and symbolic importance of centring (Couldry, 2003b) media risks being displaced – turned away from and disparaged rather than reckoned with.[2] The effect is potentially a deeply depoliticizing one, hindering our capacity to radically rethink the normative underpinnings of centring journalism (Markham, 2014). In ritually denouncing the stage of mainstream professional journalism, the question of what it "could be, or should try to be, is not addressed" (Muhlmann, 2010, p. 1).

Post-ideological neoliberalism

So, what's so different about how I approach the question of journalistic identification with neoliberalism? My answer unfolds over the course of the chapter. But let me begin in a tangential way by citing two illustrative examples of what I call the discourse of post-neoliberalism, taken from the glory days of "the Irish Celtic Tiger" (see further discussion in Chapter 8). The first is a quote from a May 1997 article in *The Economist*, on the eve of the Irish general election in June, when the magazine anticipates the political – or more like apolitical – contours of the election debate:

> ...there will be no debate between "left" and "right" in Ireland's election campaign. In Ireland those labels mean nothing... This consensus on economics, amounting in effect to an absence of economics, enabled Ireland to embark in the late 1980s on a series of national agreements on wages and taxes (Ireland Shines, 1997).

The second is from an interview with former Irish Prime Minister John Bruton on Television New Zealand in 2004. Performing what became a familiar ritual of Irish elites touring the globe revealing the secrets of the Celtic Tiger, Bruton rearticulated the basic logic of *The Economist*'s claim that conventional ideological distinctions between left and right matter little in the Irish context:

> ...Irish politicians never became ideological about economics...we were able to sort of deideologize politics as far as economics was concerned, and therefore you can have changes of government between the two main formations without that aspect of policy being changed (Bruton in Harman, 2004).

Now, one quite reasonable response to these claims, one in keeping with the critical account discussed in the previous section, might dismiss them as ridiculous, self-serving and, given their sources – *The Economist* and the right-wing Bruton – entirely predictable. The Celtic Tiger was an ideological exemplar of neoliberal capitalism, we might suggest, hardly an antidote to neoliberalism. Contrary to Bruton's claim that Irish politicians were never ideological about economics, his quote represents a near-perfect articulation of a neoliberal wish to subordinate politics to the objective of providing a stable environment for transnational capital (Harvey, 2005).

However, rather than simply dismissing these discourses, I want to develop an analytical approach that takes these "superficial" phenomena seriously and formulates an analysis of neoliberalism and journalism that passes through them. They illustrate a general condition that, as we saw in Chapters 2 and 4, goes well beyond the specific Irish case: the articulation of neoliberalized formations as "post-ideological", "post-political" and "anti-ideological" formations. Of the two ideal type neoliberal discourses considered in Chapter 2, antagonistic neoliberalism and third way neoliberalism, post-ideological neoliberalism is essentially interchangeable with the latter. It signifies a disposition that wants to distance itself from ideology, because ideology is code for a rigid and inflexible subjectivity. This disposition is often the manufactured product of public relations and political marketing strategies designed to soften the public presentation of neoliberal policies. Think, for instance, of David Cameron's "Big Society" project as an attempt to strategically distance the Conservative Party from Thatcher before subsequently embarking on a government programme arguably "more Thatcherite than Thatcher" (Defty, 2013). Post-ideological neoliberalism could therefore be dismissed as simply propaganda: all style, no substance – mere "rhetoric" in the pejorative sense. However, it is not reducible to propaganda. It captures real forms of political subjectivity that, even if they mystify, cannot be reduced to a purposeful strategy of elite mystification (Finlayson, 2003).

Recast in a critical media and journalism studies context, my key concern is: what role do centring media and journalistic logics play in enabling and naturalizing post-ideological neoliberalism – in rendering it coherent, reproducible and credible, at least *within* the logic of an elite-driven social imaginary. If post-ideological neoliberalism has become the dominant template for contemporary articulations of neoliberalism, I argue we cannot understand its naturalization independently of the mediated nature of today's social imaginary. And, most importantly here, we cannot understand its social authority independently of its specific resonances with the "journalistic habitus": the cognitive and affective dispositions generated and naturalized in the journalistic field.

The journalistic habitus

Bourdieu formulated his most purposeful analysis of the journalistic habitus in *On Television and Journalism*. Originally broadcast as a series of lectures on French public television, the book examined the "invisible structures and mechanisms" (Bourdieu, 1998b, p. 2) structuring journalists' disposition towards their practice and the wider social world. Bourdieu was, in one sense, articulating insights already well documented in the sociology of media and journalism (Corner, 1999), reinforcing the image of news construction captured in typologies of news values (Galtung & Ruge, 1965; Harcup & O'Neill, 2001). He highlighted, among other things, journalists' obsession with "scoops", "revelations" and "the new"; journalists' fixation on individuals, "especially what they do wrong"; journalists' default "readiness to denounce or indict" in

the name of accountability; journalists' "lack of time" to produce structurally sophisticated stories; and the homogenizing effects of a competitive environment where everyone in the media permanently surveys
each other (Bourdieu, 1998b, pp. 2–9). The book was not explicitly formulated as a polemic against neoliberalism, unlike some of Bourdieu's
(1998a) other popular writing. However, the question of the corrosive
effects of "the market" was central to Bourdieu's argument, at the heart
of his indictment of the kind of polity constructed in journalistic spaces.

Bourdieu formulates an account of neoliberalism and journalism not
dissimilar from the standard answer we considered earlier. Neoliberal
media regimes are defined by the economic field's growing authority
over the journalistic field. The result is the internalization of a more
sensational kind of journalistic habitus, often focused on gaining
attention as an end in itself. Journalists' capacity for field autonomy
is undermined by the privileging of audience ratings and market share
as measures of value, especially in the "most heteronomous sector of
journalism – television" (Bourdieu, 2005a, p. 42). Bourdieu emphasizes
the parallel colonizing effects of the journalistic field on other social
spaces; journalism, in effect, becomes central to the logic of neoliberal
governance. The normalization of a more aggressive journalistic habitus undermines the relative autonomy of other social fields, as measures of value consecrated in "the media" become internalized in other
social fields (see also Bourdieu, 1990). Political deliberation becomes
dominated by the relentless presentism of media logics (Meyer, 2002),
as politicians enact identities and policies adapted to the conventions,
priorities and temporalities of a media stage.

Benson and Neveu (2005) note, quite correctly, that field theory is
not simply interchangeable with critical political economy approaches
that explain "the news media's behaviour...solely with reference to their
capitalist ownership and control" (p. 10). Contrary to a critical tendency
to condemn rather than analyse journalism practice (Muhlmann,
2010), Bourdieu documents how factors often taken for granted within
the logic of the field itself impose limits on what becomes possible
and thinkable in journalistic spaces. These structural dynamics vary
depending on one's relational position within the field. Bourdieu distinguishes between relatively autonomous and heteronomous social
fields and relatively autonomous and heteronomous positions within
fields themselves (Bourdieu, 1990, 1991, 2005). The journalistic field
becomes a composite of sub-fields, each with its own particular conventions, practices and idioms, and its differential relations to other
social spaces. The political journalist cultivates "affinities of habitus"

(Darras, 2005, p. 165) with agents in the political field. The habitus of the financial and business journalist is aligned with the subjectivity of agents in the economic field, enabling a homology of dispositions that partly explains journalists' failure to anticipate the financial crisis (Manning, 2013).

Bourdieu's analysis of journalism is very rich and suggestive. That said, different critics, otherwise sympathetic to field theory, have argued that the limitations I identified earlier in the standard story of journalism and neoliberalism are sometimes evident in his work. First, Hallin (2005) discerns an economistic tendency in Bourdieu's analysis of journalism, which, like "the 'critical political economy' School" (p. 240), can collapse the distinction between the economic field and political field. The economic field becomes the privileged site of (neoliberal) power; the political field is rendered subordinate. "No doubt it is true that commercialization in many cases does have the effect of aligning the media with dominant political actors" (p. 240), Hallin suggests. "But it is too simplistic to assume that economic and political power are always in perfect alignment, and it contradicts other points Bourdieu makes about the complexity of the fields themselves" (p. 240). Schudson (2005) likewise questions Bourdieu's preoccupation with the structuring effects of market mechanisms, highlighting how American journalists regard the state as a potential threat to journalistic autonomy (see the discussion of "free press" rhetoric in Chapter 7).

Second, Lane (2006) identifies totalizing tendencies in Bourdieu's (1998a) critique of neoliberalism, equally at odds with the complex social geography of field theory. Bourdieu is over-reliant on a top-down conception of neoliberal power, he argues, insufficiently mediated by the texture of everyday life. "Throughout Bourdieu's criticisms of neoliberalism, the terms 'imposed' and 'imposition' recur with remarkable frequency" (p. 12), Lane (2006) observes. Journalists, think-tanks and other neoliberal agents are depicted as involved in a "work of imposition" (Bourdieu cited in Lane, 2006, p. 13), propagating a unitary Anglo-American ideology, and "planetary vulgate" (Bourdieu & Wacquant, 2001, p. 2), alien to French sensibilities. The agents of neoliberalism are depicted as a "genuine invisible world Government, a sort of Big Brother...deciding what we will be able to eat or not eat, see or not see on television or at the cinema" (Bourdieu cited in Lane, 2006, p. 13). Lane does not suggest that an account of neoliberalism focused on the impositional role of elite transnational institutions – the so-called "Washington consensus" – is without explanatory value. Rather, he argues Bourdieu's emphasis on a political project imposed from elsewhere obscures how neoliberal logics are reproduced in social practices that, as Hall (1988) suggested in his analysis of Thatcherism, can resonate with popular desires and subjectivities.

Finally, Bourdieu's analysis of the journalistic field is sometimes fatalistic, constructing it as a space of inevitable epistemological distortion (Ekström, 2003). Muhlmann (2010) discerns an anti-democratic sensibility in Bourdieu's work, which cannot see *any* redemptive impulses in the journalistic field's everyday levelling of social distinctions – its juxtaposition of the scientific and the vulgar, the knowledgeable and the opinionated, the specialist and the non-specialist, in the same public space (pp. 22–28).[3] Muhlmann (2010) recognizes the productivity of Bourdieu's sociology; indeed, like Hallin, she suggests Bourdieu's critique of journalism sometimes "runs counter to the complexity of his own analyses of the notion of the field" (p. 27). What she dislikes are the normative consequences that follow on from his one-dimensional valorization of field autonomy (Schudson, 2005). Bourdieu's critique of journalism feeds an inclination to retreat from the publicness of the journalistic field, she suggests, leaving us with little option but to carve out whatever autonomy we can from repressive media regimes that conceal and obscure under the pretence of "seeing". Bourdieu "doesn't just criticize bad journalism, but all kinds of journalistic practice" Muhlmann (2010, p. 24) insists; he communicates "a certain distaste for public space" (p. 22) and the journalistic values of popularization, openness and accessibility. Muhlmann argues Bourdieu ultimately has to fall back on the simplistic idea of a "pure public" (p. 28), because "the public" and "audience" constructed in media spaces are dismissed as little more than self-serving "journalistic construction[s]"; names journalists "give to their own wishes" (p. 27). His critique holds out for the fantasy of a "full communication" (p. 23), a "true" measure of public opinion that escapes the distorting effects of journalistic representation.

Here is not the place for critical reflection on these readings of Bourdieu. Instead, I want to affirm their polemical productivity as antidotes to certain tendencies in work that Bourdieu wrote primarily for a wider audience. Field theory concepts are not, as Hallin and Muhlmann suggest, exhausted by Bourdieu's own reflections on journalism and neoliberalism. Indeed, Bourdieu affirmed this methodological principle himself, cautioning against a formulaic application of "field theory" analyses from one social context to another (Bourdieu & Wacquant, 1992). Concepts like journalistic habitus, field and doxa need to be adapted to the particular social conjuncture, rather than mechanically applied in accordance with Bourdieu's own empirical analyses. And they need to be dialectically alert to a wider hegemonic universe, beyond the self-contained orbit of the journalistic field.

Journalism, ideology and politics

I am especially interested in critically understanding an enduring journalistic tendency to assume an ideologically charged stance that is enacted as ideologically or politically indifferent. This habitus embodies the basic discourse of post-ideological neoliberalism: neoliberal logics and assumptions are internalized but construed as objectively necessary and politically neutral. The argument recalls the Birmingham School's work of the 1970s. Hall, Critcher, Jefferson, Clarke and Roberts (2013) likewise insist on the need for an analysis of journalism and media that passes through journalists' own professional ideologies and practices, instead of simply casting them as the servants and dupes of capital. They argue the media's role in producing a regime of social objectivity is best explained as a systematic product of mundane journalistic routines and practices, rather than through journalists' explicit identification with a unitary political ideology. Journalists consecrate an existing social imaginary not simply by parroting the discourses of the ruling class, but by practicing the codes of objective and impartial journalism: balancing different sources against each other, but in a fashion that implicitly constructs some perspectives as more agreeable and reasonable than others. Political differences within the social formation are repeatedly staged, but backgrounded by the assumption of a fundamental social consensus that represses the conflictual logic of the political (Muhlmann, 2010).

The allusion to the journalism culture of 1970s Britain perhaps suggests some immediate objections. Doesn't my line of argument miss one of the most obvious legacies of neoliberal political economy: the emergence of a hyper-commercial news culture that increasingly rewards theatrical, opinionated and partisan styles of journalism (Hallin, 2006)? How does it account for the more explicitly antagonistic character of contemporary journalism? Much has certainly changed since journalism's "high modernist" (Hallin, 1992) period. The principles of journalistic objectivity and neutrality are no longer the straightforward propositions they might have been in the past, for either journalists or audiences. And the image of the journalist as a trusted public servant, a professional identity that "appear[s] to most of the society to be genuinely 'above politics'" (Hallin, 1992, p. 15), is now rather quaint. However, it would be a mistake to cast the old modernist imaginary as irrelevant, especially if we look beyond the US context that exemplified the changes identified by Hallin. Cross-national surveys document journalists' ongoing affinity to modernist logics in different countries. Objectivity, accuracy, balance, political detachment and the watchdog principle are still important tenets of journalism practice (Hanitzsch et al., 2011), even within a journalistic universe transformed by neoliberalism. As Zelizer (2004) suggests, appeals to "truth", "facts", "reality" and "objectivity" continue to be crucial "God-terms" of journalism practice, despite decades of cultural studies research highlighting the ideologically embedded nature of journalists' epistemology (pp. 186–187).

The cultural studies critique of journalism has, in one sense, become common-sensical. Savvy and cynical audiences (Andrejevic, 2010) deconstruct and ironize journalism's "naïve" epistemology. Students come to class already knowing journalistic objectivity is a sham. However, even if these impressions capture something, professional journalism cultures are still internally regulated by the assumption that a commitment to the professional and occupational ideology of journalism (Deuze, 2005) should override identification with any *political* ideology. The notion that journalism should aim to be objective, impartial, balanced and neutral is still inculcated in the education and socialization of journalists, even if most have absorbed enough post-modernist doxa to ritually concede that absolute objectivity is impossible. These normative commitments hold even when journalists move between reportorial and opinionated registers, the fidelity to a journalistic habitus outlawing any crude identification with political ideology. What endures across genres, as a misrecognized form of political and ideological commitment, is journalistic identification with "the public" (Higgins, 2008) – still the "God term of the press, the term without which the press does not make any sense" (Carey, 1997c, p. 218). The appeal routinely conceals the fundamental political antagonisms within the public (Dahlberg, 2007; Mouffe, 2005), obscuring conflict and differences behind the mythical image of a unified polity (Muhlmann, 2010).

Journalism and market realism

Aune's concept of market realism offers a productive resource for analysing a mode of neoliberal identification that speaks to a realist, rather than ideological and doctrinal, sensibility (see also Fisher, 2009). Indeed, he troubles the distinction between realism and ideology, arguing that a realist style is a marked feature of market ideologies. "Realism is the default rhetoric for defenders of the free market" (Aune, 2001, p. 40), he suggests, discernible in a rhetorical style linking Adam Smith, Richard

Posner, Ronald Reagan and Newt Gingrich. Economic arguments in favour of the market are typically *"styled* in a 'realistic' way. They reflect a worldview pleased with itself for 'seeing through' the pretensions of poets, dreamers, and romantics" (p. 40). By definition, there is nothing abstruse or ornate about the "realist style"; rather it works through "familiar topoi or rhetorical templates" (p. 39) articulated in a "plain style" that "profess[es] to see the world clearly" (p. 41). Realism is, consequently, an "antirhetorical rhetoric", because it "denies...its own 'rhetoricity'" (p. 42): by claiming direct access to how things really are, conscious persuasion is deemed redundant. "Within the realist imaginary, the 'rhetorical' is always the 'merely rhetorical' and the attribute of one's political opponents: those 'prisoners of verbal illusions' (p. 40) who lack the 'no-nonsense' (p. 41) clarity of the realist worldview".[4]

Aune did not purposefully explore the relationship between journalism and market ideology, but, if he did, he might have highlighted the resonances between the realist style and the journalistic doxa and habitus. Journalists' normative commitment to an anti-ideological ideology bears an obvious affinity to Aune's notion of an "antirhetorical rhetoric". Within a journalistic imaginary, "ideology" and "rhetoric" are signifiers of that which distort and obstruct the pursuit of journalistic truth. They represent two of the most offensive slights imaginable within the universe of the professional journalist, for they signify exaggerated truth claims and manipulative "agendas" that should be anathema to the truth-seeking journalist. The journalist should protect "the public" against such tendentiousness, not by ignoring it, but by making sure that the contestability of such truth claims is challenged. My portrait may seem removed from a world of polarized journalism and labour conditions where many journalists have time for little more than modifying press releases. Yet, this doxa endures even in journalistic identities that would otherwise make a nonsense of the idea of a journalism that disavows ideology. Think of the "straight-talking, no bullshit, tell it like it is" realist posture of a journalist/broadcaster like Fox News's Bill O'Reilly (see Connolly, 2008). His signature "no-spin zone" interviews, alongside Fox's general branding slogan of "fair and balanced", suggests an enduring identification with a modernist style, however absurd its enactment. Modernist logics are articulated with aggressive watchdog logics (Louw, 2005), spawning a routinized combination of personality-driven, opinionated and traditional journalistic registers.

The resonances between journalistic and neoliberal logics can be partly understood, therefore, as a convergence of realist styles and dispositions. The claim necessitates disarticulating elements of Aune's analysis from its primarily US bearings. American political and cultural identification with the free market is embedded in a particular national mythos (Connolly, 2008; Gray, 1998a) that cannot be transposed mechanically to other cultural contexts. If the excesses of American cultural identification with free-market capitalism were to be taken as the benchmark for "neoliberalism in action", practices in other countries would be too quickly read as antidotes to neoliberalism (much like the explicit codes of the UK class system allow other countries to tell themselves they do not have class systems of their own). We would simply point to an American denunciation of welfare-state entitlements available elsewhere and console ourselves that we are not really neoliberal(ized) at all.

Aune's concept of market realism also needs rethinking from the perspective of post-ideological neoliberalism. We can differentiate between two ideal type realist styles: a belligerent realism aligned with a discourse of antagonistic neoliberalism (the combative realism of Bill O'Reilly) and a pragmatic realism aligned with the third way logic of post-ideological neoliberalism (see Chapter 2). Those articulating a post-ideological identity have a particular interest in communicating their realist credentials as a point of difference from the evangelical free-market identity of others. Their realism is articulated as conciliatory and consensual, lest a more aggressive realist style appear too zealous and overbearing. The journalistic habitus enacts an analogous mix of the realist and the pragmatic, similarly inclined to eschew the zeal and inflationary claims of others. Both dispositions have little time for those who question the common-sense antenna and economic correctness of the realist imaginary: its grasp of "realities" and "facts" obscured and wished away by others. And both are inclined to deny their own rhetoricity, inhabiting an imaginary where the realist assertion is always juxtaposed with the "merely" rhetorical arguments of others (p. 42).

The crisis and the market realist style: *The Irish Times's* Stephen Collins

This section brings the different conceptual elements of the chapter together in an empirically grounded way. I want to explore how a version of Aune's market realist style, adapted to the logic of post-ideological neoliberalism, informs how the Irish journalist Stephen Collins has represented the economic and social crisis.

Collins occupies a prestigious place within the Irish journalistic field, as the political editor for the de facto national "paper of record" *The Irish Times*. The paper is routinely attributed with a mythical "left-liberal" identity on social and economic issues, partly given credence by high-profile columnists like Fintan O'Toole and Vincent Browne. Moreover, its independent trust-based ownership structure gives it a relative journalistic autonomy from economic field pressures, at least compared to media outlets embedded in transnational corporate structures (Ellis, 2011). However, during the Celtic Tiger years, the paper's institutional and editorial habitus exemplified the logic of post-ideological neoliberalism (Phelan, 2009). It shunned the "vulgar" embrace of market ideology, while at the same time pragmatically affirming the rightness of neoliberal policies. And its fortunes were deeply embedded in the wider political economy, its property and business supplements booming in tandem with unprecedented economic growth (see further discussion in Chapter 8).

A MA politics graduate from University College Dublin, Collins joined *The Irish Times* staff in January 2006, having previously worked as a political correspondent for the *Irish Press* and *Sunday Tribune* (*The Irish Times*, 2005). His journalistic disposition as political editor is structured by its relative closeness with agents in the political field. On the one hand, his political journalistic habitus assumes an official distance from government and the state in keeping with fourth-estate conventions. Yet, on the other hand, the political journalist's "semi-insider" status cultivates a "de facto symbiotic relationship with politicians" and their press handlers, often rendering journalists "accomplices in the impression management game" (Louw, 2005, p. 29; see also Champagne & Marchetti, 2005; Darras, 2005).

Collins's closeness to the political field is illustrated by his authorship of a number of books on Irish political parties and leaders (*The Irish Times*, 2005). One traced the history of the now disbanded Progressive Democrats: the minor party of two coalition governments in the 1990s and 2000s and Ireland's most ardently pro–free-market party of the last 30 years. The affinities of habitus between the political and journalistic fields were further evident in the biographical circumstances governing his appointment. Collins was appointed to *The Irish Times* under the editorship of Geraldine Kennedy, a member of Parliament for the Progressive Democrats from 1987 to 1989, later serving in her own right as the paper's political correspondent and political editor. The period of Collins's appointment coincided with a more general impression of a shift to the "right" at the paper (H. Browne, 2006), symbolized in recent times by the appointment of two economics editors with neoliberal-friendly CVs, their backgrounds arguably closer to the economic field than the journalistic field. Marc Coleman was the paper's economics editor from 2005 to 2007, having previously worked as a policy official at the Irish Department of Finance and the European Central Bank

(Coleman, 2014). And Dan O'Brien was economics editor from 2010 to 2013, formerly working as "a senior economist and editor at the intelligence unit of the *Economist* magazine" (*The Irish Times*, 2014).

To get a representative sense of how market realist signifiers are operating in Collins's journalism, I constructed a sample of 457 *The Irish Times* articles from January 1, 2008 to May 25, 2103, sourced from the Factiva database using the search terms "Stephen Collins" and "economy". The sample includes a mix of textual genres consistent with the different aspects of Collins's political editor role. Some are news reports written or co-authored by Collins. Others are explicitly coded as analysis or opinion pieces, typically weekly assessments of the latest political news – the space where Collins offers his most pointed contributions. The sample covers a period of major economic and social dislocation in Ireland, intersecting with the dynamics of the wider financial crisis. Some of the most notable events included "the Irish government's historically unprecedented decision, in 2008, to offer a blanket guarantee on deposits and bonds in six banks" (Titley, 2013, p. 293); the November 2010 "bailout" of the Irish banking system (now reconstituted as a sovereign debt crisis) by the troika of the European Commission, International Monetary Fund (IMF) and European Central Bank; and the Irish state's exit from the bailout scheme in November 2013, generating news hype about the miraculous "Irish turnaround" (see further discussion in Chapter 8).

I examined the 457 articles, amounting to a corpus size of 367,344 words, using the concordance software Wordsmith.[5] This enabled me to quickly establish how often particular signifiers were used and how they were articulated in context. This elementary quantitative method has its obvious epistemological limits; my selective searches can hardly claim to capture the internal heterogeneity of Collins's journalism. Nonetheless, this approach allows me to document how key signifiers of a market realist style are inscribed in Collins's construction of the crisis. And it provides a useful empirical platform for making sense of an individual Collins article before I critically assess the neoliberalized character of his journalistic habitus and doxa.

Absences and omissions

The term "neoliberal" – including its various hyphenated and lexical variants – is used only once in the sample. It is not voiced by Collins directly, but attributed as a direct quote to Greek Prime Minister Antonis Samaras. In one sense, this is quite predictable: neoliberalism is more commonly cited in critical academic and activist contexts than in mainstream media discourses. Nonetheless, the near invisibility of the term is interesting given the impression that it had a new prominence in media discourses at the time – as a name for the ruptured social formation and, later, as a name for the political regimes reconstituted in the name of "austerity". The relative absence suggests a journalistic habitus averse to grand theoretical talk about "isms", an impression reinforced by Collins's single reference to "capitalism".

The terms "free market" and "capitalism" are only used once each, while "capitalist(s)" is used five times. The term "free market" is attributed to a source, while Collins cites the nominalized phrases "crony capitalism" (2009, April 25) and "crony capitalist" (2009, June 8) to criticize the excesses of the Fianna Fáil–led governments during the Celtic Tiger years. Three of the other four references to capitalist(s) refer to the Irish government's 2008 plan to introduce a new tax regime for international "venture capitalists" (as a remedy to salvage the collapsing economy), while the fourth describes how parties affiliated to the United Left Alliance are "highly critical of the capitalist system" (2011, November 23). The single reference to capitalism suggests an absence of any epochal framing of the crisis as a *capitalist* crisis. However, "crisis" is certainly a keyword of Collins's journalism, cited 421 times, alongside eight references to pluralized "crises" and 53 references to "austerity". The general categories of "economy" and "market" are cited 845 and 212 times respectively, consistent with, as we will see, Collins's repeated insistence that "the economy" is the number-one political priority.

The term "ideology" (including its lexical variants "ideological", "ideologies" and "ideologue") is used only five times. The term is either attributed directly or indirectly to sources – and on four occasions to the Labour Party leader, Eamon Gilmore. In each instance, the term is articulated pejoratively, either disavowed by a particular speaker ("this is not a matter of ideology" asserts Gilmore [2009, May 13]) or used to discredit a rival political identity. These sporadic references capture a post-ideological atmosphere that regards ideology as a negative force and refrains from naming the crisis as an ideological crisis. Tellingly, the most significant expression of global opposition to the ideological and political management of the financial crisis – the Occupy movement – was never mentioned in Collins's journalism.

The semblance of a realist style

Collins's single reference to the "free market" suggests an identity markedly different from the free-market cheerleaders analysed by Aune. Yet the outlines of a distinct market realist style are more discernible when we look at how Collins articulates the category of "realism". Even if only cited six times in the sample, the category is always signified in an affirmative way, as a virtue of good governance and sound political thinking – a virtue threatened by the unreasonable expectations of others. For example, writing in the early days of the Irish crisis in April 2008, Collins underlines the need for "a return to the realism displayed in the period after 1987", the year typically cited as a defining moment in the embryonic emergence of the Celtic Tiger:

> Social partnership [code for Ireland's neo-corporatist model] has been a cornerstone of policy for two decades but, unless there is a return to the realism displayed in the period after 1987, it could become a millstone around the Government's neck (2008, April 12).

Anticipating the December 2010 budget that took place immediately after the Troika bailout, Collins wishes for a set of "measures [that] will, hopefully, bring a sense of realism in public debate about how we get out of our grave difficulties" (2010, November 22). And, citing a February 2012 article from *The Financial Times* that favourably compares the Irish situation to Greece, he suggests "it should induce an element of realism here about how far we have come as well as how far we still have to go" (2012, February 11).

The terms "reality" (used 102 times) and "realist/realistic/realistically" (used 30 times) are articulated in diverse ways, not all of them emblematic of a market realist style. However, when linked to assessments of Irish political economy, as they often are, the message is similar. The "realist" expectation is commended over the fanciful expectations of others, and Collins leaves his imagined reader in little doubt that *now* is a time for realism in Irish politics.

To cite one micro-illustration, the declarative phrase "the reality is" is used 12 times in the sample: four times directly by Collins, seven times by government ministers and once by a Fianna Fáil parliamentarian. In each case the phrase is invoked to justify different austerity measures in the name of a collective and classless "we", perfectly capturing an affinity of journalistic field and political field subjectivities. Reflecting on the bailout conditions imposed on Ireland, Collins suggests: "The reality is that we have got to implement the EU-IMF programme as any alternative will be far worse" (2011, April 9). And, on another occasion, his frustration with those in denial of "reality" is palpable:

> The reality is that the Frankfurt way [pejorative code for the punitive bailout conditions] rather than Fine Gael or Labour way was always going to prevail, except in the fevered imaginations of those who don't know how the real world works (2011, April 1).

Anti-rhetorical rhetoric

Now, in themselves, Collins's appeals to "reality" and "realism" only tell us so much. "The real" is a God term of journalistic practice (Zelizer, 2004), and simply appealing to "reality" does not neoliberalize Collins. However, the wider political implications of his stance come clearer into view in how he articulates the category of rhetoric. Collins exemplifies "the antirhetorical rhetoric" of the realist style, because "rhetoric" is persistently attributed to those who obscure or deny his own realist assumptions. The signifier does similar policing work to the category of ideology: both are always the attribute of the "Other" (Eagleton, 1991).

The term "rhetoric" (the variant "rhetorical" is not cited) is used 28 times in the sample, nearly always constructing unflattering representations of those unanchored in "reality".[6] Collins has little time for politicians who engage in what his *Irish Times* colleague Harry McGee calls, in a similar vein, "hyperbolic and ramped-up rhetoric" (2012, July 27). Before his entry to government in 2011, the "anti-Frankfurt rhetoric" of Labour Party leader Eamon Gilmore is a target of regular criticism: "Gilmore's anti-Frankfurt rhetoric…may win some votes for his party, [but] it will be no help when he gets into government and the actual attempt to renegotiate the deal begins" (2011, February 5). Collins worries that Fine Gael has been infected with a similar virus in May 2010, in what one headline describes as "Fine Gael's dangerous flirtation with populist rhetoric" (2012, May 15).[7] And after the election of a new Fine Gael/Labour coalition government in 2011, and the announcement of a €755 million cut to a capital expenditure programme, Collins affirms the wisdom of his own worldview under the headline "Pre-election rhetoric meets post-election reality": "the Coalition parties are finding out now that the kind of choices they are faced with in office is making their pre-election rhetoric look foolish" (2011, November 11).

The "common good" against the "vested interests"

As a supplement to the corpus-assisted results, let us look at how this reality/rhetoric dualism textures a July 2011 opinion piece by Collins, published under the headline "Political leaders must stand up to vested interests" (2011, July 1). The article puts the "current crisis" in national historical context, maintaining that "despite all the doom and gloom of the past few years the atmosphere today is not nearly as hopeless as that which prevailed in the 1950s or the 1980s, and living standards are immeasurably better". At the same time, Collins suggests "courage" and "resolute action" are needed to face up to the current crisis and "our political system would benefit if politicians start telling voters the facts".

He constructs a clear discursive antagonism between those committed to the "common good" and unnamed "vested interests" making unreasonable demands against the state:

> Of course, the challenge involved in getting the country to that happy state when the economy is back on an even keel should not be underestimated. Nonetheless, it can be achieved as long as our political leaders have the courage to stand firm in the face of vested interests who seek to put sectional advantage ahead of the common good.

Collins's denunciation of "vested interests" folds into a criticism of how Irish media have represented the crisis, a theme repeatedly voiced in his journalism (see 2013, June 1). Vested interests are essentially indulged by the media, normalizing an exaggerated atmosphere of "doom and gloom" in Irish "public discourse" (2011, July 1). "The problem is that vested interests of all kinds often put forward hard cases to cloak their aspirations and tend to win media sympathy in the public relations battles with government". Against the media's easy identification with sectional interests, Collins underlines the importance of "identifying the common good and pursuing it relentlessly". And "in order to achieve a political consensus on the kind of action required, the Government needs to ensure that the measures taken are fair and perceived to be fair". He underlines the latter point: "ensuring that those at the top are seen to take a hit is very important in paving the way for a consensus on the wider budgetary action".

Collins's intolerance of exaggerated talk extends to other targets, already familiar to us from earlier illustrations. He has no time for those who want to "play the blame game" (Dyer-Witheford & Compton, 2011). "The tendency to blame the EU and the International Monetary Fund for our difficulties has become a dangerous trend which only obscures the fact that swingeing cuts in Government spending are necessary for the country's survival" (2011, July 1). Thankfully, "since confronting the reality of office", the Coalition has "dropped that kind of talk", which "fostered the notion that we had become victims of some malign conspiracy by the EU or the European Central Bank designed to punish us". Even so, that talk has now "taken on a life of its own fuelled by the needless row over the interest rate the country is paying on the bailout". Collins ends the article by affirming his favourite realist trope, suggesting that reform of the Irish political system "might encourage all of those elected to the Oireachtas [the Irish Parliament] to behave responsibly and stop fostering unrealistic expectations".

Neoliberalization and the politics of the journalistic habitus

So, what can we take from this brief analysis of Collins's journalism? How can we extrapolate from a specific example, embedded in Irish particulars, to say something more general about how a mainstream journalistic habitus identifies with neoliberal logics?

Collins's journalism exemplifies the discourse of post-ideological neoliberalism. On the one hand, he refrains from any self-consciously ideological commitment to the free market, capitalism or neoliberalism. Indeed, his supplementary emphasis on policy measures that are "fair and perceived to be fair" articulates a moral concern for the collective, quite distinct from an archetypal neoliberalism hostile to the public good.[8] However, on the other hand, his steadfast support for austerity policies signifies a journalistic identity (see Andersson, 2010; Dyer-Witheford & Compton, 2012; Harvey, 2010) that envisions a reconstituted version of "business as usual" as the only viable response to the crisis. His neoliberalism is of the naturalized rather than the normative kind (Hay, 2004) – the product of a journalistic habitus attuned to "how the real world works", rather than some abstract ideological and doctrinal prescription. He internalizes a logic of market determinism in a pragmatic, if fatalistic, register, symptomatic of what Fisher (2009) calls the imaginary of capitalist realism.[9]

In Collins's view, politics must now prioritize the problem of fixing "the economy" (see Chapter 8): as he observes in a July 2012 article, "everything else pales into insignificance in the face of that overwhelming task" (Collins, 2012). But politics is also construed as separate from the market and economy (O'Rourke & Hogan, 2014), his "modernist" inclination to assume separate ontological domains (Grossberg, 2010, p. 103) collapsing into a neoliberal desire to keep politics out of the economy (see Chapter 7). Collins's radar as a political journalist is focused on addressing the concrete problem of Ireland's "sovereign debt crisis". He has only impatience for those who want to keep pointing out how, as Blyth (2013a) puts it, the problem "started with the banks and will end with the banks" (p. 5). In the temporal horizon of the journalistic field (Meyer, 2002), these observations are "old news": facts to be dealt with rather than existentially contested and debated. At the same time, Collins tries to assuage anxieties about the current crisis with a comforting narrative of Irish modernity: a story of how far "we" have progressed. His primary referent for the current crisis is the Irish austerity regime of the late 1980s, constructing a political morality tale that can only see the Irishness of the story and annihilates the differences between past and present (Kinsella, 2012). Critical questions about the structural condition of contemporary capitalist societies have no place in his analysis. "The dominance of capitalism constitutes a sort of invisible horizon" (Fisher cited in Fisher & Gilbert, 2013, p. 90) beyond the factual purview of the political journalist.

Collins articulates an identity consistent with the normative codes and doxa of political journalism, eschewing overt support for any particular political party. Yet, his realist style is deeply political. It signifies a political logic "directed towards anti-political ends" (Barry, 2002, p. 268), which depoliticize the economy and delegitimize the critics of austerity.[10] Within Collins's universe, anyone envisioning alternatives to austerity is either fooling him or herself or is a cynical opportunist, happy to cultivate a "rhetorical" and "populist" hysteria for his or her own self-serving strategic ends. The implication seems to be that politics itself should be regarded with suspicion, because it risks amplifying an irresponsible public mood that, ramped up by a knee-jerk anti-austerity media, thinks it can break from the "realities" of the present. For Collins, the "common good" is an object to be factually determined, rather than a site of fundamental political contestation over how the common good is to be articulated.

Previous research suggests Collins's journalistic subjectivity is a representative one. Contrary to Collins's image of an anti-austerity media,[11] Mercille's (2013a) analysis of reportage and opinion pieces in three Irish newspapers documents how the majority of articles voiced support for austerity policies, with scant coverage of alternative perspectives (see also Silke & Preston, 2011). Titley (2013) discusses how the activist media collective "crisisjam" set out to interrogate "five key mantras" (p. 298) of the dominant neoliberal narrative ahead of the 2010 Irish budget, all clearly discernible in Collins's journalism: "The country is broke (bankrupt); We're all in this together; We have to move on, going forward; The tough love of the IMF/EU is actually good after a period of 'mismanagement'; [and] (the Ur-mantra) There is no alternative" (p. 299). Critical interrogation of Collins's journalism is routinely evident in readers' online comments, which are sometimes scathing about its ideological complicity.[12] And, in a popular-culture setting, the hackneyed nature of the Irish media and political establishment's appeal to "reality" was mocked in a high-profile television appearance by the comedy troupe Après Match (RTE, 2010) a few weeks after the November 2010 bailout, in the figure of a buffoonish finance minister appealing to "the reality of the situation".

Situated within the cultural politics of the present, Collins's journalism is, in one sense, the very embodiment of the neoliberal doxa "there is no alternative". He is so embedded in the rationality of a neoliberalized reality that he cannot see any outside and disparages those who think they can. His realist antenna is focused on pragmatically negotiating a given terrain of institutional politics – the empirically concrete world where the banking crisis has been politically remade into a crisis of the state (the reasons why this happened magically disappearing in the appeal to "reality"). Abstract reflections on the question of the political are not his thing, as symbolized by his indifference to the Occupy protests. He might be better described, following Ranciere (1999), as *The Irish Times*' "police" editor, rather than political editor, because of his stuckness in a "social vision that cannot see beyond the given ways of doing, ways of being, and ways of saying" (p. 29).

Yet, Muhlmann (2010) reminds us how the wish to escape the conflictual logic of the political has been part of journalism's history. It is embodied in a normative vision of journalism that privileges a logic of unity and consensus over a logic of division and conflict. And it is articulated in a particular normative vision of democracy, embedded in the pluralist conventions and assumptions of liberal democratic regimes (Karppinen, 2008). Differences and conflict within the community are acknowledged, consistent with a journalistic ideal of representing "a perfect plurality of points of view" (Muhlmann, 2010, p. 222). But these differences are ultimately incorporated into an institutional expression of the "public interest" and "common good", which all sectional interests are rendered subordinate to (except, in Collins's case, the "vested interests" of capital). Producing a reasoned consensus in the name of the democratic community is presupposed as the telos of mediated political deliberation, grounded in a liberal democratic confidence that the different "parts" of the community have been "counted" (Ranciere, 1999, 2009) and that all the journalistic "facts" have been considered.

Muhlmann helps us grasp dimensions of Collins's habitus that go beyond the charge of neoliberal collusion. Collins is not identifying with any neoliberal credo or doctrine or such, even if he privileges "the economy" as a social object and even if he renders the national polity subordinate to the "likes" and "dislikes" of "the market" (Silke & Preston, 2011). Rather, he is identifying with a logic of the "common good", a logic of the "national interest" and a logic of the state that has *internalized* a logic of market determinism (see Chapter 8). He wants to align those logics with the "unified public" – the "we" – of journalism (Jutel, 2013), even reading the "surge in the birth rate" revealed in the 2011 census as a sign of how "the broad mass of people have more faith in the country's future than the prophets of doom who so often dominate the public discourse" (2011, July 2). Political divisions within the national community are clearly still apparent, amplified by what he sees as the media's exaggerated portrayal of the crisis (2013, June 1). Yet, these divisions are accounted for in a *moralizing register* that discredits their political standing, for one side of the argument has the monopoly on reality, reason and "the facts", the other side amounts to little more than incoherent noise and braying – the "rhetoric" of fantasists unhinged from reality and "vested interests" cloaking their self-interested aspirations in the language of publicness. As Mouffe's (2005) discussion of post-politics suggests, "in place of a struggle between 'right and left' we are faced with a struggle between 'right and wrong'" (p. 5) – a clear-cut antagonism between a reasoned political subjectivity that accepts the reality of the world as it "is" and a deluded subjectivity that denies "the facts" of the situation. In Collins's universe, to be opposed to austerity is to be *for* the "vested interests" and against the "common good", the differences between one interest and another annihilated in Collins's antagonistic representation.

Collins's journalism is embedded in the political and ideological rationality of neoliberalism. Yet, politicizing this journalistic habitus and doxa will require us to do more than naming it as "neoliberal". Rather, it will necessitate the politicization of a wider set of dispositional tendencies that structure journalistic and public identification with the discourse of post-ideological neoliberalism and which regulate the journalistic field more generally. Most importantly, it will require us to politicize how journalists and others articulate "the public" and the "common good" – sometimes by obscuring political divisions within the community in the name of a false unity, sometimes by recasting legitimate political divisions as a morality play between right and wrong, sometimes by locking the enactment of political differences into theatrical spectacles that "entrench" the political (Bloom & Dallyn, 2011) and sometimes by embedding the discussion of political economy into an inward-looking national frame that, in the Irish case, is paradoxically tied to a discourse of modernization (Cleary, 2007). What might be enabled, as a normative and ethical counterpoint, is the possibility of a radical pluralist (Connolly, 2005) journalism: a truly *"political* community" (Muhlmann, 2010, p.185) capable of staging its legitimate political divisions within the common space of journalism (Markham, 2014). Opposition to austerity might be recognized as embodying a collective desire for a radically different kind of society, rather than morally condemned for its failure to submit to the realist imperatives of the existing social order and the outrageousness of its appearing on the media stage without a fully formed political alternative. The journalistic field becomes a space of enabling the political imagination (Connolly, 2008; Norval, 2007) rather than policing and repressing it.

Conclusion

This chapter explored how we might critically understand the relationship between neoliberalism and journalism, questioning the adequacy of the typical political economy analysis. I drew on Bourdieu's concept of habitus and Aune's concept of market realism to examine the particular resonances between journalists' realist sensibilities and the realist logics of post-ideological neoliberalism. I then explored the argument empirically, based on a selective analysis of how the economic and social crisis has been represented by *The Irish Times'* journalist Stephen Collins. Rather than one-dimensionally reading Collins as a neoliberal, I suggested his identification with neoliberal logics is grounded in an anti-political logic that is emblematic of post-ideological neoliberalism but also historically embedded in the political rationality of the journalistic field. Instead of being a caricatured cheerleader for "the market", Collins identifies primarily with the condition of an Irish state, locked into the structures of neoliberal internationalism (Harmes, 2012).

The relationship between national logics, internationalist logics, neoliberal logics and the object called "the economy" will be revisited in Chapter 8. However, let us now consider the relationship between neoliberalism, media and the political from a different angle, already prefigured in Collins's image of a public discourse dominated by vested interests. Chapter 6 reflects on the authority of logics of self-interest in contemporary media cultures via an analysis of the mediated construction of the so-called "climategate" scandal in November 2009.

6
Media Cultures, Anti-politics and the "Climategate" Affair

The hacking of thousands of emails from the Climate Research Unit (CRU) at the University of East Anglia in November 2009 was widely represented as a scandalous moment for climate change scientists. According to the narrative originally articulated in the blogosphere, the documents showed how CRU researchers had "manipulated" data to conceal evidence at odds with the assumption of anthropogenic climate change. The revelation resulted in the widespread publication of news stories questioning the integrity of climate change scientists, though "multiple investigations concluded that no fraud or scientific misconduct had occurred" (Maibach et al., 2012, p. 289). The event dubbed "climategate" exemplified the "cultural politics" of climate change (Boykoff, 2013, p. 800), the "gate" suffix communicating the intended aura of scandal and wrongdoing.[1] It gave new life to the idea of a vibrant debate between an "imperious" scientific establishment and "brave" heterodox scientists, belying the impression that the science has been "settled". And it politicized the domain of scientific practice itself, eliding any meaningful distinction between science and politics among those most gripped by the scandal.

This chapter explores how neoliberal logics structured the blogosphere and mainstream media representation of the CRU controversy. I begin not with a discussion of previous research on media and climate change. Rather, I reflect on the negative standing of politics and politicians in contemporary culture and the role of media practices in normalizing a culture of political cynicism. Why preface the analysis of a media controversy about climate change science by reflecting on contemporary perceptions of politics? Because it allows us to explore a structural homology between media discourses that position agents in the political field and scientific field as self-interested actors. Both discourses are, I argue, partly made possible by the hegemonic authority of neoliberal logics. Politicians are, in the familiar refrain, simply "in it for themselves", engendering a general cultural scepticism about the possibility of deliberating on and institutionalizing the common good. Scientists may, in comparison, be regarded as more trustworthy, despite a "certain de-sacralization of science and scientific institutions in the media" (Carvalho, 2007, p. 236) in recent times. Yet the climategate scandal was driven by an analogous construction of scientists as self-interested creatures, manipulating research data for their own venal reasons. Both representations are implicated in the rise of neoliberalism, especially in the form of a rational choice theoretic worldview that intellectually consecrates the assumption of self-interested action (Hay, 2007). And both are emblematic of a neoliberal antagonism to agents aligned to the state (see Chapters 2 and 7), exemplified in the CRU case by discourses highlighting scientists' interest in maintaining taxpayer-funded research regimes.

The representation of climate change scientists as self-interested agents was most forcefully articulated by the so-called climate change "sceptics" and "deniers" who broke the story. The charge was articulated in strident opposition to a state-centred regime of climate change "hysteria" and "alarmism": the harbinger of what some have called, in an appropriate nod to Hayek, a "green Road to Serfdom" (Bradley, 2012). The climategate scandal transcended a narrow focus on questions of scientific communication.[2] Rather, it gave publicity to quintessentially neoliberal arguments about the nature of the state and the corrupting effects of governmental regimes, amplified by their resonances with hegemonic news values (Berglez, 2011; Carvalho, 2007). And it was institutionally mediated by the same libertarian and conservative think-tank infrastructure that had facilitated the neoliberal political ascendency of the 1970s and 1980s (see Chapter 2) – the constituency that, as the ventriloquists of corporate interests, has been most vocal in belittling climate change science over the past 20 years (Banning, 2009; Mirowski, 2013; Nerlich, 2010). Following Carvalho (2007), my approach addresses the relative neglect of the "role of ideology in the media representation" (p. 225) of science, interrogating a sensibility that wants to expunge politics and ideology from the discussion of climate change. On the contrary, I argue that we cannot understand the climategate scandal independently of the generative power of neoliberal and rational choice logics and the anti-political dynamics of neoliberalized regimes.

Before I look at the mediated construction of the CRU controversy more closely, my argument takes two turns. First, I reflect on the relationship between rational choice theory, neoliberalism and politics, drawing on Colin Hay's (2007) analysis of how rational choice assumptions engender a culture of anti-politics. And, second, I examine how media and journalistic practices amplify a culture of public cynicism, intuitively projecting self-interested motivations onto politicians and other public actors. That groundwork complete, I then return to the CRU case, beginning with a discussion of existing research on the controversy. I follow that with an analysis of how neoliberal and rational choice logics structured its initial blogosphere and mainstream media representation – in constructing the event as a "scandal".

Politics, anti-politics and rational choice theory

As discussed in Chapter 1, neoliberalism represents a composite of different economic theories: neoclassical economics, Austrian economics, supply-side economics and monetarism. Among them is rational choice theory, a contemporary reformulation of a 19th century neoclassical view of human beings as utility-maximizing agents. Rational choice theory is not simply interchangeable with neoliberalism. Nor does it take the form of a "monolithic theory that all practitioners are presumed to accept" (Green & Shapiro, 1994, p. 13). Topper (2005) cautions against making "sweeping generalizations" (p. 207) about the ideological temper of rational choice analysis (see also Hay, 2004). Like its methodological cousin "game theory", rational choice sometimes advances "interpretative and transformative aims" (Topper, 2005, p. 207) aligned with hermeneutic, critical realist, poststructuralist and Marxist (Aune, 2001) sensibilities. At its best, Topper suggests rational choice analysis illuminates the problem of "collective action" (Heath, 2000), highlighting the rational dimensions of actions that might otherwise be dismissed as irrational. The problem is when rational choice principles assume the standing of a "'grand' or 'universal' theory", where everything is explained "in terms of market logic" and instrumental motives (Topper, 2005, p. 209; see also Bourdieu, 2005b; Green & Shapiro, 1994). When elevated to a "metaphysics" aligned to free-market ideology, Aune (2001) suggests they "become dangerous" – exemplars of a "realist style" (see Chapter 5) that is "fundamentally corrosive to public order" (p. 46).

Hay (2007) traces the normalization of an anti-politics culture to the intellectual ascent of "public choice theory", the variant of rational choice theory used to analyse politics.[3] He argues we cannot understand contemporary antagonisms to politics and politicians independently of the generalized common-sense authority of a theoretical paradigm that – as evidenced by the field of political marketing (Savigny, 2008) – "models political behaviour on the simplifying premise that political actors [including voters] are instrumental, self-serving and efficient in maximizing" their own desired interests (p. 96). Public choice theory and neoliberalism have "something of a natural affinity" (p. 97), he contends (Mirowski, 2013). Cleverly reappropriating a Keynesian rhetoric of "market failure", Buchanan branded public choice theory a "science of political failure" (cited in Hay, 2007, p. 96), documenting how public policies, nominally intended to serve "the public good", fail on their own terms. Hay recognizes how, in one sense, public choice theory encourages a "healthy cynicism" (p. 100) about the motivations of politicians and public officials – an antidote to overly optimistic discourses about the state's capacity to deliver on its commitments. However, as it gained authority during the capitalist and state crises of the 1970s, it helped naturalize a neoliberal portrait of the state, fomenting a general cultural "scepticism over the inherent meaningfulness of 'the public', 'public interest', or 'general welfare'" (Amadae, 2003, p. 4). From the perspective of the present, Hay (2007) suggests public choice theory's suspicion of politics has been universalized: "to attribute 'political' motives to an actor's conduct is now invariably to question that actor's honesty, integrity or capacity to deliver an outcome that reflects anything other than his or her material self-interest" (p. 1).

In its neoliberal articulation, the rhetoric of rational choice theory is anti-political and anti-state. However, institutionalizing its logics within the field of the state was itself a deeply political process. Hay (2007) identifies two distinct phases in the hegemonic convergence of public choice theory and neoliberalism which overlap with the Chapter 2 distinction between antagonistic and third way neoliberalism. First, during the period of neoliberalism's political emergence in the 1970s and 1980s – the phase of "normative neoliberalism" (p. 98) – public choice analysis provided a diagnostic of the social conjuncture that constructed the state as the problem and energized popular media narratives (Hay, 1996). Second, during the period of "normalized neoliberalism" (p. 98) – the neoliberalism of the third way – the institutional embedding of public choice logics symbolized a depoliticization of economy, but on necessitarian grounds, quite different from the combative ideological prescriptions of normative neoliberals like Thatcher and Reagan. One important theoretical supplement to rational choice theory was the so-called new public management regulatory approach, which prescribes the application of "private business methods" within the provision of public services (Crouch, 2011, p. 16). It installed "the audit" as the master instrument of what Shore (2008) calls a new "generalized model (and technology) of governance" (p. 290) symptomatic of a society where everything must be checked because no one can be trusted (Power, 1997).

Hay (2007) wonders about the cumulative cultural effects when discourses "animated...by a rather pessimistic conception of the human subject" (p. 99) become hegemonic. He does not suggest we should simply "trust politicians and public servants more" (p. 161), inverting a default cynicism with a carefree optimism. Rather, he wants to "politicize" the common-sense authority of public choice logics and "make them the subject of public deliberation" (p. 161). Hay flips the standard argument about political disengagement around. Instead of blaming citizens for their political apathy (a familiar refrain in the literature), he asks: how might the image of politics normalized in public choice and neoliberal rhetoric explain why politics is seen as a "dirty word" (p. 1)?

Aune (2001) identifies two reasons for the generalized "rhetorical appeal" (p. 22) of rational choice theory as an analytical device for explaining an entire spectrum of human behaviour. First, it embodies the characteristics of what "Kenneth Burke (1968) referred to as the 'syllogistic form', in which a text appeals to a reader simply because it ties up all the loose ends, much as the classic mystery story" (p. 22). We might say it's a form especially well suited to the performative constraints of media discourse, the quick projection of a self-interested motivation seeming to immediately explain an agent's argument. Second, "it taps into the student's capacity for irony" (p. 22), nurturing an aesthetic appreciation of the unanticipated consequences of human action (Hirschman, 1991; see Chapter 7). Rational choice principles "become all-purpose templates, or rhetorical topoi, for making complex cases of political and economic behaviours understandable and explainable" (Aune, 2001, p. 46), adaptable to different contexts, extendable to new domains. Aune's description reads like a prophetic anticipation of the Freakonomics literature: neoclassical and rational choice logics repackaged into a popular culture form (Fine, 2010) that promises to "explor[e] the hidden side of everything" (Freakonomics, 2014).

Rational choice rhetoric is often articulated as a particular affective style: embodied in a performative knowingness about the true sources of human motivation.[4] There is, in one sense, nothing inherently neoliberal about this disposition. The left is just as likely as the right to project self-interested motivations; and, whether from left or right, the projection is often entirely valid. Whatever form they take, my concern is with the ideological authority of these self-interested projections as a taken-for-granted doxa for talking about the social world.

The naturalized authority of these projections cannot be understood independently of their neoliberalized resonances. Nor can they be grasped separately from their ontological and epistemological affinity with the logic of journalistic representations, namely their shared tendency to privilege explanations of individual motives over structural explanations (Bourdieu, 1998b; Carey, 1997b; Green & Shapiro, 1994).

Anti-politics and media cynicism

Hay's (2007) argument in *Why We Hate Politics* is not focused on media. Yet, he recognizes the role of media practices in reproducing a culture of anti-politics (see Hay & Stoker, 2009) and connecting popular subjectivities to "formal political processes" (Hay, 2007, p. 75). His understanding of politics does not limit itself to formal institutional domains. Similar to Laclau's generalized conception of the political (see Chapter 2), he embraces a more open-ended view of politics, breaking from "rigid disciplinary and sub-disciplinary" (Hay, 2002, p. 5) approaches that "confine themselves to the narrowly political analysis of narrowly political variables" (p. 3). In contrast, politics is sometimes narrowly equated with electoral politics in the political engagement literature, obscuring how "politics may occur in contexts not conventionally understood in such terms" (p. 77). A similarly delimited conception of politics has structured the subfield of political communication, historically more concerned with how media cover formal political events like elections, rather than the generalized political condition of the social (Barnhurst, 2011; Dahlgren, 2004).

Nonetheless, the role of media and journalistic practices in fostering a culture of political cynicism has been widely discussed in the political communication literature (Lilleker, 2006). Cappella and Jamieson (1997) criticize news media for reporting on politics in a pejorative fashion that intuitively projects morally dubious motives onto politicians. Crude psychological interpretations of politicians' behaviours become staples of political reporting, reducing politics to a strategic "game" and elections to the archetypal "horse-race" (p. 33). This journalistic disposition is symptomatic of a general "escalation in public cynicism about institutions", the cumulative outcome of a "corrosive individualism" (p. 29). These cynical projections are reinforced by journalists' fixated "focus on strategy, conflict and motives" (p. 31), displacing a healthy scepticism about public officials with a climate of "sensational watchdogism" (Louw, 2005, p. 60).

The spirit of Cappella and Jamieson's argument about US media cultures has been echoed in analyses of the spectacle-driven and aggressive nature of political journalism in other countries (see, for example, Atkinson, 2010; Blumler & Coleman, 2011; Comrie, 2012). Others offering their own version of Hay's "defence of politics" argument have attributed particular culpability to the media in debasing politics. Reflecting on the 2009 MPs expenses scandal in the UK[5], Flinders (2012) maintains the dominant media narrative constructed politicians as modern-day "folk devils": figures to be relentlessly demonized and castigated, the personification of opportunism and venality. He argues media representations of politics have become vivid symbols of a pathological tendency to cast "all politicians [as] corrupt, self-interested and untrustworthy" (p. 605). Journalistic excesses are rationalized by a regime of "monitory democracy" (Keane cited in Flinders, 2012, p. 11) that theatrically pursues its target in the name of "accountability" (p. 11). Flinders captures an aggressive journalistic posture, acting in the name of democracy, equally applicable to the bloggers who broke the climategate story. The logic of the traditional fourth-estate model was generalized, the "fifth estate" of the blogosphere insisting that the previously autonomous field of science needed to be held accountable (Holliman, 2011).

Cappella and Jamieson understand the intuitive storytelling appeal of journalistic shorthands that explain public actors' behaviour in narrow self-interested terms. They cite James Carey's observation about the long-standing importance of agents' motives and intentions in journalism narratives (Cappella & Hall Jamieson, 1997, p. 27); as Carey (1997b) puts it, "in American journalism, names make news, and explanations in the news pretty much come down to the motives of the actors in the political drama" (p. 153). There is nothing historically novel about the charge that politicians and others act in self-interested ways, Cappella and Jamieson suggest. Nor is there anything new in laments about journalistic cynicism. But these elements have been amplified by a press culture preoccupied with dramatizing conflict and scandal and reciprocated by aggressive political campaigning strategies that generate a "spiral of cynicism" between one domain and another. In this culture, winning is rendered "equivalent to advancing one's own agenda, one's own self-interest, so the actions stand not for themselves but for the motivational system that gives rise to them – narrow self-interest" (p. 34). Knee-jerk media cynicism becomes symptomatic of a crisis in the concept of the "public good" (p. 237), reinforcing the impression that politics is just another domain of marketing hype and aggressive competition.

Cappella and Jamieson recognize the emergence of a generalized culture of anti-elitism (see also Blumler & Kavanagh, 1999). Yet, they make little effort to systematically connect changes in the media representation of politics to wider social and political changes – the very changes signified by the term "neoliberalism". The register of their analysis is essentially moral: primarily concerned with the normative question of how the press might better perform its fourth-estate role within a given liberal democratic infrastructure. Chang and Glynos's (2011) examination of similar terrain takes a more expansive approach. In some respects, their analysis of how the UK MPs expenses scandal was represented in the British tabloid press supports the standard media cynicism thesis. Justified indignation about the abuses of the expenses system by particular MPs was transfigured into a media demonization of all politicians (for a first-hand account, see Mullin, 2011). Yet, unlike the media-centric critiques of Cappella and Jamieson and Flinders, Chang and Glynos (2011) balk from interpreting the anti-politician media rhetoric as symptomatic of a blanket anti-politics (see also Segbers, 2012) – as if there were not good politically engaged reasons for the popular hostility to the expenses regime. Instead, they ask: *how* were the tabloids political and *how* was the mediated construction of the scandal underpinned by particular normative fantasies of how society should be organized?[6]

Chang and Glynos's (2011) approach is suggestive. Instead of simply morally condemning sensationalized media discourses, they encourage us to think about their political valence. Put another way, if events like the MPs expenses scandal are indicative of a generalized distrust of politics, they ask us to consider: how might we understand the *politics* of anti-politics (see also Newman, 2011a)? Reoriented to the empirical concerns of this chapter, this means grasping the political conditions of possibility of the climategate scandal as a mediated political event. Rather than simply dismissing the affair as the predictable work of climate change "sceptics" and "deniers", we need to grasp the regime of truth that made the event possible and gave it traction as a news story, giving it some credibility among those otherwise convinced of the fact of anthropogenic climate change. That regime cannot be grasped independently of the neoliberal turn and the naturalization of an anti-politics and anti-elitist imaginary. In short, the projections of venal self-interest documented in the political and media cynicism literatures were transposed to climate change scientists and the entire infrastructure of climate change policy.

Previous research on climategate

If there are obvious differences between the media representations of politicians and the media representations of climate chance scientists, there were also clear parallels in the climategate scandal. In the initial blogosphere framing of the story, "scientists were portrayed as being in cahoots with politicians, with both reaping financial benefits" (Nerlich, 2010, p. 423). The impression was of a scientific "scam" and "fraud", ultimately at the expense of the taxpayers (Nerlich, 2010). Six subsequent investigations exonerated the scientists from any charge of malpractice, though their "bunker mentality" and lack of openness was censured (Grundmann, 2013, p. 86; Ravetz, 2011). Evaluating the email transcripts from an ethical perspective, Grundmann (2013) finds several failings, concluding the scientists sometimes "acted strategically, showing self-interest and zeal" (p. 86). Here is not the place for a detailed overview of the CRU scandal or a comprehensive analysis of all the elements that might interest media scholars. However, let's briefly consider the basic details of the case with reference to previous research on the issue.

The hacked files were initially posted to a Russian server on November 17, 2009, and then brought to the attention of different climate science blogs (Pearce, 2010). The files contained private email correspondence between a team of CRU scientists over a 13-year period, extending to conversations with international collaborators. One scientist, Phil Jones, the director of the research centre, became the focal point of media attention (Pearce, 2010). The original story was widely attributed to the blog *Watts Up With That*, a site popular with climate change sceptics (see further discussion below). The initial blog post of November 19 contained the email extracts that dominated the media narrative. They included colourful passages where the CRU scientists reflected on the machinations of the academic peer review process; offered candid observations about fellow scientists; talked about how they might collaborate to discredit a journal that gave too much credibility to sceptics' arguments; and discussed how their research data could be cordoned off from freedom of information requests previously made against the Centre (Grundmann, 2013; Pearce, 2010; Ravetz, 2011). Most provocatively, Jones invoked the word "trick" to describe how different data sets could be reconciled for presentational purposes: "to hide the decline" that would otherwise be apparent (cited in Pearce, 2010, p. 2249). Nerlich (2010) suggests Jones was simply using "standard mathematical jargon" (p. 422), consistent with the predominately scientific register of the email exchanges. Likewise, Ryghaug and Skjølsvold (2010) maintain the emails were evidence of "business as usual" (p. 304) in the world of high-achieving scientists. Yet, not surprisingly, the impressions of trickery and concealment became key motifs in the mediated construction of the story, encouraging well-known authorities in the field of climate science like Sarah Palin to conclude that what was being hidden was a decline in global temperatures (Pearce, 2010). The carefully selected emails were taken from a much larger sample, most of which contained little to excite the narrative of scientific corruption. Nonetheless, these fragmented extracts became the story, in what many saw as a blatant attempt to derail the already weak momentum towards a policy agreement ahead of the 2009 United Nations Climate Change conference in Copenhagen. The author of the hack was never identified. Some wondered if it might have been a whistleblower from within the University of East Anglia (Pearce, 2010). However, the public presentation of the story was marked by a clear strategic intent. Lahsen (2013) suggests it was "made subject to an orchestrated campaign by the same conglomerate of backlash actors behind a series of similar public relations orchestrated controversies witnessed since the early 1990s" (p. 548).

The narrative initially constructed in the blogosphere was primed to secure wider media attention. The "media-literate critics of anthropogenic explanations of climate change" used the blogosphere as a platform to package the story for wider audiences (Holliman, 2011, p. 832). The story arrived with its own built-in interpretation; as Pearce suggests, the bloggers "knew that, as in most breaking news stories, whoever grabs the agenda first has a home run" (p. 228). The scandal illustrated "outliers'" well-documented capacity to strategically exploit mainstream news values, enabling a level of media visibility for sceptics' arguments vastly at odds with their standing in the scientific field (Boykoff, 2013). The story could be inserted into the hegemonic "media logic", easily adapted to the most commonplace news presentation styles and framing schemas (Berglez, 2011, p. 451). The story was individualized and personalized, casting doubt over what – to a general audience – would have otherwise been unimpeachable scientific reputations: people directly involved in the authorship of previous reports by the United Nations Intergovernmental Panel on Climate Change (IPCC). It was timely, the interest in climate change stories intensifying ahead of the Copenhagen summit. It had the hint of an elite conspiracy, at odds with the journalistic values of openness, transparency and accountability. And the story's news value was perfected when, a day after it broke, *The Daily Telegraph* journalist James Delingpole published a story under the "climategate" banner. Nisbet suggests the name immediately communicated the impression of "wrongdoing, politicization, and a cover-up on the part of mainstream scientists" (cited in Nerlich, 2010, p. 423), inscribing the story in a collective memory of stories tied to the "gate" suffix, all the way back to the original "Watergate" (p. 423). This powerful naming device rendered an alternative framing of the event as a story about the illegal hacking of a university computer server less tenable, encouraging mockery of those who initially reported the news as a criminal story. The blogger critics were the "investigative journalists" (Holliman, 2011, p. 838), leaving mainstream media playing catch-up. Even stories that led by questioning the motives of the bloggers could not but give some life to the perception of wrongdoing encapsulated in the "climategate" frame.

Leiserowitz, Maibach, Roser-Renouf, Smith and Dawson (2013) surveyed the impact of the scandal on the level of public trust in climate change science in the US, the nominally UK-centric story gaining its initial footing in the US blogosphere. Their results showed a "significant decline" in the belief that "climate change is happening, human-caused, and a serious threat, along with declines in public trust in climate science and scientists" (p. 821) broadly corresponding with the timeframe of the scandal. 56 per cent of survey respondents said they had not heard of the story. But the 47 per cent of those who had said it "had made them somewhat (18 per cent) or much more certain (29 per cent) that global warming is not happening". Perceptions were strongly determined by political ideological affiliations. 80 per cent of "self-identified conservatives" indicated the affair had decreased their trust in scientists, compared to a modest 9 per cent of liberals (p. 826). Thus Leiserowitz et al. (2013) attribute the declining "public trust in scientists" to the "strongly individualistic worldview" of those on the conservative and libertarian right – those most inclined to see climate change as a ruse for a new regime of governmental power (p. 828).

The politicization of climate change research is routinely decried by both the scientific establishment and climate change sceptics, if for wildly different reasons. From an establishment perspective, politicization is code for the delay tactics of those with a vested interest in stalling the development of adequate policy responses. It represents a politics directed towards anti-political ends, strategically designed to normalize a condition of "political paralysis" (Nerlich, 2010, p. 219). The politicization of the issue is partly explained in terms of the distorting effects of media reporting conventions. Media critics highlight journalists' fidelity to a "he said/she said" formula of journalistic objectivity and balance that essentially prefabricates a space for sceptics' arguments (Boykoff, 2013). However, Lahsen (2013) questions the default pejorative connotations typically signified by the collocation of politics and science. Instead, she argues climate change science is inevitably marked by social, cultural and political factors. Lahsen does not crudely reduce the science to politics. Yet, she wonders if climate change scientists' vulnerability to periodic "backlashes" is partly down to their reluctance to acknowledge the inherently political nature of the processes institutionalized in the IPCC. "Work highlighting the social dimensions of climate science...remains marginal in the academy" (p. 550), she observes. And it has "even less influence in environmental politics and policy-making beyond the academy" (p. 55). Accordingly, public perceptions of science continue to be dominated by a crude objectivist discourse that demands total certainty, potentially rendering science – and politics – impossible. Ryghaug and Skjølsvold (2010) maintain many journalists "judged the e-mail conversations on a kind of Boy Scout image of science" (p. 304), treating any hint of subjective commitment as inherently suspicious, as if the mere suggestion of self-interested and political motives *within* the social logic of the scientific field (Bourdieu, 1990; Grundmann, 2013) is cause for scandal.[7] Journalists thus "appear to be surprised that scientific facts are made and not just discovered, that they emerge as products of deliberation and persuasion, that methodological doubts may be resilient, and that scientists' trustworthiness is important" (Ryghaug & Skjølsvold, 2010, p. 304). Similar epistemological assumptions were replicated in sceptics' appeal to the "simple facts", even if the demand for "better science" was paradoxically intermixed with representations of climate change scientists as religious zealots (Nerlich, 2010).

Neoliberal logics and the initial media construction of the CRU scandal

Now that I have considered some of the previous research on climategate, let's examine how neoliberal logics and arguments structured the initial mediation of the controversy. My analysis focuses on two media spaces already identified as important agents in the construction of a scandal narrative: the blog credited with breaking the story, *Watts Up With That*, and the blog of *The Daily Telegraph* journalist James Delingpole. Both occupy quite different spaces within the media field, even if they cross-reference each other. *Watts Up With That* was created in 2006 by Californian meteorologist Anthony Watts as a "soapbox for mainly sceptical news and views on climate science" (Pearce, 2010, p. 174). From its modest beginnings, Pearce suggests it is now "perhaps the most visited climate website in the world" (p. 174), "with more than two million unique visitors a month" (p. 2155).

Delingpole is directly aligned to a traditional fourth-estate media identity, *The Daily Telegraph* newspaper, positioned at the right-wing pole of the British journalistic field. He blogged regularly on the scandal; his early dissemination of the term "climategate" made his blog an integral part of the networked journalism logic energizing the story. Delingpole has written several book-length critiques of the green movement, including his 2011 book, *Watermelons: The Green Movement's True Colours*. Playing off the metaphor of "green on the outside, red on the inside" (Delingpole, 2011, p. 1509), Delingpole sees the entire green movement, including the case for anthropogenic climate change, as simply a front for a socialist attack against the capitalist system. Self-described as a "libertarian conservative", his coverage of the CRU scandal was officially commended in neoliberal circles (Delingpole, 2014). He won the 2010 "Bastiat Prize": a journalist award conferred by the "free-market International Politics Network", whose previous judges included Milton Friedman, James Buchanan and Margaret Thatcher (Thompson, 2010). Delingpole replicates a distinctly American media habitus constructed around a mix of libertarian polemic and left-liberal baiting, humorous and aggressive registers (Chambers & Finlayson, 2009). These affinities were crystallized in February 2014 when he left the *Telegraph* to write full-time for the London edition of breitbart.com, the site established by an American libertarian hero – the now deceased Andrew Breitbart. Delingpole embodies the logic of media commodification discussed in Chapter 3, fashioning a self-commodified journalistic identity perfectly aligned with the habitus of his neoliberal readers.

The climategate story did not lend itself to extended eulogizing on the free market. Instead, I examine how neoliberal logics structured the antagonistic representation of the story, consistent with the supposition that neoliberal logics are often most effectively articulated as a strategy of political disidentification (see Chapter 2). I am especially interested in how politics, government, state and media were implicated in antagonistic constructions of the CRU scientists. I focus on one blog post from both sites, each published within two days of the original story. And I look at readers' comments on both pieces to see how the story rearticulated an existing set of neoliberal antagonisms, amplifying a subjectivity averse to the state and averse to politics.

Watts Up With That: Two days on[8]

Consciously asserting its journalistic credentials, the blog's founder, Anthony Watts, first published the story as a "breaking news story" on November 19 under the heading of "CRU has apparently been hacked – hundreds of files released" (Watts, 2009). The post examined here

(Spencer, 2009) was published two days later and written by Roy W. Spencer, after Watts forwarded a post from Spencer's own blog. A meteorologist and the author of a book called *Climate Confusion*, Spencer's post was the most explicitly political article posted to the blog in the immediate aftermath. Watts gave it the headline of "Spencer on elitism in the IPCC climate machine" (cited in Spencer, 2009). The same thematic was given a different inflexion in Spencer's own preferred headline of "Climategate and the Elitist Roots of Global Warming Alarmism".

Spencer constructs a discursive antagonism linking a number of different elements to the CRU scandal. Elitism is the master signifier enabling a chain of equivalence that links the CRU scientists, Real-climate.org (a website endorsed by the scientific establishment), "bureaucrats", "George Soros", "global governance", "the most authoritarian means", "mainstream journalists", "the latest environmental craze", "alarmism", "data spin" and, above all, the IPCC. The metaphorical construction of the IPCC signifies a deep antipathy to politics, redolent of the anti-collectivist and anti-statist logics of neoliberal discourse (see Chapters 2 and 7). The IPCC are the ones who think they know best: the "IPCC machine is made up of bureaucrats and scientists who think they know how the world should be run". They are repressive and authoritarian: anyone that "departs from the IPCC party line" or "casts doubt on their tidy worldview" risks being silenced. They subordinate everything to politics: "most climate research now being funded is for the purpose of supporting the IPCC's politics". And, like the lampooned figure of the "champagne socialist", they are hypocrites: "IPCC folks jet around the world to all kinds of exotic locations for their UN-organized meetings where they eat the finest food; their gigantic carbon footprints stomp[ing] around the planet...". Spencer escalates the particular CRU story into a universalizing attack against anyone or anything aligned to the IPCC. "Elitists" becomes code for a regime of power tied to the state. These antagonisms dramatize the globalized nature of this emerging state infrastructure, symptomatic of how "the globalists" have become exemplary fantasmatic figures for US libertarian conservatives (see, for example, Nimmo, 2007).

Spencer (2009) articulates, on the one hand, a strong moral condemnation of the IPCC, both in its own right and as a proxy for the CRU scientists. Yet, on the other hand, he constructs the scientific establishment's confidence in its own morality as part of the problem, because, in the CRU universe, "manipulati[ng]...climate data" is "ok" since "apparently, the ends justify the means". The argument recalls Hayek's (1944) suspicion of political agents guided by moral objectives because they seek to organize society towards a unitary end (see Chapter 7). Spencer

(2009) emphasizes the moral priggishness at the heart of the scientific establishment, insisting "these scientists look upon us sceptics with scorn". The scientists' identity as *scientists* is displaced by constructing them as oppressively moral figures that simultaneously live off the indulgent lifestyle enabled by the IPCC regime.

138 comments were posted in response to Spencer's article. They take different forms, in keeping with the relatively chaotic organization of the blog's comment sections. Some offer extended reflections on the CRU scandal. Some repost extracts from Spencer's article or other posters' comments, adding short supplementary observations of their own. And some link to articles circulating elsewhere, in some cases republishing articles in full. Most comments are consistent with the sceptical editorial stance of the blog, though some question Spencer's rhetorical escalation of the CRU affair into a generalized anti-elitism. Taken as a whole, the comments extend Spencer's chain of equivalence to a wider set of targets, many of them familiar neoliberal antagonists.

CRU scientists and the IPCC are constructed as equivalent to among other discursive antagonists: "political fanaticism in general"; environmental psychology research designed to "convince the population to 'buy in' to more government control of their lives"; idolatry of government and the UN; the "propagandizing [of] 'global' warming"; scapegoating of "the private sector"; government officials who want to "lord over others"; a culture of "belief" and "religion" over science; "blind fanatical environmentalism"; the "political correctness...infesting the universities and other public institutions"; the "ALP [Australian Labor Party] and its socialist fellow travellers"; "politically motivated science"; plans to "change our life with socialistic law"; "academic hierarchies"; anti-capitalists; "progressive fellow travellers"; teachers and professors who punish students who don't agree with them; "World Government"; "vested interests"; the "organs of the state"; "economically-ruinous eco-alarmism"; the "AGW scientific-consensus dogma"; and the authoritarian rule of the Church "in Europe in the 1300's".

Usurping the conventional research assumption that the media give disproportionate attention to the arguments of climate change sceptics, the blog community constructs mainstream media, or what is also glossed as "MSM", as a clear Other. The comments identify a diverse cast of mainstream media antagonists. All are taken to be "complici[t] in this farce" and accused of "largely" "ignor[ing] or distort[ing]" the story, partly because "the MSM thinks its [sic] superior to the blogosphere". Public service broadcasters aligned to the state come in for particular flak, cast as simple "teleprompters" of government. "Still a complete stone wall of silence here in Australia...[about] the hacking from the ABC [Australian Broadcasting Corporation]," suggests one poster; its "elitism knows no limits". Another poster accuses the BBC of "having brushed the whole Climategate incident well under the carpet", though, later, another notes how "I suspect under pressure [the BBC] have finally caught up and covered this on the Daily Politics show and on Newsnight with Prof Singer". The discursive antagonism is extended to a wider set of media targets, including the *Huffington Post, The Globe and Mail*, the *New York Times* and even the Murdoch-owned *Sunday Times*. Nonetheless, the mainstream media is still positioned as an important battleground: one poster wonders if someone is "creating a talking points list for the media". Different individual journalists aligned to the sceptics' argument are lauded, including Andrew Bolt, Paul Sheehan, Alan Jones in Australia and Melanie Phillips in the UK. And, if hardly a regular ally, the environmental campaigner and *Guardian* journalist George Monbiot's call on Phil Jones to resign from the CRU because of the damaging emails is mentioned too (see Pearce, 2010).

Different posters speculate on the base pecuniary motives of the CRU researchers: they are "looking out for number one" and "making stuff up on the taxpayer's dime". One posts the entire transcript of an article by Tim Blair, a journalist for the Sydney *Daily Telegraph*, highlighting how one of the hacked emails had noted how Phil Jones had "collected 13.7 million in grants since 1990". Doing his bit to confer journalistic authority on the commentsphere, Blair cites the street-level observations of a comment posted to America's National Public Radio: "I've been working around scientists milking this scam for a decade for grant money. Most will admit it's BS when you pour enough beers into them, but hey, the money's good". And, like Delingpole (see below), he draws a direct analogy with the MPs expenses scandal in the UK, emphasizing the "great public hunger" for both stories – the metaphor signifying an atmosphere of democratic awakening.

James Delingpole at the *Daily Telegraph*

Delingpole's investment in the story was a product of his previous writing on climate change and his key role in disseminating the "climategate" label. Widely credited with coining the term, he attributed it to a poster to *Watts Up With That* called Bulldust who asked: "Hmm how long before this is dubbed Climategate?" (Delingpole, 2009d). The name was a remarkably potent framing device. It energized the "media rituals" (Couldry, 2003b) driving the story (see Chapter 8). Writing in *The Spectator* magazine a few weeks later, Delingpole (2009d) admitted that watching what he dubbed "the greatest scientific scandal in the history of the world" made him "feel like a proud parent". At that stage, the name "climategate" had "clocked well over 30 million Google hits", helped by its circulation throughout mainstream media outlets.[9] Delingpole's construction of the story was wildly hyperbolic. One headline declared the scandal "our Berlin Wall Moment", the pronoun speaking on behalf of a universe of "sceptics" heretofore "considered freaks – almost as bad as Holocaust deniers – beyond the pale of reasoned balanced discussion" (Delingpole, 2009c). Delingpole gave particular attention to the media politics of the scandal. He devoted his second blog post to summarizing "how the MSM had reported the scandal", deriding those media organizations who initially constructed it as a "routine data-theft story" (Delingpole, 2009b).

Delingpole (2009a) published his first post on November 19, sufficiently early in the drama for him to wonder "if" the emails are "genuine". Even with the caveats and question mark, the headline was emphatic, immediately moving from the particular story to a sweeping universal claim: "Climategate: the final nail in the coffin of 'Anthropogenic Global Warming'?". Delingpole explicitly embedded himself in the networked construction of the story, transcending national journalistic fields and any old media/new media distinction. He credits the story to *Watts Up With That* and quotes Australian journalist Andrew Bolt's observation that "the scandal could be 'the greatest in modern science'". The post highlights six quotes from the emails (billed as "a few tasters"), each listed under headings that construct a narrative of scientific "conspiracy" and "manipulation". And he points to the scientists' previous "form", referencing a story he published in September claiming CRU researchers had "'cherry-picked' data".

Similar to *Watts Up With That*, Delingpole links the CRU researchers to a wider discursive antagonism directed against, among others, "ecofascist activists" and "hysterical (and grotesquely exaggerated) stories... in the Mainstream Media". All references to the theory of anthropogenic climate change are derisory. He describes it variously as a "myth", "Al Gore's Anthropogenic Global Warming theory", and "aka ManBearPig", the latter a reference to a *South Park* episode that satirized Gore's climate change activism. Delingpole speaks of the "global warming industry", amplifying an image of moral projects being pursued for self-interested reasons, analogous to the use of "the poverty industry" label to mock poverty campaigners and activists. The thematic is reinforced when he draws a direct parallel to the "Telegraph MPs' expenses scandal" (the *Telegraph* had broken the latter story), insisting "warmist scientists" "manipulation" or "suppression of evidence" in "order to support their cause" is the "scientific equivalent" of the political scandal. And he does not forget to taunt the liberal-left, suggesting the "cheap swipes from Libtards" he receives in the comment thread are a source of enjoyment because "their discomfort and rage are my joy".

Delingpole ends by explicitly discussing the political economy of climate change. He constructs his position as an inherently democratic one, for "the so-called 'sceptical' view...is now also, thank heaven, the majority view". Dismissing the criticism that his lack of a "science degree" precludes him from commenting on the issue, he retorts: "I just happen to be a believer in empiricism and not spending taxpayers' money on a problem that may well not exist". "Electorates are increasingly reluctant to support eco-policies leading to more oppressive regulation, higher taxes and higher utility bills", he suggests; "the tide is turning against Al Gore's Anthropogenic Global Warming theory". However, to his disappointment, he adds:

> Unfortunately, we've a long, long way to go before the public mood (and scientific truth) is reflected by our policy makers. There are too many vested interests in AGW, with far too much to lose either in terms of reputation or money, for this to end without a bitter fight.

Delingpole's argument is a quintessentially neoliberal one, dramatized by his self-conscious participation in a war of ideas between the defenders of liberty and idolaters of the state. Yet it is more than simply a neoliberal argument. It is anchored in a journalistic appeal to the public and the democratic majority (the implication being that climate change policy should be determined by opinion polls). He stages a journalistic identification with the logics of accountability, transparency and information (the same holy trinity built into the governmentality of audit regimes[10]). And he asserts a self-regarding journalistic "empiricism" that fetishizes "the facts" and is hostile to "theory" (see Phelan, 2011b).

In Delingpole's world, scientists are simply another "vested interest" and, like any vested interest, they will milk the public purse for all it's worth. The scientific issue of anthropogenic climate change is recast as a routine political one. Any distinction between the political field and scientific field disappears. And the claim to scientific field autonomy is annihilated by a blogosphere ideology acting in the name of openness, transparency and democracy. Delingpole gives the climategate scandal the form of a familiar journalistic drama and accountability narrative (see Montgomery, 2008), where "we", the "public" and "taxpayers", are once again being ripped off by government and "policy makers". As he narrates it, it *is* the scientific version of the MPs expenses scandal, energizing a political subjectivity that loathes the state and hates politics (the two typically conflated).

Delingpole's blog posts had a large audience, "generating in some cases over a million page views each" (Thompson, 2010). His first post amassed 469 comments, resulting in a corpus of over 72,000 words. Here is not the place for a comprehensive overview of the comments. But let's end by briefly considering how anti-politics logics structured commenters' own construction of the scandal. Based on a corpus-assisted analysis of all lexical variants of the word, the comments included 58 references to "politics" (cited in Delingpole, 2009a). Most were pejorative, though there were a few exceptions. One poster suggests the views in the comment thread are "representative of the people in society who haven't a clue about science...politicians, to their credit, trust science". Another criticizes the scientists, but highlights "the extraordinary political will [that will be] required to face up to the challenge [of climate change] effectively". And even if not explicitly affirmative of politics, another interrogates the general drift of the comments by noting how "climate changes has nothing to do with who you find annoying and which Political party you hate".

However, most of the comments are textbook illustrations of a culture that hates politics. Scientists and politicians are articulated as part of the same discursive antagonism. Consider the following examples:

This is politicised science, akin to the Soviet version...this climate dogma basically is a free pass to politicos on the cultural left to raise taxes at will.

Put governments in charge of "improving the environment" and you will get nothing but expensive, wasteful and corrupt politics.

The end game is political power and huge sums of money.

What we are seeing is the hijacking of junk science for a political revolution.

Now will the world demand that these criminals, the liars who manipulated data to steal government money be punished? I doubt it. The media is still in bed with them, and politicians are thieves.

This is only an issue about money now. Science, politics, construction, autos, appliances, it doesn't matter, its [sic] only about money...

Are politicians batsh*t insane? We need a return to logic and reason, and that includes the many fields of scientific research currently tainted by political interference.

The result is that science is no longer run by scientists but by politicians – i.e. by bureaucratic administrators who dish out money according to their own agendas.

...the media, education institutions at all levels and politicians are responsible for this unbelievable mountain of lies and use these lies as a vehicle toward redistribution of wealth and "social justice".

And adding some variation to the theme, another poster affirms an anti-politics logic while otherwise going against the grain of the other comments:

...unless you have lived under a rock, you will know what is meant by climate denial – this creationistic like contortions to reality to deny how climate actually is affected. Generally politically motivated by swivelly eyed conspiracy theorists.

The representation of politics and politicians in the comment thread reinforces Delingpole's equivalence with the MPs expenses scandal. The formula of "politics + state + money = corruption" is rearticulated as "science + politics + state + money = corruption". And in a customary neoliberal fashion, the chain of equivalence is routinely extended to the "mainstream media", as if the latter had nothing to do with the *Daily Telegraph*. This discourse is energized by a view of human motivation as narrowly self-interested. It captures a political subjectivity that implies "that this sort of event was entirely expected" (Chang & Glynos, 2011, p. 218) because what else would we expect scientists to do but game the system. The self-consciously neoliberal nature of the argument is sometimes apparent, illustrated in one poster's scare-quoted reference to "social justice" (see above), a concept interrogated by Hayek and other neoliberals. But these projections sometimes draw explicitly on other sources, some counter-intuitive for the comments section of a right-wing newspaper: one poster cites Noam Chomsky to support the claim that anthropogenic climate change is a project for "controlling the public".[11] Whatever the source, politics is regarded with antipathy, symptomatic of its naturalized condition in a neoliberal ecology.

Conclusion

This chapter began by considering Colin Hay's argument that projections of narrow self-interest, intellectually legitimized by rational choice theory, texture a contemporary hatred of politics. I examined how these projections are embedded in cynical media representations of politicians and other public figures, and I argued that these sedimented discourses are pertinent to the climategate scandal. After briefly reviewing literature on the scandal, I then examined how the hacked emails were represented in two media spaces disseminating the "scandal" narrative, one aligned to a traditional newspaper identity and a second aligned to the climate sceptics' blogosphere. I documented how the antagonistic representation of climate change scientists was made possible by the neoliberal "truths" already established in other domains, energized by a ready-to-hand representation of politicians and the entire "public sector" as self-interested actors. I showed how the journalistic construction of the scandal appealed to the logics of accountability and transparency, helping to give the story traction beyond a universe of climate change sceptics. And I showed how antagonistic representations of climate change scientists were embedded in discourses deeply hostile to politics: cast as a byword for corruption and self-serving behaviour.

Wherever we look, the discussion of climate change seems to signify a cultural aversion to politics and the political. The proponents of the climategate scandal denounce the world of "politics as usual" (Wodak, 2009), as institutionally represented in the intergovernmental panel on climate change. And they are anti-political in a more radical sense: determined to ideologically repress any fundamental contestation of a capitalist social order. This anti-political logic is, at the same time, deeply political, because of a desire to politicize the domain of climate science itself. Those aligned to the scientific consensus counter by lamenting the "politicization" of science, reinforcing the perception that politics is a dirty word that should have nothing to do with the "pure" world of science. This anti-political logic bears at least some family resemblance to what Berglez and Olausson (2014) call the "post-political condition of climate change" (p. 1): the supposition that climate change can be satisfactory addressed *within* the logic of neoliberal capitalism (also see Mirowski, 2013), without politically interrogating the causal role of the capitalist system itself. The links between these different domains are complex and multidimensional. And they need to be navigated without annihilating the crucial differences between the politics of the science field and the politics of the political field. However they are approached, the need for a more affirmative conception of politics is surely central to the cultural politics of climate change and the project of articulating a collective political will to radically address the problem.

Our argument now moves to a very different empirical context, the 2011–2012 Leveson Inquiry in the UK press, though the condition of the public good and the negative representation of politics are again key concerns. There is also some empirical overlap in the form of a second *Daily Telegraph* journalist making arguments with an affinity to Delingpole's in a different domain – this time in the name of "press freedom".

7
Neoliberal Imaginaries, Press Freedom and the Politics of Leveson

The 2011 Leveson Inquiry into the "culture, practices and ethics of the [UK] press" (Leveson Inquiry, 2012, p. 1) invites critical reflection on the problematic of neoliberalism, media and the political for at least two reasons. First, the events that led to the establishment of the Inquiry – *The Guardian*'s revelation of systematic phone hacking at the *News of the World* newspaper – symbolized the abject condition of journalism in a corporate media system. Neoliberal regimes are officially governed by the assumption that the organization of social life is best served by the market: in Hayek's (1960) famous formulation, the "spontaneous order" of the market should be the primary mechanism for constituting the social. However, within the realpolitik of "actually existing neoliberalism" (Brenner & Theodore, 2002, p. 349), things often function differently. The appeal to "free market orthodoxies" acts as a "smokescreen" for policy regimes that "optimize the power and influence" (Puttnam cited in Gaber, 2012, p. 637) of corporations. Crouch (2011) suggests actually existing neoliberalism is "devoted to the dominance of public life by the giant corporation" (p. viii), ironically privileging a paternalistic and collectivist logic of "consumer welfare" over the individualist logic of "consumer choice" (p. 55). Choice, it turns out, is not that important at all – not even to Chicago School economists. So long as there is a "*general* gain in efficiency across the economic system" (p. 56), how the gain is socially distributed or organized does not matter much. Two newspapers in a city might give us more choice. However, if merging them produces economic efficiencies, the interests of the (rational) consumer will have been served within the Chicago School imaginary.

The Inquiry crystallized the image of Rupert Murdoch, the founder and former chief executive officer of News Corporation, as the defining figure of a neoliberalized media system. Following previous revelations by *The Guardian* that the paper had hacked celebrity phones, the news that an investigator working for Murdoch's *News of the World* had hacked a murdered teenager's phone symbolized a regime of media power unaccountable to no one but itself (Freedman, 2012). The criminal transgressions involved in the phone-hacking scandal were in one sense exceptional, even if anecdotal evidence presented at the Inquiry suggested they had a wider currency. However, the scandal raised "deeper structural questions" about the political economy of British media (Wring, 2012, p. 632) and the institutional norms that enabled such practices (as well as questions about the institutional relations between the police and News Corporation journalists, given the failure of the police to adequately investigate the initial phone-hacking claims). Fenton (2013) suggests it exemplified journalism's fate in a "thoroughly marketized" (p. 173) news system where "the mission...to gain competitive advantage and increase newspaper sales" (p. 175) overrides all other concerns.

Neoliberalism is routinely defined through shorthand binaries of market versus state, regulation versus deregulation. Yet the Inquiry illuminated how the construction of a neoliberal media policy regime necessitated a "political project of state-crafting" (Wacquant, 2012, p. 66), forging what Franklin (2012) calls "a relationship between media and political power which allowed the former to exercise political advantage in the pursuit of corporate profit at the expense of democratic decision making" (p. 671). Murdoch's UK media power was enabled by a regulatory regime that re-engineered state media policy rather than dismantled it, rearticulating the state as an agent of capitalist ambitions. The Inquiry revealed an extraordinary "story of complicity" (Wring, 2012, p. 631) between News Corporation and successive UK governments. In the case of the Cameron government alone, 27 meetings took place between Cameron and News Corporation executives in his first year of office, augmented by an additional 86 meetings between different government ministers and News Corporation staff (Gaber, 2012). Freedman (2008) notes how the Inquiry cast new light on Murdoch's capacity to "terrifi[fy] politicians who dared even to contemplate challenging Murdoch owned papers" (p. 19). But Murdoch's political support brought strategic political benefits too, sometimes enabling a perfect alignment of political field and journalist field perspectives. And none were more emblematic of the neoliberal turn than Murdoch and Thatcher's parallel wars against the trade unions in the 1980s (Wring, 2012), all ramped up by a persistent campaign of anti-union demonization in the Murdoch-owned press.

Leveson's bearing on the problematic of neoliberalism, media and the political opens up a second line of inquiry, however, one dialectically linked to questions of political economy. It points to the resonances between a neoliberal logic of freedom and an idea central to the cultural politics of the Inquiry: the concept of the free press. Fenton (2013) regards the *News of the World* scandal as symptomatic of how the "cosmopolitan ethics of the 'freedom of the press' have become distorted by a thoroughly commercialized tabloid media, to mean little more than freedom of the market to do as it pleases" (p. 172). A commitment to press freedom can no longer be read as a universal tenet of democratic progress, she argues, because of the concept's "contemporary neoliberal translation" and embeddedness in a particular "political-economic system" (p. 173). Dawes (2013) likewise interrogates how the concept of press freedom has been colonized by neoliberal logics and the property rights of media owners (see also Steel, 2012). The concept is primarily defined as "freedom from government and state" (Dawes, 2013, p. 12): a right claimed by prototypically individual subjects, even when the subject takes the form of a global media corporation. This obscures how freedom is potentially threatened by corporate power – a regime of censorship beyond the image of a heavy-handed state. And it cultivates a logic of "the public interest" "all too easily conflated with the private interests of the powerful": those best positioned to orchestrate an appeal to "individual freedom" that serves their own business interests (p. 30).

   This chapter pursues this second line of thought, culminating in an analysis of how the discourse of the free press was articulated in critiques of Leveson. Many have noted the enduring importance of a classic 19th century liberal imaginary to the hegemonic discourse of press freedom: the myth of the press as a "free marketplace of ideas" (Peters, 2005, p. 15). I ask: how might we understand contemporary claims about the neoliberalization of press freedom as a point of departure? My analysis of the antagonisms generated after the November 2012 publication of the Leveson report takes a circuitous route. I centre the discussion on a critical examination of how freedom is conceived in the work of Hayek and Friedman, highlighting how their commitment to market freedom was tied to an antagonistic representation of the socialist/social democratic state, generating political antagonisms that still texture contemporary debates about state and market. I then analyse the place of neoliberal logics in the rhetoric of some of the journalists and journalism academics most opposed to Leveson's proposal for a "statutory verification process" (Leveson Inquiry, 2012) to support the new regulatory regime – a recommendation that much of the UK media, indeed, many in the international media too, represented as nothing less than a proposal to "end" the free press.

Journalism and freedom of the press

The rhetoric of the free press is clearly open to different political and discursive articulations. Steel (2012) reminds us of the young Marx's homage to the free press as "the embodiment of a people's faith in itself, the eloquent link that connects the individual with the state and the world" (cited in Steel, 2012, p. 1). Press freedom has been established as a default principle of "all significant national and international statements of human rights" (McQuail, 2013, p. 34). Robert McChesney, one of the best-known critics of media neoliberalization, incorporated the term "free press" into the name of the media reform and democracy organization he co-founded in 2003. And in the context of the Leveson Inquiry, all those lined up as the enemies of press freedom – the British political establishment, the Hacked Off campaign, Judge Leveson himself – have asserted their commitment to press freedom. As an abstract idea, the principle of a free press has "few actual opponents" (McQuail, 2013, p. 35), much like the concept of freedom itself.

The idea of the free press has been primarily aligned with a "liberal narrative" (Curran, 2002) of journalism, historically strongest in Anglo-American journalism cultures (Hallin & Mancini, 2004). It has typically been treated as interchangeable with the concept of free speech. Steel (2012) emphasizes the philosophical heterogeneity of the liberal tradition (see also Peters, 2005). He locates liberalism's "roots in the European Enlightenment when the principles of reason were asserted to provide an intellectual challenge to established authority – the monarchy and the Church – during the late sixteenth, seventeenth and eighteenth centuries" (Steel, 2012, p. 9). The emergence of the rhetoric of press freedom paralleled the emergence of a bourgeois "public sphere" and the effective invention of "public opinion" as a master category of liberal and democratic cultures (Habermas, 1989). From the mid-19th century onwards, Conboy (2004) suggests "this freedom was to be increasingly couched in economic terms" (p. 110), hostile to the state's capacity to thwart the logic of the "free market". The concept became hinged to the principle of the "fourth estate" (p. 110) and the notion of the press as a "watchdog" holding the powerful to account. The discourse of the fourth estate became an important mythical prop for the enactment of journalism's freedom from power, naturalizing a claim to journalistic autonomy within a liberal democratic infrastructure. Yet, it also signified "the incorporation of journalism into [a] political and economic status quo" (Conboy, 2004, p. 110) focused primarily on the state, not the market, as the site of power (Louw, 2005).[1]

Journalism's structural dependency on the market has long been inter-rogated by critical theorists. However, within the professional ideology of journalists, journalism's commercial orientation has been regarded more favourably. The market has been seen as a facilitator of freedom, because of the distance it enables from the state. Dawes (2013) notes how the story of press freedom is usually narrated as one "of gradual independence from state power and public authority, with the market in the role of guarantor of its democratic potential" (p. 5). It folds into a general free speech story. The press assumes a privileged role in the constitution of "a marketplace of ideas", where "any notion, good, bad, or ugly, could be evaluated on its own merits and whose price would be set by nothing but free and open competition" (Peters, 2005, p. 15). Trust in the market's capacity to enable a free interplay of ideas is tied to an ideological belief in "the necessity of publicity" as a central "organ-izing element of democratic politics" (Dean, 2001, p. 625). Gripped by the dream of a "panoptic light penetrating every nook and cranny", Peters (2005) emphasizes liberals' quasi-religious "faith in the power of the airing of ideas to reveal truth over the din of public relations and the dullness of public ignorance" (p. 17). The "self-righting public" (p. 17) is exalted, mirroring an ideological confidence in the self-regulating market's capacity to facilitate a regime of media pluralism (Karppinen, 2008). Faith in the "court of public opinion" and the peo-ple's capacity to "make up their own minds" is ritualistically affirmed, deflecting serious analysis of the potentially corrosive and anti-democratic effects of journalistic practices justified in the name of free speech (Peters, 2005, p. 17).

Petley (2012) insists this liberal narrative of press freedom rooted in a 19th century imaginary is in "serious need of updating" (p. 532). One problem is that the concepts of "freedom of expression and freedom of the press are all too readily conflated": too quickly reformulated as the "right of the press to publish" what it wishes (p. 532). The two concepts need to be distinguished, Petley argues, to acknowledge how readers' information rights as citizens "places certain obligations on the press" (p. 532). Steel (2012) accepts the "good historical and philosophical rea-sons for connecting freedom of speech with freedom of press" (p. 4). However, in a world of corporatized media power, he also worries about their contemporary conflation: the *"principle* of freedom of speech" has been debased because of the news media's commercial orientation (p. 5). Statutory regulation of the press may be necessary to support a democratically vibrant media, Steel contends, such are the threats to freedom of speech from a contemporary regime of "market censorship"

(p. 6). Benson (2007) makes a similar argument in the US context, where cultural identification with a free-market ethos is encoded in a legal interpretation of the First Amendment that is equally protective of corporate and commercial speech (Freedman, 2008; Steel, 2012). The construction of a more robust media infrastructure may necessitate a curtailing of journalists' "market" freedom, he suggests: the imposition of "constraint[s] that will need to come from the democratic political system – the State" (Benson, 2007, p. 6).

The question of how a neoliberal articulation of press freedom might differ from a generic liberal imaginary will be explored later in the chapter. However, before I move to a discussion of how neoliberals conceptualize freedom, let me quickly clarify a philosophical distinction already implicit in the discussion. McQuail (2013) identifies two distinct conceptions of liberty in debates about press freedom, one negative and one positive.[2] The negative view, the one that interests us most here, treats the market as the best instrument for protecting freedom, defined primarily as individual freedom from state coercion. In contrast, the positive view conceptualizes freedom as a capacity to be nurtured and enabled (see Sen, 1999), a value "conditional on the pursuit of the good of society as well as the self" (McQuail, 2013, p. 35). McQuail aligns the positive liberty tradition with the institutions of public service broadcasting, exemplified by the institutional pursuit of public communication objectives beyond the logic of the market (Cushion, 2012). Dramatizing an antagonism between these two conceptions of media freedom has been a central element in the neoliberalization of media policy regimes since the 1980s. Gaber (2012) underlines how these political tensions were embodied in Murdoch's antagonism to the BBC, the institution that "represents, par excellence, everything that he is opposed to" (p. 644), because of what he took to be its paternalistic desire to "improve" its audience. And they were articulated in Murdoch's "freedom in broadcasting" lecture at the 1989 Edinburgh Television Festival (p. 644): "perhaps Murdoch's best articulation of [a] faux anti-elitism" that, in a revolutionary vein, purported to reclaim broadcasting on behalf of "the people" (p. 644).

Neoliberal freedom

Freedom is one of the master signifiers of neoliberal thought. Hayek (1960) describes his influential book *The Constitution of Liberty* (1960) as a "comprehensive restatement of the basic principles of a philosophy of freedom" (p. 3), a proclamation of "the criteria by which particular measures must be judged if they are to fit into a regime of freedom" (p. 5). Milton Friedman accorded the term a similar weight in *Free To Choose* (1990) and *Capitalism and Freedom* (1962), the latter asking "how can we keep the government we create from becoming a Frankenstein that will destroy the very freedom we establish it to protect?" (p. 2). Neoliberals conceded – if reluctantly – that they did not have a monopoly on the term: Hayek (1944) laments, in *The Road to Serfdom*, how the meaning of "freedom" has been corrupted, claimed by even the most vehemently anti-liberal of political ideologies (p. 118). What distinguishes Hayek's (1960) conception of freedom is its negative character: "it describes the absence of a particular obstacle – coercion by other men" (p. 19). Freedom "refers solely to a relation of men [sic] to other men, and the only infringement on it is coercion by men" (Hayek, 1960, p. 12). Construed as an inherently individualistic concept, "freedom thus presupposes that the individual has some assured private sphere, that there is some set of circumstances in his environment with which others cannot interfere" (p. 13).

Hayek (1960) demarcates his account of freedom from all other uses of the term, those typically aligned with the positive liberty tradition. Rival discourses of freedom and liberty "are not different species of the same genus but entirely different conditions, often in conflict with one another, which therefore should be kept clearly distinct" (p. 12).[3] These antithetical conceptions include "what is commonly called 'political freedom', the participation of men in the choice of their government", ruled out because it applies "our concept to groups of men as a whole which gives them a sort of collective liberty" (p. 13). And, even more ominously, they include a conception of freedom as "collective power" (p. 16), in which, citing Dewey, liberty becomes the "effective power to do specific things" and the "demand of liberty is the demand of power" (Dewey cited in Hayek, 1960, p. 17). Conflating the distinction between liberty and collective power can legitimize "measures which destroy individual liberty", Hayek argues, "trick[ing]" people to "give up their liberty" in "the name of liberty" (p. 16). It forges an illegitimate link between liberty and a "demand" for wealth distribution, because, in his account, "we may be free and yet miserable. Liberty does not mean all good things and the absence of all evils" (p. 18).

Hayek's reflections on freedom lay the groundwork for the construction of the market as the "impersonal mechanism" (p. 4) that best guarantees a free social order. Conversely, the state, closely followed by trade unions, is constructed as the exemplary site of potential coercion. Hayek does not deny the legitimacy of the state or its need for coercive powers. Giving the state the authority to police the coercive actions of others is unavoidable and necessary: "a free society demands...that the government have the monopoly of coercion" (p. 222). His concern, rather, is when the state assumes an unreasonable degree of coercive power, crystallized in the image of a "fully socialist state...[that] would possess unlimited powers of coercion" (p. 137). The borderline between reasonable and unreasonable coercion is determined by the question of how the state comports itself as a rule- and decision-making body. Does it seek to govern like the prototypical socialist state in the name of *the collective*? Or, as neoliberals hope, does it act as a "consumer" and "producer" of market-based and individualized freedoms (see Foucault, 2008, p. 63)?

"It is the character rather than the volume of government activity that is important" (p. 221) in a free society, Hayek (1960) suggests, rejecting a "habitual" laissez-faire "appeal to the principle of non-interference" (p. 221). "A functioning market economy presupposes certain activities on the part of the state...provided that they are of a kind which are compatible with the functioning market" (p. 222). These activities are essentially legalistic in nature (see Foucault, 2008): the constitution of a set of legal rules that "apply equally to everybody" and "do not name any particulars" (Hayek, 1960, pp. 153–154). Law is conceived as a necessarily abstract and impersonal mechanism, replicating the "impersonal" (p. 4) logic of the market. Naming particulars – "to single out any specific person or groups of persons" – would be anathema to a regime of general legal principles (pp. 153–154). It would cultivate an arbitrary use of law, allowing subjective determinations of "merit", driven by the moral demands of particular interest groups and constituencies, to undermine a market-based regime of "objective" reward and value (p. 94). Neither the state nor the law should concern themselves with pursuing universal social or moral ends, Hayek suggests, an argument later developed into a strong critique of the concept of social justice (p. 93; see also Gray, 1998b).[4] The pursuit of social and moral ends is reimagined as the proper domain of the individual, or groups of individuals voluntarily constituted, since they are best placed to determine what particular ends are appropriate for them.

Hayek recognizes that a regime of freedom, embedded in the market, needs to be politically institutionalized. However, once established, the logic of politics and economy must be kept separate, because any governmental intervention, beyond the domain of general-rule setting, risks undermining the logic of the market: the institution that is the "precondition for the evolution of all our democratic freedoms" (Eastman cited in Hayek, 1944, p. 78). The establishment of a market order as a social "end" in its own right is therefore depoliticized, obscured by the technocratic pursuit of the institutional "means" that best allow individuals to pursue their own ends. Friedman's theory of political economy is premised on a similar logic. "Economic freedom" is not only "an end in itself", it is also "an indispensable means towards the achievement of political freedom" (Friedman, 1962, p. 8). The two kinds of freedom are, with one notable qualification, largely congruent: "For most citizens of the country, *if not for the intellectual* [italics added], the direct importance of economic freedom is at least comparable in significance to the indirect importance of economic freedom as a means to political freedom" (p. 8).

Friedman's antagonistic division between "most citizens" and "the intellectual" is a marked trope of his and Hayek's work. The category of the intellectual is consistently Othered by both – code for socialist intellectuals who want to collapse the distinction between political freedom and economic freedom, but by a different route: by rendering economics subordinate to *politics*.[5] Intellectuals are those who think they know better than regular folk – cultural elites "inclined to regard their own pursuit of allegedly higher values as on a different plane of significance and as deserving of special attention" (Friedman, 1962, p. 8). Hayek (1944) concedes their ideas often hold moral appeal: the arguments in favour of a planned economy "appeal to our best instincts and often attract the finest minds" (p. 66). However, these "single minded idealists" (p. 40) ultimately threaten a regime of freedom, because of their over-confidence in the capacity of the world to be rationally constructed. Hayek (1991) reformulated the argument in explicitly epistemological terms (Mirowski, 2013), transposing his 1930s critique of the economics of central planning (see Gray, 1998b) into a critique of the factual errors of socialism. He saw intellectuals as especially prone to the fallacy he dubbed "constructivist rationalism": a rationalist mindset that thinks social institutions can be "deliberately designed" and constructed to serve human purposes (Hayek, 1982, pp. 8–9). This fallacy fails to see how the "social order cannot be the product of anything resembling conscious control or rational design" (Gray, 1998b, p. 27). And it generates an unjustified confidence in the state's capacity to mould the social. Against this rationalistic tendency, Hayek (1944) insists the "growth of reason" (p. 123) depends on a social ecology paradoxically free from rational control: exemplified in what Mirowski (2013) characterizes as a belief in the market's "superhuman qualities of information processing" – its status as the "Ultimate Cyborg" that "is literally taken to be smarter than any human being" (p. 334).

Neoliberalism and the rhetoric of press freedom

So what can we say about the specific neoliberalization of press freedom in light of our engagement primarily with Hayek and secondarily with Friedman? Much in the neoliberal account of freedom is clearly consistent with a generic free-market, free-press imaginary. As with the liberalism of the 18th and 19th centuries, the state is conceived as the principal threat to freedom. The coercive potential of market actors is obscured by the identification of the state as the primary site of power. And human subjectivity is prefigured through the image of a collection of self-contained individuals, each with their assumed autonomy from the others.

Yet, there are different reasons why it might be productive to speak of a neoliberalization of free press rhetoric. Let us start with the rather simple chronological observation that neoliberalism *came after* liberalism, at least in a Euro-American context. Liberalism had its historical origins in a particular set of cultural and political antagonisms. Different political factions asserted their autonomy vis-à-vis the monarchy and the church: the agents of modernity pitched against the forces of superstition and tradition. Neoliberalism likewise had its origins in a particular historical conjuncture (see Chapter 2), but one structured by a markedly different set of antagonists. Instead of casting the proponents of enlightenment against the believers of divine or royal authority, the antagonisms took place within a common enlightenment tradition (Gray, 1998b) – as political and ideological contestation over the very meaning of modernity, progress, reason and human freedom.

Different interlinked antagonisms structure the identity of Hayek and Friedman: an antagonism to socialism, an antagonism to collectivism, an antagonism to the state, an antagonism to Keynesian social democracy and an antagonism to intellectuals. They represent the key antagonistic outsides of neoliberal discourse: the rejected identities that, paradoxically, give coherence to the neoliberal's identity (Laclau, 1990). These antagonisms are inscribed in the official neoliberal imaginary from its historical origins in Hayek's critique of socialist economics in the 1930s, to the conviction politics of Thatcher, to the comic-book excesses of the Tea Party. However, these antagonisms are also hegemonically encoded in more subtle forms that disavow the politics of antagonism and ideology (see Chapter 2). And they can be creatively adapted to different historical and social conjunctures, reconfigured into rhetorical forms that speak to the cultural politics of the particular context.

Hayek and Friedman were both writing from a self-consciously marginalized position, at odds with the collectivist atmosphere of a historical conjuncture that linked free-market ideology to the causes of the Great Depression. Their register was an explicitly political one: mapping out the terrain of a "war of ideas" (see Chapter 2) against what Hayek saw as "the dogmatic ideology of our antagonists" (Hayek, 1960, p. 2). To adapt Karl Polanyi's (1944) term, neoliberalism emerged as a countermovement to the "counter-movement" (p. 132) institutionalized in the post World War II system of political economy. Polanyi originally coined the concept of the counter – or double – movement to describe the diverse forms of political opposition to laissez-faire policies that spontaneously emerged in the second half of the 19th century. Different legislative reforms mitigated the devastating social impact of market commodification, creating the embryonic grounds for the emergence of the welfare state. The countermovement became a second "organizing principle of society", counterbalancing a utopian faith in the logic of a "self-adjusting market" (p. 132). Polanyi argued laissez-faire ideology paradoxically undermined the stability of the market system, because it disregarded the need to "embed" economic relations in "social relations", treating "social relations" as subordinate to the economy (p. 3). In pursuing an "illusionary idea of freedom", economic liberals denied "the reality of society" (p. 257) and the limits of the market as a principle of social organization.

In *The Road to Serfdom*, Hayek (1944) implicitly challenged Polanyi's argument that the market utopianism of the 19th century had been a causal factor in both world wars. On the contrary, he attributed responsibility to the logic of the countermovement, because it ultimately spawned a totalitarian imaginary and the fantasy of a "planned" economy subordinate to social and moral ends. The historical and political context governing Hayek's reformulation of a new liberal argument was therefore crucial. It embedded the neoliberal imaginary in a profoundly anti-socialist and anti-collectivist mindset, rooted in a sharp opposition between the emancipatory logic of the market and the image of a social colonized by the state. Gray's (1998b) retrospective assessment of Hayek's work, in which he largely renounced his earlier enthusiasm, is perceptive on this point. Gray suggests Hayek's most significant legacy is embodied in a politics of *disidentification*, because "it is as a critic of socialism, not a philosopher of liberalism, that Hayek will be remembered" (p. 146). Even if he "failed entirely to comprehend how unfettered markets can weaken social cohesion in liberal cultures" (p. 147), Hayek still convincingly showed that "successful central economic planning was an epistemological impossibility" (p. 149).

Here is not the place to critically reflect on Gray's rearticulation of a Hayekian portrait of socialism. Let us instead consider how the discussion of neoliberal antagonisms might be linked back to the question of press freedom. My simple claim is that Hayek and Friedman offer a set of rhetorical resources that texture contemporary arguments about the respective roles of market and state as freedom-enabling and coercive institutions. The official neoliberal account of freedom may be easily gainsaid by highlighting how corporate actors like Murdoch assert their coercive authority, against Hayek's quaint image of an impersonal market of abstract, disembedded individuals.[6] And the normative claim that the immanent rationality of the market should be devoid of direct political interference is, as we know, a malleable principle in times of crisis. Nonetheless, the ideas articulated by Hayek, Friedman and others are not simply abstract ideological claims at odds with the political economy of actually existing neoliberalism, "merely" rhetorical cover for what happens in practice. Rather, they embody a "system of dispositions" (Hilgers, 2013) that have circulated throughout the social ecology since the 1970s and 1980s and become central to the political rationality of neoliberal regimes. They represent a set of dispositions that help make neoliberal regimes possible, internalized in the affective and cognitive sensibilities of an everyday life wedded, if often ambivalently (Clarke & Newman, 2012), to the imperatives of a market-based order (Connolly, 2013). And they are perhaps most effective of all when they do not parade themselves as neoliberal, giving an aura of common-senseness to what might otherwise be dismissed as ideological grandstanding.

Other reasons for speaking of a neoliberalization of free-press rhetoric follow on from this attention to historical context. As I discussed in Chapter 6, Hay (2007) traces the logic of anti-politics to the grip of a neoliberal imaginary and the naturalization of a rational choice discourse that explains political behaviour in narrow self-interested terms. Politicians themselves have internalized a distrust of politics, he argues, exemplified by their outsourcing of political decision-making to technocratic and quasi-judicial bodies.[7] The doctrinaire neoliberal's disidentification with the socialist and social democratic state is transfigured into a popular disidentification with the very idea of politics. And it becomes encoded in the analysis of politics itself: in the axiomatic assumption of self-interested action and a deep suspicion of those purporting to speak on behalf of collectives (Bourdieu, 1998a). Thus any political attempt to reinvigorate a positive conception of media freedom, motivated by a concern for the public interest, inevitably triggers the countercharge that the appeal masks a self-interested motive. The discursive differences between the categories of state, government and public are elided in the knowing assumption that the weasel word "public" is a cover for political power and ambition. Or the scary prospect of a state-determined public is rebutted by the image of a public already well catered for within a system of market-based media.

Finally, debates about state and market are energized by the presence of certain fantasmatic figures as archetypal enemies of freedom. Glynos and Howarth (2007) characterize the fantasmatic as a logic of ideological fantasy that structures an individual's affective attachment with a particular discourse and their corollary disidentification with its enemies. Hayek and Friedman's hostility to intellectuals becomes the template for a gallery of antagonists: the "dangerous ideologue", the "critical academic", the "priggish moralist", the "well-intentioned do-gooder" and so on, all of whom are constructed as equivalent enemies. These antagonists purport to represent the public and the public interest, having an elevated sense of their own moral judgment. However, within the neoliberal imaginary, their concerns are represented as rarefied ones, removed from the concerns of regular people or hostage to special interests acting in the name of the collective. Writing about the US "new economy" of the 1990s, Frank (2000) characterized this phenomenon as "market populism". In place of the image of a market elite, "elites" becomes code for anyone who dares question the "democracy" of the market.

From Leveson to the Royal Charter

A comprehensive review of the Leveson Inquiry's deliberations, and the trajectory of events that followed the November 2012 publication of its report, is beyond my focus here (see Barnett, 2013a). But even a casual observer could discern how the report's recommendation for the establishment of a new "independent self-regulatory regime", "independent of the industry and the Government" (Leveson Inquiry, 2012, p. 33) amplified latent political and cultural antagonisms. The main source of controversy concerned the proposal that the regulatory regime should be supported by legislation that would "facilitate its recognition in legal processes" (p. 18). Leveson insisted the recommendation "is not, and cannot be characterized as, statutory regulation of the press" (p. 18). Rather, the legislation would establish "a statutory verification process" (p. 18) to ensure a genuinely independent regulatory body that would encourage the uptake of publisher-members through different financial incentives. Leveson also proposed that the legislation "enshrine, for the first time, a legal duty on the Government to protect the freedom of the press" (p. 18), hoping to appeal to British journalistic envy at the absence of a local equivalent of the US First Amendment.

Leveson's prediction that his recommendation would be distorted in subsequent news stories proved accurate. Greenslade (2012) characterized the British press's immediate response to the report as, "in the main", one of surprising "humility", most accepting the need for a new regulatory regime. Yet, "trenchant, occasionally defiant, opposition" (Greenslade, 2012) to the prospect of a statutory guarantee was evident from the outset, especially among the right-wing press. These antagonisms intensified over subsequent months. And they reached a crescendo when the British Parliament ratified a reconstituted version of Leveson's proposal in October 2013. The coverage was often apocalyptic, decrying the "end" of the free press. The distinguished former editor of the *Sunday Times*, Harry Evans, characterized "the misrepresentation of Leveson's main proposal [as] staggering. To portray his careful construct for statutory underpinning as state control is a gross distortion" (cited in Barnett, 2013a, p. 355). The British film producer and Labour peer David Puttnam suggested much of the press coverage was "straight out of the Joseph Goebbels propaganda rulebook" (cited in Barnett, 2013a, p. 355), such was the determination of the right-wing press to bind the recommendation to the image of a state takeover.

In contrast, the *Guardian/Observer*, *Financial Times* and *The Independent* responded in a generally favourable way to Leveson's legislative proposal, seeing it as an opportunity to institutionalize the principle of press freedom and enable a form of public redress for abuses of media power. However, their enthusiasm was dulled by the subsequent decision of the Conservative/Liberal Democrat coalition to bypass the normal legislative mechanisms of Parliament. Instead, the core of Leveson's regulatory proposal was reconstituted as a Royal Charter: a monarchical legal instrument administered by the Privy Council, the latter a privately convened sub-committee of government ministers. Nowhere envisaged in the Leveson report, a *Guardian* editorial ("Leveson vote", 2013) rubbished the Royal Charter mechanism as a "medieval piece of constitutional nonsense", but without renouncing support for Leveson's original proposal. The cultural politics of the Inquiry was further complicated ahead of the sealing of the Royal Charter by the right-wing press's criticism of *The Guardian*'s role in the National Security Agency (NSA) files released by whistleblower Edward Snowden for allegedly threatening Britain's national security. The NSA story increased journalistic scepticism about the "secret state's" (Freedland, 2013) respect for the principle of media freedom. Writing in the *Guardian*, Freedland (2013) drew a

direct parallel to the secretive nature of the Privy Council. He also highlighted the selective nature of the right-wing press's crusade for press
freedom, the archenemies of a statute-based regulatory regime happy to
submit to the imperatives of state security.

Neoliberal logics and the cultural politics of Leveson

Now that I have given some context to the cultural politics of Leveson,
let us examine how neoliberal logics, arguments and projections were
operating in some of the strongest journalistic critiques of the proposal
for a statutory underpinning, whether in the form of Leveson's original
proposal or a Royal Charter. As I discussed in Chapters 2 and 3, to speak
of neoliberal logics, as opposed to a singular neoliberalism, is simply
to recognize that neoliberal reason is articulated in fractured and fragmentary ways that do not preclude its articulation with other discourses
and sensibilities. It is more accurate to speak of a *neoliberalization* of
journalistic identities, rather than the pure journalistic enactment of a
neoliberal identity. Even if our analysis presupposes resonances between
journalistic and neoliberal articulations of freedom, the two should not
be conflated.

I focus primarily on a single comment piece by four critics of Leveson,
all published before the ratification of the Royal Charter. Two are working journalists, Andrew Gilligan and Mick Hume, and two are journalists
turned academics, Tim Luckhurst and Paul Lashmar. I do not offer an
exhaustive account of each individual position here. Nor do I interrogate their factual representation of the report in the purposeful fashion
of Barnett (2013a). Rather, I focus on three interlinked thematics that
resonate with my earlier claims about the neoliberalization of free-press
rhetoric: a Hayekian fixation on the (socialist) state as *the* threat to freedom; the articulation of an anti-politics and anti-collectivist imaginary;
and the fantasmatic construction of various enemies of press freedom.
Much of the press coverage was deeply propagandistic: media outlets
exploited their publicness to pursue their own institutional interests.
Nonetheless, the hegemonic free-press argument is not reducible to
propaganda. The ongoing impasse over the fate of the Royal Charter
regulator in early 2014 indicates its ongoing symbolic power, despite its
interrogation during the Leveson Inquiry.

Each author writes from a particular field position(s) that shapes and
inflects his stance. A journalist with the flagship Tory papers, the *Daily
Telegraph/Sunday Telegraph*, Gilligan's suspicion of the state assumes
a first-hand experiential authority from his previous life as a BBC

journalist. He became a high-profile news subject in 2003 for his controversial reporting of the UK government's case for invading Iraq, later resigning from the BBC after a judicial inquiry criticized the journalistic processes underpinning his claim that the UK government had "sexed up" the supporting dossier. Hume occupies a less clear-cut position within the UK journalistic field. His columns on Leveson were published in a number of papers aligned to the right-wing pole of the field, including the *Times, The Sunday Times* and *The Sun*. Some were syndicated in international papers like the News Corporation-owned *The Australian* (interesting in itself given the parallel debates then taking place in Australia).[8] Within UK journalistic circles, Hume is perhaps best known for his editorial affiliation with the radical libertarian online magazine *spiked*. The magazine was launched in 2001 after its direct predecessor, *Living Marxism*, historically affiliated with the British Revolutionary Communist Party, lost a 2000 libel case taken against it by the UK television channel ITN (Independent Television News) (Monbiot, 2003). Hume's (2012a) avowal of a left-wing libertarian identity ("I am a man of the left", he affirmed in September 2012) may, on first glance, suggest a clear point of distinction from a "right-wing" neoliberalism. However, *spiked* has been critiqued as opportunistic and "cultish" (Monbiot, 2003) by some left-liberal journalists, accused of, among other things, aggressively promoting an absolutist free-speech agenda that legitimizes the interests of "big business" (Pallister, Vidal & Maguire, 2000). Conversely, Hume's (2012a) well-timed polemic, *There Is No Such Thing as a Free Press…and We Need One More Than Ever*, was praised by journalists affiliated with the right-wing press. However, he had supporters elsewhere too, such as the former editor of *The Guardian*, Peter Preston (2012).

A former BBC journalist and editor of *The Scotsman* newspaper, Tim Luckhurst officially speaks from an academic field position, aligned to his current role as a professor of journalism at the University of Kent. However, like many journalists turned academics – what some have playfully, if pointedly, dubbed "hackademics" (Harcup, 2012) – Luckhurst articulates an academic field identity that, in many respects, is closer to the journalistic field. This fidelity to a journalistic habitus is partly enabled by journalism's place within the academy (Phelan, 2011b). In many cases, if certainly not all (Harcup, 2012), the teaching of journalism continues to be dominated by a habitus more aligned with the training needs of industry rather than academic research or critical theoretical reflection on journalism. These structures give ongoing life to a long-established antagonism between journalist practitioners and critical theorists, which, as we will see, Luckhurst (2010) is not averse to inflaming.

Luckhurst was a prolific media contributor on the Inquiry, publishing commentary in, among other outlets, *The Telegraph*, *The Daily Mail* and *The Sunday Times*. He was also a widely used source, cited, as we see below, by Gilligan. And a month before the publication of the Leveson report, his pamphlet on press freedom (Luckhurst, 2012) was launched by the Free Speech Network (2014), a publisher-funded body directly opposed to the introduction of "a statutory backstop to press regulation".

Our final figure, Paul Lashmar, is another journalist turned academic, currently a lecturer in journalism and PhD candidate at Brunel University. However, his habitus is more methodical and reflexive than the opinionated Luckhurst, his "investigative journalist" background (in print, radio and television) enabling greater critical distance from elite industry perspectives. Lashmar (2013) condemns the unethical practices he's encountered "for three decades" among journalists "many from the Murdoch empire"; he even links the deterioration in journalistic ethical standards to the "post 1979 neoliberal climate". Unlike our other three contributors, Lashmar wrote a single article on Leveson published in both the *openDemocracy* website and the newsletter of the Media, Communication and Cultural Studies Association. Notably, Steven Barnett (2013b), one of the academic members of the Hacked Off campaign (see below), directly replied to Lashmar's piece, commending him for formulating his critique in a "restrained and dignified manner without resorting to the vitriolic and sometimes deeply personal abuse which has characterized so much of the outpouring from those who claim that 'freedom of the press' is under attack".

The (socialist) state as the threat to freedom

Leveson (2012) may have insisted his legislative proposal should not be construed as "statutory regulation". Yet, any meaningful distinction between "statutory regulation" and the concept of "a statutory verification process" to support a system of "independent self-regulation" was elided in much of the press commentary. For instance, Gilligan (2013) reformulates, without qualification, the pro-Leveson Hacked Off campaign's description of itself as an advocate "for a free and accountable press" as a "campaign for a controlled press". The campaign's demand for "statutory verification" is rearticulated as the firmer demand for a "state-backed regulator". Gilligan conjures up the image of a media system subordinate to the state, matter-of-factly observing how "the royal charter... has just ended 300 years of an unregulated press" (the nominalized phrase "unregulated press" inadvertently conceding that the previous regime of industry self-regulation was not really a system of regulation at all).

Luckhurst (2013) articulates a similar anti-statist logic. The distinction between "statutory regulation" and Leveson's proposal for a system of "independent self-regulation" supported by statute is collapsed, the latter perfunctorily dismissed as an "obviously irreconcilable" mix of objectives. "Statutory underpinning" is provocatively reformulated as "government power over newspapers" and "the clunking fist of statute". It is represented as a departure from the cosmopolitan conventions operating "throughout the developed world", rooted in "the principle of separation between the state and journalism". Luckhurst voices a strong confidence in the ability of the "newspaper industry" to "put its own house in order", metaphorically reworking the image of a "self-regulating market". Talking up the possibility of an industry alternative to Leveson,[9] he even insists the proposal for a new voluntary regime of self-regulation has "nigh universal approval" (the universe now magically rendered synonymous with the orbit of the news industry).

Hume's (2012b) stance assumes an even more absolutist form, consistent with *spiked*'s house style as a militant propagandist of unreconstructed enlightenment values. "A free press and freedom of expression are indivisible rights that belong to all or none at all", he insists. There should be no "buts", outside the rule of law, in upholding the twinned principles of free speech and press freedom. Hume constructs a logic of equivalence between free speech, press freedom *and* a radical anti-statist politics, because "historically, of course, it was those who sought radical and democratic change in Britain who fought to free the press from any form of licensing, taxation or interference by the state". His primary critical target, in the context of Leveson, is "the pro-regulation" left: a left that has given up on the value of press freedom; a left defined by its "disastrous attachment to the state and detachment from demos, the people"; a left "so attached to the state as the agent of progress that they can see nothing wrong with a judge proposing how far to turn the clock back on press freedom". Hume's appeal to the demos communicates the echo of a radical left-libertarian identity. Yet, bracket that out, his pro-regulation left essentially folds into the left of Hayek and Friedman: a left fixated on the state, hostile to liberty and removed from the concerns of ordinary people.[10]

Lashmar (2013) writes in a self-reflexive voice, departing from the hyper-self-assuredness of our other authors. He acknowledges his initial struggles with articulating the reasons for his misgivings about the Leveson report – an unease "resid[ing] in the gut and not the intellect". Tellingly, the moment of "clarity" comes from attending a public meeting on Leveson where "unexpectedly" he finds himself identifying most with Mick Hume. Lashmar refrains from a knee-jerk anti-statute logic. However, "by unequivocally supporting Leveson", he thinks Hacked Off and others will bring in "more and more regulation that will, unintentionally, restrict good journalism as it is really done". His main concern is that some of the "add-ons" in the report might undermine the practice of investigative journalism, an interpretation which Barnett (2013a) challenges on factual ground. On its own terms, Lashmar's piece conjures up the image of well-intentioned proposals drafted by those with no appreciation of the street smarts needed to do good investigative journalism. His argument recalls Hayek's (1960) privileging of the tacit forms of knowledge that cannot be adequately captured in abstract rationalistic terms, the intuitive forms of judgment embedded in individuals' own "response[s] to the events that immediately act upon them" (p. 160).[11]

Anti-politics and anti-collectivism

"Politics" is a dirty word for Gilligan (2013), a byword for nefariousness and opportunism. The existing regime of "the press" is implicitly represented as an apolitical phenomenon, as if the emergence of a corporate-driven media system dominated by Murdoch had nothing to do with politics. In contrast, the agenda of the all-powerful Hacked Off is represented as a wickedly political one: "For all the routine disclaimers that no one wants political interference with the press, it is clear that is precisely what Hacked Off does want". Gilligan binds politics to an "authoritarian" logic, positioning Hacked Off as motivated by a straightforward political desire "to force the press to serve defined social and political objectives – at the expense, if necessary, of the right to free expression". Hacked Off purports to "act in the name of the victims of the press, [but] victims are not its central concern". Instead it acts in the name of a "left-wing ideology", its influence constituting "a sort of coup, by people even more unaccountable and unrepresentative than the average newspaper owner".

Gilligan explicitly interrogates a left-wing conception of the "public good" and "public interest", reflecting on his attendance at a public meeting co-organized by Hacked Off and the Co-Coordinating Committee for Media Reform. His portrait is a quintessentially neoliberal one: a textbook illustration of Hayek's depiction of the rationalistic and moralizing hubris of left-wing intellectuals. Gilligan sets out to illustrate the incoherence of the desire to institutionalize a commitment to "the public good" at the heart of the media system by reporting different groups' views about how the "press regulator" should operate:

Keep our National Health Service (NHS) public, a ban Page 3 campaign, Youth Media Agency, Trans Media Watch and anti-discrimination group Engage. The intention, within the logic of the article, is a wry, comical one. The different demands are articulated as emblematic of a political rationality where, as Hayek feared, the subjective moral claims of different actors become internalized in the structures of government. The Leveson report may have made no prescriptive recommendations about media content, belying the impression of a left-wing coalition that wants to control output. But, not to mind, Gilligan draws on Luckhurst to put the moralizing agents in their place, reminding them of elementary distinctions between journalism and advocacy.

Hume's critique of the concept of the "public interest" follows a similar script, wedded to his aversion to the "pro-regulation left". "What does this oft-cited concept mean?", he asks. He initially answers by citing Hacked Off's Brian Cathart's articulation of a familiar distinction: that the public interest is "obviously not the same thing as what interests the public.... That would legitimise all kinds of gratuitous cruelty and dishonesty, reviving the morality that permitted bear-baiting and public executions" (Cathcart cited in Hume, 2012b). Hume takes the quote as evidence of the "pro-regulation left's real view of the people", embodied in the condescending image of a "cruel public" who are a step away from "demanding hangings in the street". The appeal to the public interest becomes a prop allowing a privileged elite of "experts, judges – and journalism professors" to act as moral guardians to a public they essentially "fear and loath[e]". A Hayekian critique of the public interest is articulated with a radical libertarian one, both averse to the very notion of institutionally *representing* collective interests.

Luckhurst likewise depicts Hacked Off as a "self-appointed elite", pursuing a definition of the "public interest" removed from the sensibilities of "common men". He does not disparage the concept of the public interest, even if "the distinction between the public interest and what the public is interested in defies accurate definition". We can have "a journalism capable of serving the public interest and holding power to account", he insists, if everyone would simply reaffirm the principle of industry self-regulation. In Luckhurst's schema, the "public interest" remains the definitional prerogative of the industry, because any state-affiliated definition – at least when it comes to journalism – inevitably censors. Power is accordingly tied, in a fourth-estate mode, to the power of government and the state, bracketing out the concerns about unaccountable corporate power at the very heart of the inquiry.

Lashmar stresses the importance of "public interest" arguments to investigative journalists, especially when their work sometimes necessitates breaking the law. However, the proverb centring his assessment of Leveson is more revealing: that "the path to hell is paved by good intentions". The proverb recalls all three tropes structuring Hirschman's (1991) analysis of the "rhetoric of reaction": the tropes of perversity, futility and jeopardy.[12] It most obviously resonates with the trope of perversity; encapsulated in the argument that *"the attempt to push society in a certain direction will result in its moving all right, but in the opposite direction"* (p. 11). The trope is a marked feature of neoliberal rhetoric: embodied in a suspicion of the concept of the public interest, an ironic scepticism about the effects of morality in politics and Hayek's critique of a constructivist rationalism. Lashmar fears the report's well-intentioned attempt to address unethical aspects of the press could undermine the work of investigative journalism, because of "the almost inevitable intervention of the law of unintended consequences". The argument therefore reinforces (if unintentionally!) a certain neoliberal logic: that even if the report is trying to do the right thing and address unethical journalism practices, it might result in a perverse outcome that leaves us with a media system less free than the one we have now. Taken to its extreme, the perversity argument becomes an argument for doing nothing at all, inculcating a resigned fatalism about a collective democratic capacity to change society.

The fantasmatic Other(s)

As will already be clear, the Hacked Off campaign is persistently represented as a elite group of do-gooder moralizing types who will, whether they intend to or not, take us on *The Road to Serfdom*. The fixation on the campaign's power over the Leveson Inquiry accords perfectly with Glynos and Howarth's (2007) concept of fantasmatic logics, exemplified by the fantasy narrative that the "elite", "unaccountable" and "sanctimonious" Hacked Off are the only ones really demanding a different regulatory regime (thus obscuring how even opinion polls commissioned by the right-wing press suggested solid public support [see Ramsay, 2013]). This Othering logic is less pronounced in Lashmar's (2013) case. He communicates a moral sensibility that wants to identify with Hacked Off, implicitly apologizing for his instinctive aversion to the prospect of a statutory role ("I admit I am reluctant to see the state involved in media regulation not least as I have no doubt the licence fee is used to pressurise the BBC"). However, in recalling his attendance at a meeting where he identified with the "pugilistic" and "abrasive" Mick

Hume over "the beatific" and "doubt-free" Hacked Off campaigner Evan Harris, Lashmar captures the outlines of a fantasmatic figure developed more purposefully by our other authors.

Gilligan (2013) and Luckhurst (2013) construct a straightforward anti-left antagonism, ramping up the fantasmatic image of Hacked Off and their allies as dangerous ideologues in what is otherwise coded as an ideology-free world. Gilligan (2013) cites Luckhurst to support his depiction of the campaign and its affiliates as a "profoundly ideological" (Luckhurst in Gilligan, 2013) project, intent on "claim[ing] the country for the authoritarian left". Hacked Off's clear ideological objectives are juxtaposed with a depiction of Judge Leveson as a passive and unworldly figure: a well-intentioned dupe "cut[ting] and past[ing]" from the Hacked Off campaign script, in Luckhurst's assessment "embrac[ing] unquestioningly" an agenda "previously held only by a small group of Left-of-centre academics". Parliament is implicitly represented in an equally passive fashion, such is Gilligan's fixation on a group that has "come from nowhere to write perhaps the most important constitutional change yet of the 21st century". Decontextualized quotes from different media scholars affiliated in some way to Hacked Off – James Curran, Natalie Fenton and Chris Frost – are cited to support Gilligan's case, all primed as signifiers of an illiberal, undemocratic and authoritarian disposition.

Luckhurst (2013) rearticulates his frustration with left-wing media academics in his own article. Their failure to support free-press orthodoxy has severely disappointed him: "Nothing in my career in academia has depressed me as thoroughly as the absence of vocal hostility to statutory underpinning from fellow journalism academics". The generalized image of Hacked Off as a "self-appointed" elite, combining authoritarian and moralizing logics, is reinforced, this time supported by an Orwell quote. Luckhurst represents the campaign as a priggish force which desires a "newspaper market constrained by sanctimony" and "shorn of scandal and glamour", combining the "worst instincts of Whig imperialism and Democratic Centralism".

Hume (2012b) likewise reflects on "the remarkable rise of Hacked Off's three-academics-and-an-actor[13] outfit", casting Judge Leveson in a similarly passive role. Unlike Gilligan, he dismisses the narrative of a "left-wing conspiracy". Hacked Off's political success is symptomatic instead of a culture where the mainstream no longer believe in the concept of the free press, another emblem of the risk-averse and politically correct culture – the enfeebled liberalism – that *spiked* has railed against since its inception. Hume's own version of Hayek's socialist intellectual is again discernible: the members of Hacked Off want to see their own moral codes embedded in the fabric of the social order because they ultimately know better and do not really believe in the values of a free society. Once more, the state, buoyed by the wrong-headed statism of left-wing intellectuals, is recast as the primary existential impediment to human freedom.

Conclusion

This chapter explored how we might justifiably speak of a neoliberalization of free-press rhetoric as a variation on a historical coupling of free-press, free-market imaginaries. I argued the neoliberal account of freedom is inscribed in a set of political antagonisms markedly different from the antagonisms governing a generic liberalism. Hayek and Friedman not only reinvigorated a negative conception of liberty that defines freedom as individual freedom *from state coercion*, they also brought the enemies of freedom sharper into view, constructing socialists, collectivists, intellectuals, indeed the whole tradition of positive liberty, as political antagonists. I showed how the second-hand imprint of these antagonisms was internalized, to varying degrees, in four journalistic critiques of the Leveson report. They were articulated through a logic that fixated on the (socialist) state as *the threat* to freedom, a logic hostile to politics and suspicious of the state's capacity to represent the public interest, and a logic of Othering Leveson's "elite" supporters.

Hayek famously argued in *The Road to Serfdom* that there can be no "'middle way' between competition and central direction" (cited in Cockett, 1995, p. 79). This absolutist logic has been central to the most antagonistic representations of neoliberal identity ever since, enacted through a default denunciation of the prospect of state "interference" in the market. It would be a mistake to suggest that journalists, in the main, consciously submit to this doctrinaire neoliberal script; as I have argued throughout this book, if we want to satisfactorily understand the political and ideological resonances between journalism and neoliberalism, we need to pass through an analysis of a journalistic habitus that "doesn't do ideology". Nonetheless, a version of this absolutist logic is clearly inscribed in journalistic critiques of the prospect of a "statutory underpinning" as a threat to press freedom. It constitutes a deeply ideological representation, which, all disclaimers aside, cannot see beyond the logic of the antagonism (see Chapter 2). Within this discourse, there can be no escaping from the clarity of the basic proposition: either one is in favour of a market-enabled "free press" (faults and all) or one is in favour of a regime likely to lead to state coercion.

Luckhurst (2013) inadvertently shows us what is obscured by this fundamentalist logic. Frustrated that his academic colleagues will not get behind the case for a "free press", he urges them "to recognise that the state should have no greater involvement in the regulation of journalism than in the peer review of submissions to scholarly journals". The analogy is an instructive one, if not for the reasons Luckhurst intends, because, within the political economy of academic publishing, the system of peer review is, of course, heavily dependent on an infrastructure of publicly funded education to subsidize the requisite academic labour. Moreover, this labour is effectively free at the other end, helping generate huge profits for the global corporations who control academic publishing. The example serves to illustrate a more complex geography of state, market and economy that *cannot be represented* within the logic of an interminable ideological antagonism between state and market, but which will need to be articulated if journalism is to secure a vibrant democratic future (a point regularly cited by our authors to reproach Leveson's impact on an already beleaguered industry). Journalists may be suspicious of such strong antagonisms in other contexts; the "middle way" is, in many respects, their default setting. Yet, a distinctly Hayekian antagonism between state and market remains embedded, if more precariously than before, in contemporary iterations of press freedom.

8

Media Rituals and the Celtic Tiger: The Neoliberal Nation and its Transnational Circulation

Neoliberalism is sometimes represented as synonymous with globalization. Activists condemn the ideology of "neoliberal globalization" and its policy inscription in the "Washington consensus". The critique morphs into a story of declining state power: of how the political agency of nation-states has been undermined by the creation of a politico-judicial architecture beholden to the principles of "free trade" and "free markets". The nation-state is positioned as a bulwark against the external forces of neoliberalism, a site of democratic and sovereign resistance to the politically unaccountable masters of our neoliberal age.

There is much truth in this story. Yet, simply equating neoliberalism with internationalism, and nationalism with "social democratic and other more interventionist approaches" (Harmes, 2012, p. 60), is too neat. Studies show how "nationalists can employ neoliberal policies for nationalist reasons" and, conversely, neoliberals can use "nationalist discourses to universalize and promote neoliberal policies" (p. 60). But Harmes takes the argument further: "not only" are "certain nationalist policies...compatible with neoliberal values, but...these values may actually be dependent on certain nationalist policies" (p. 59). Neoliberals espouse, on the one hand, a particular model of internationalism that exalts the global mobility of capital. Yet, on the other, this is coupled with strong opposition to the development of anything resembling a social democratic infrastructure at a transnational level. Harmes concludes that, as left-wing activists increasingly embrace transnational forms of political organization, the phenomenon of "neoliberal nationalism may be on the rise" (p. 59). Neoliberals deploy the language of national sovereignty to counter the possibility of a different model of globalization.

We will come back to Harmes's argument in the final section of the chapter. Here I want to take his interrogation of a one-dimensional conception of the spatial geography of neoliberalism as a starting point for exploring the relationship between neoliberal logics and national and transnational media logics. Our case study is already familiar to us from Chapter 5: we can call it the "Irish" case, though simply naming it as such, as unavoidable as that might be, carries a political valence. The name deemphasizes the role of a wider set of transnational actors in the rise and fall of the "Irish Celtic Tiger". It attributes national actors with achievements and failures that cannot be adequately explained in national terms. In its dominant iteration, the Celtic Tiger was a story about the "reinvention" and "modernization" of the Republic of Ireland (Kirby, Gibbons & Cronin, 2002), one encoded in "a very particular and essentially hegemonic reading of the nature of contemporary Irish society" (Coulter & Coleman, 2003, p. 4). In critical appraisals, it became a story synonymous with the neoliberalization of Ireland. Yet, it was also an inherently transnational story: its model of political economy tailored to the interests of transnational corporations (among them Apple, Google, Facebook, Pfizer, Intel, Dell and Hewlett Packard) enticed by the country's exceptionally low corporate tax rates (officially 12.5 per cent since 1998). And the Tiger metaphor was rooted in discourses articulated elsewhere: first coined in a report on the Irish economy by an American stockbroking firm that established a direct equivalence with the Tiger economies of Southeast Asia.

This chapter examines the mediated politics of the Celtic Tiger regime. Our object of analysis is a transnational one; it demands we move between national and international contexts, rather than locking the discussion into a national frame and nation-centred epistemology (Berglez, 2013). I do not present a comprehensive list of political economy themes relevant to the Irish case. Nor do I offer a detailed analysis of particular empirical events. Rather, I analyse a particular conjunctural representation of Ireland from the mid-1990s onwards, moving between different empirical illustrations so as to grasp the multiplicity of contexts, relations and connections (Grossberg, 2010) mediating the Celtic Tiger.[1] I offer a necessarily partial account of the period before the post-2007 "collapse" of the Irish economy, when it was still celebrated as one of the defining success stories of globalization. I examine, among other things, the media visibility of the Celtic Tiger label itself, Irish media institutions' structural dependency on the property market, media representations of Ireland in *The Economist* magazine and elsewhere and the media construction of the privatization of the state-owned telecommunications company in 1999. I show how a narrative of Irish success was appropriated to do discursive and ideological work at home and abroad – bolstering a story of Irish modernity, while also offering a model for other countries to follow. I end with a postscript reflection on the Ireland of the present, now exalted as a model of austerity.

Before I explore the Irish case further, I first need to introduce two concepts informing the discussion: Nick Couldry's (2003b) concept of "media rituals" and Michael Billig's (1995) concept of "banal" rhetoric. The concept of media rituals highlights the role of everyday mediated practices in the naturalization of social formations. The concept of banal rhetoric, not dissimilarly, captures the ideological nature of discursive practices that do not seem especially ideological, echoing the discussion of post-ideological neoliberalism in Chapter 5. Later, I extend the discussion of the banal to Timothy Mitchell's work on the early 20th century emergence of "the economy" as a social object. I use Mitchell to analyse the place of media rituals in constituting the Celtic Tiger imaginary, in rendering the name itself a defining object of Irish economic and social transformation.

Media rituals and banal neoliberalism

The concept of media rituals has been a long-standing concern of media and communication researchers, inspired by Durkheim's analysis of the role of rituals in constituting group identities (Couldry, 2003b). The precise nature and scope of media rituals has been disputed. Some insist that ritual is best understood ceremonially – that the concept of media rituals, or what Cottle (2006) calls "mediatized rituals", is best reserved for the analysis of "those exceptional...media phenomena that serve to sustain and/or mobilize collective sentiments and solidarities" (p. 415). Others question the coupling of ritual with exceptional communicative events, if still attentive to ritual's sacred dimension. Carey (1997a) famously developed a ritual view of communication against the theoretical hegemony of message-transmission models of communication. And Couldry (2003b), my main reference here, reorients the focus of media rituals on "banal practices of ordering": everyday practices of categorizing the social world in which large-scale media representations assume a generalized power and authority (p. 47).

Power dynamics have, Couldry contends, been relatively neglected in previous media rituals research. Analyses have been hampered by functionalist assumptions: too inclined to treat media practices as instrumental vehicles for the reproduction of social order, and too quick to take the very concept of social order for granted. What is obscured is the political question of how the social order is constituted and the role of media practices in concealing or revealing the fundamentally contestable nature of the social. Couldry's argument recalls our Chapter 2 discussion of Laclau, and both Laclau and Bourdieu are among his sources. Laclau is cited to emphasize the enduring importance of media in the production of social order, reconceptualized as a hegemonized order structurally vulnerable to dislocation and rupture. Bourdieu is used to reinforce how the basic linguistic categories of social life operate as forms of symbolic power, acting in the name of the universal.

Couldry treats media rituals as a form of power often socially invisible as power-laden.[2] They signify the power dynamics of media naming and framing: the capacity of media representations of the social world to determine how other social actors understand, talk about and act on social reality. Couldry (2003b) focuses on the power of "central" or "centring" media: those mass-media circuits and channels aligned with a society's common-sense antennae, those signified by the everyday construction of "the media" as a single object (Couldry, 2009). He interrogates what he calls the "myth of the mediated centre: the belief, or assumption, that there is a centre to the social world and that, in some sense, the media speaks for that centre" (Couldry, 2003b, p. 2). Media constructions of the social world assume a universal authority that is ultimately mythical and impossible, because – as Laclau (2005) would put it – universality itself is structurally incomplete. Media-centric ways of naming the social become common-sensical and naturalized (even if their common-senseness can always potentially be called into question and politicized). Think, for instance, of the routinized anthropomorphization of "the market", as if it really was a person (Mirowski, 2013), with its own intuitions, inclinations and feelings (Silke & Preston, 2011).

Couldry (2003b) highlights – in one instance citing Billig – how media's symbolic power can manifest itself in banal ways that do not register as political or ideological because they "bypas[s] explicit belief" (p. 24). Billig (1995) formulated an argument about the banal nature of ideology in his influential book *Banal Nationalism*. He shows how discourses of national identity are reproduced through everyday textual artefacts such as weather reports, news bulletins, television adverts and so on: in banal appeals to the "we" and "here" of nation, and the "they" and "there" of elsewhere. Written in parallel with the Balkan wars in the early 1990s, Billig (1995) questions the tendency to reduce nationalism to "hot nationalisms": belligerent, triumphant and vitriolic expressions of national identity. Conceptually privileging the latter obscures how discourses of national identity work in relatively invisible ways, socially imperceptible because they are already sedimented into the common-sense fabric of everyday life.[3]

I want to bring Couldry's concept of media rituals and Billig's concept of banal rhetoric together to analyse the political significance of "the media", as a centring force, in constituting the imaginary of the Celtic Tiger. If we can speak of a banal nationalism, it is equally appropriate to speak of a banal neoliberalism: a neoliberalism constituted more through mundane social logics, rather than through overt and evangelical commitments – a neoliberalism that intersects with a banal nationalism in the mediated construction of the nation as a "brand" identity (Jansen, 2008; Volcic & Andrejevic, 2011). Focusing on the banal nature of media power should not exhaust our attention; we can hardly ignore the political economy power of media institutions. Nonetheless, the concepts of media ritual and banal rhetoric sharpen our alertness to symbolic practices that may not obviously seem powerful or political, but which can have immense reality-producing effects on how the social order is named, articulated and configured.

Bringing the Celtic Tiger into being

The Celtic Tiger became the most commonly used shorthand for describing Irish social and economic change in the 1990s and 2000s. The term was often invoked ironically. Even during the boom period, it was articulated as a signifier of material transformations that bypassed the lived experience of many Irish people. And the irony was universalized from 2008 onwards. In its initial articulation, the term signified the emergence of a new wondrous Ireland that had finally escaped a historical legacy of economic and social failure. It became central to the official representation of national identity. Yet, it was not always eulogized by political elites. Fine Gael, then the main opposition party, attempted (and ultimately failed) to gain political capital in 2000 with its "Celtic Snail" campaign, an ironic commentary on the effects of unprecedented economic growth on the country's infrastructure. Irrespective of how it was articulated, the Celtic Tiger became an absolutely central category for making sense of Irish identity. Couldry (2008a) suggests that the political and cognitive power of particular linguistic categories is signified as much by their social dissemination as their precise semantic referent: their taken-for-grantedness as categories for talking about the social. Put in context, whatever they thought or felt about it, people living in Ireland, or indeed Irish people living elsewhere, could not but talk about something called the Celtic Tiger from the late 1990s onwards.

The Celtic Tiger was, of course, about more than language (it's not as if the category itself could magically bring the social formation into being). This is not the place for a comprehensive discussion of the political economy of the Irish case; such analyses have already been done by others (see, for example, Allen, 2003; Kirby, 2002; Kitchin et al., 2012; Smith, 2005). Instead, our focus is on a dimension relatively under-analysed in the existing literature: the media's role in the construction of a Celtic Tiger imaginary and the neoliberalization of Irish identity.

To give the theoretical discussion an empirical anchor, I searched for the prominence of the term "Celtic Tiger" on the Factiva news and information database from 1994 till 2011. The database does not capture all citations of the term in the sampled publications. Nor does it archive publications consistently across the timeframe of the sample. There seems to be some obvious anomalies in the sample, such as the non-inclusion of Ireland's best-selling newspaper, *The Irish Independent*, in the early years. Nonetheless, for our purposes here, it gives us an indicative sense of the term's visibility and trajectory in print media over the relevant timeframe.

The term first appeared in print on September 2, 1994, in an *Irish Times* business report about a "detailed review of the Irish economy and markets" (B. McGrath, 1994a) published by the London office of the American investment bank Morgan Stanley and widely attributed to the UK economist Kevin Gardiner (Coulter & Coleman, 2003). Gardiner coined the Celtic Tiger metaphor to laud the growth potential of the Irish stock market and, according to *The Sunday Times*, the country's exemplification of an economic "dynamism similar to the emerging markets of southeast Asia" (Nuki, 1994). *The Irish Times* called the report an "extraordinary bullish" assessment of the Irish economy, even if it described the bank's endorsement of the Celtic Tiger label as tentative (B. McGrath, 1994b). The paper's "markets editor" was immediately attributing the report's call "on investors to increase their exposure" to Irish stock markets with material effects (B. McGrath, 1994b). The report was cited the day after to explain a sharp rise in Irish market prices, noting the specific "10p" price rise at Bank of Ireland – what an offshoot of *The Financial Times* described a few weeks later as "Morgan Stanley's favourite Irish stock", under the imaginative headline of "Luck of the Irish" (1994).

What is striking, in retrospect, was the relatively low print media visibility of the term after its initial naming, especially when it immediately circulated beyond a strict financial sphere. Irish Taoiseach

(Prime Minister) Albert Reynolds invoked the metaphor on a visit to Australia in September 1994 ("Irish Premier", 1994), and Irish president Mary Robinson did likewise at a dinner given by the Federal Reserve Bank in Atlanta, Georgia, a few weeks later ("Irish Workforce", 1994a). However, despite these high-profile citations, the term only featured in 15 articles in my Factiva search for 1994. Scepticism about the descriptive value of the term was apparent from the outset. An *Irish Times* (1994) editorial of September 1994 wondered about the "'illusory" nature of the glowing economic forecasts, observing that, until "the Republic's most pervasive economic problem" of unemployment is improved, "those filing the labour exchanges can be forgiven for regarding the 'Celtic Tiger' as more of a paper Tiger". The stockbroking firm MMI was even more disparaging, insisting that "Celtic Tortoise" (Linnane, 1994) would be a more appropriate epithet for growth figures obscuring the amount of profits repatriated by multinational companies from the Irish domestic economy (for discussion of the differences between Irish GNP and GDP, see Kirby, 2002).

The term seemed to have even less visibility in 1995: my Factiva sample records a mere 12 articles. As in 1994, the term featured primarily in financial journalism: the business sections of newspapers, specialist financial publications or news agency business reports. Its citation in 33 articles in 1996 was higher, if still very low in the context of the overall sample. Yet, here we start to see the outlines of a trend that became more salient in subsequent years: the citation of the term in popular journalistic genres and idioms beyond the comparatively abstruse world of financial journalism – its ever-expanding circulation in a "logic of equivalence" (Laclau & Mouffe, 2001) for everything Irish.

For example, a December 1996 news report in the Irish edition of the British tabloid newspaper the *Daily Mirror* ("Celtic Tiger", 1996) described the announcement of 600 new jobs in Dublin as "another vote of confidence in the Irish economy, now known around an envious globe as 'the Celtic Tiger'". The term was cited in an *Irish Times* television preview of the 1996 Atlanta Olympic games, which playfully speculated about the potential distractions to workers in "our own" Celtic Tiger economy (Linehan, 1996). And the opening line of an article in the *Australian Financial Review* – "A Celtic Tiger is leaping out of the Irish bog" – encapsulated a metaphorical contrast that became a staple feature of international media representations: its packaging as a story about the belated emergence of Irish modernity and national liberation from a backward peasant history (Brenchley, 1996).

The media visibility of the term increased dramatically in 1997: from 33 citations in 1996, Factiva records 603 citations for 1997. It gained increased traction in Irish publications like *The Irish Times*, but it was also cited in international newspapers like *The Wall Street Journal*, *The Guardian*, *International Herald Tribune*, *The Boston Globe*, *The* [Melbourne] *Age*, *The Toronto Star* and *The Washington Post*. I cannot properly account for the term's increased prominence here. However, the figures suggest that one media event – a media ritual in the ceremonial sense – was an important contributory factor: *The Economist* magazine's glowing front-page tribute to the Irish economy in May 1997. Under the cover title of "The Celtic Tiger: Europe's Shining Light", and back-dropped by the image of a haloed Ireland and a Europe draped in green, the magazine dedicated two lengthy articles (see further discussion below) to describing and explaining the fundamentals of Irish economic success. The magazine's consecration of the Irish case seemed to have amplifying effects throughout the media ecology. Prior to May 1997, Celtic Tiger was cited in only 61 articles, compared to 542 citations for the rest of the year and 62 citations for May alone. Another factor affecting the term's increased circulation from May onwards was the Irish general election of June 6, 1997, which invited media speculation about the impact of the election outcome on the fate of the Irish economy.

The detail only needs summarizing here. But the term achieved a consistently high level of media visibility from 1997 onwards, becoming a taken-for-granted object of Irish public discourse and, to a lesser degree, international media representations of Ireland. The Factiva results from 1998 to 2011 (see Table 8.1 below) show a consistent increase in citations from 1002 in 1998 to 1352 in 2001. The figure dipped marginally in 2002 and more significantly in 2003. However, this was followed by another consistent bump in citations from 2004 until 2010, the year of the IMF-led bailout of the Irish economy – the year that most vividly symbolized the Irish economy's collapse. The 2011 and 2012 figures illustrate the enduring currency of the term in the paradoxical form of an ongoing post-mortem about the Tiger's "death" alongside recent speculation about its miraculous recovery.

"The economy" as a social object

So what, we might ask, is the point of empirically tracking the media circulation of what became a trite category for talking about Irish economic and social transformation? To answer this, we need to take a brief detour through Mitchell's work on the historical emergence of something called "the economy" as a social and discursive object. Counter-intuitively, Mitchell (2002) locates its origins in the 1930s, arguing that

Table 8.1   Search results for the use of the "Celtic Tiger" label on the Factiva database: 1998 to 2012

Year	Number of articles
1998	1002
1999	1129
2000	1327
2001	1352
2002	1315
2003	1156
2004	1399
2005	1504
2006	2194
2007	2438
2008	2878
2009	3789
2010	4135
2011	3516
2012	3128

"no political economist of the eighteenth or nineteenth century wrote about an object called 'the economy'" (p. 4)[4]. Against Karl Polanyi[5] and others, he maintains that

> [t]he idea of the economy in its contemporary sense did not emerge until the middle decades of the twentieth century. Between the 1930s and 1950s, economists, sociologists, national statistical agencies, international and corporate organizations, and government programs formulated the concept of the economy, meaning the totality of monetarized exchanges with a defined space. The economy came into being as a self-contained, internally dynamic, and statistically measurable sphere of social action, scientific analysis and political regulation (p. 4).

"The economy" is more than a "social construction", Mitchell argues, anticipating the charge of idealism. It is not just an "invention of the social imagination" (p. 4) disembedded from the material constitution of the social world. Nor is it a "new word...for something [that] always existed" (p. 5). Instead, drawing on Foucault and Actor Network Theory, Mitchell attributes the emergence of "the economy" to the discursive interplay of a diverse set of events, moments and practices, such as the writing of Keynes; the emergence of macroeconomics; the invention of econometric models for mathematically analysing national economies; the Great Depression; the development of state models for managing economic production in the 1930s; the growth of transnational corporations; and the outbreak of World War II. These different logics and elements worked together to produce "the economy", in particular "the national economy" (Mitchell, 2005a), as an object of everyday social circulation, institutionally embedded in the practices of different fields and in the relational dynamics between one field and another. The result was the naturalization of an object that radically transformed the conditions of political and social life. It became the primary object of politics: an object that practices in other domains were rendered subordinate and accountable to.

Mitchell's account of a networked economy, structured by mediated connections and linkages between different social fields and horizons, is immediately suggestive in a media and communication studies context (see Couldry, 2008b). There are some fragmentary references to media in his work.[6] He recognizes the importance of branding and marketing practices to contemporary capitalism (Mitchell, 2005a). However, there is no specific acknowledgement of the constitutive role of "the media" – a social object that emerged in a later period of Western modernity – in bringing the economy into being. This omission is all the more surprising given Mitchell's (2005b) surely correct insistence that "to understand the work of economics, we need to expand our conception of its reach" beyond the confines of the narrow "academic discipline" (p. 298). To understand "how facts about the economy are produced" (p. 297), we cannot grasp how those facts gain authority, beyond a horizon of technocratic, corporate and political elites, independently of their popular mediation and circulation. And if constituting "the economy" as a regime of facticity means different social "locations must be well connected to one another" (p. 304), it is difficult to see how that discursive labour can be understood independently of the media's role in mythically centring the social (Couldry, 2003b).

Mitchell interrogates a reified conception of the economy: analytical discourses that speak of "it" as "though it were a free-standing object" (Mitchell, 2005b, p. 298) independent of the social logics and agents enabling its constitution (see also Bourdieu, 2005b). Economists claim "only to describe" the economy, "but in fact they participat[e] in producing it" (Mitchell, 2008, p. 1116). In the 20th century "economy no longer referred to a way of exercising power and accumulating knowledge; it now referred to an *object* of power and knowledge" (Mitchell, 2008, p. 1117). Mitchell's argument can be easily recast in a media studies context: media do not simply describe the economy, they also participate in constituting it as an object of a shared social reality (Richardson, 1998). Much like Anderson's (1991) analysis of the historical role of the printing press in making "the nation", it follows that media should be equally prominent in our efforts to understand the social circulation of the economy; indeed, our three objects intersect in the sedimentation of the media and the economy in a nation-centred frame. Some media theorists go even further in underlining the imbrication of media and economy. Cubitt (2011) describes the ontological condition of 21st century capitalism as "a complex collection of mediations", for "both power and economy require media to complete their tasks, media without which they cannot function" (p. 9).

Media rituals and the Celtic Tiger

The key insight I want to take from Mitchell will therefore be obvious: media did not simply describe the Celtic Tiger, they also participated in making it a social object that seeped into the texture of Irish social life and placed the economy at the heart of a feel-good, often narcissistic, national narrative. This new imaginary marked, on the one hand, a full-circle departure from the bleak narratives of economy that structured the Ireland of the 1980s. Yet, on the other hand, the collective memories of "the bad old days" were still politically salient, regularly invoked to disparage any criticisms of the new Ireland (Phelan, 2007a). The Irish past was, in effect, an antagonist to the Ireland of the present. And what kind of object was the Celtic Tiger? Well, we could call it a discursive or metaphorical object, recognizing how both are constitutive of social reality. But it is perhaps best described as a reified object that gave a "thing-like" name and shape to a complex set of socio-economic processes, dynamics and logics (Hay, 2001). It became a "thing" that acted on other things: framed as an agent in its own right, with causal effects on a diversity of objects, subjects and processes. To its supporters, it was a thing to be celebrated, nurtured and defended; to its critics, a thing to be denounced, interrogated and ironized. Whatever "it" was, media rituals played a crucial role in naturalizing its "thingness", in articulating it as a social object that had real material effects on how Irish political and social life was constituted at a particular historical moment.

To cite the most obvious case, one cannot satisfactorily understand the material dynamics of the Irish property market in the 1990s and 2000s without understanding the role of media rituals in inculcating, normalizing and amplifying the subjectivity and fantasies that drove the desire for property (Kitchin et al., 2012; Mercille, 2013b). The period saw a proliferation of property sections and supplements in Irish newspapers, advertising properties not only in Ireland, but all over the world as large-scale and small-scale Irish investors asserted their right to be landlords elsewhere (and nowhere more triumphantly than in London, the metropolitan centre of the old empire). Newspaper property supplements helped give a mythical social centre to the Irish property market, facilitating a regime of connections between bankers, property developers, builders, urban planners, property agents, solicitors, farmers, economists, politicians and financial advisers. They became objects of detailed scrutiny for aspirational homeowners, sellers and investors. And they became objects of fascination for wider communities of readers (the Tiger's spectators), bedazzled by the seemingly interminable increases in property prices.

These social logics were structured in part by media institutions' own direct participation in a particular regime of political economy that from 2003 onwards became even more dependent on an expanding property market, rather than the productivity gains and export-led growth of the 1990s (Kitchin et al., 2012; O'Rourke & Hogan, 2014).[7] The 1990s saw a huge spike in advertising revenues at Irish media outlets, especially in property and recruitment advertising. Increased media profits enabled journalistic innovations that were not always commercially sustainable (Brady, 2005). The economic vulnerability of media institutions was clearly evident in 2001, after the comparative economic slump that followed the 9/11 attacks. *The Irish Times* was forced to take an unprecedented set of cost-cutting measures in 2002, which then editor Conor Brady (2005) justified by noting how "our advertising revenue was ominously over-dependent on property and appointments" (p. 218). However, like the Irish state, the paper was slow to learn about the dangers of over-depending on revenue from property. Anxious to claim a foothold in the online advertising market, it purchased the "myhome.ie" property website for $50 million in June 2006, a year out from the collapse of the Irish property market (Phelan, 2009).

The structural dependency on a booming economy was internalized in the habitus of Irish journalists, torn between an impulse for journalistic autonomy and the expectation that, as one financial journalist put it, "they not run against the tide when everyone is getting rich" (anonymous journalist cited in Fahy, O'Brien & Poti, 2010, p. 15). Another cited in the same study recounted a more direct form of pressure, believing "that journalists 'were leaned on' by their organisations not to talk down the banks [and the] property market because those organisations have a heavy reliance on property advertising' (p. 115). A third recalled how "reporters who were critical were excluded from receiving exclusive off-the-record information and were often 'shouted down' by politicians or special interests" (p. 16). Irish politicians sometimes resorted to very aggressive tactics in closing down any questioning about the well-being of the Tiger. The defining Minister of Finance of the Celtic Tiger period, Charlie McCreevy, an Irish embodiment of "market populism" (Frank, 2002), denounced those he deemed to be insufficiently appreciative of Irish success as "left-wing pinko" commentators in 2000 (Phelan, 2007a): the cranks and bedgrudgers who, in his view, were given far too much airtime in the media. More darkly, Taoiseach Bertie Ahern wondered in 2007 if those intent on "talking down" the economy should "go and commit suicide", such was their uselessness to his desired national vision ("Ahern Apologizes", 2007).

The dominant media imaginary therefore fused neoliberal and nationalist logics, appealing to an entrepreneurial and risk-taking subjectivity (Holborow, 2012a) that simultaneously evoked a tribal collective, mythologized as a classless celebration of newfound wealth. Media rituals constructed the Celtic Tiger as an object that implicated "everyone" living in Ireland, that "we all" apparently reaped benefits from. These rituals were not confined to news and current affairs spaces. They were also enacted in the cultural politics of chat shows, reality television programmes, advertising and elsewhere. Bertie Ahern was particularly adept at exploiting his (pre-crash) media image as the archetypal "man of the people", once appearing as a pundit on a Saturday-evening soccer programme. The annual summer pilgrimage of politicians, bankers and property developers to the Fianna Fáil tent at the Galway races became a defining media image of Celtic Tiger excess, later cancelled when Ahern's successor, Brian Cowen, sought to convey a new proto-austerity spirit. But the spectacle of the tent also appropriated, however outrageously, a particular myth of "the people": grounded in a tribal identification with land and the Irish "west" as the site of national belonging, a myth shaped by the disproportionate impact of the 19th century Irish famine on the poorer western counties.

Media rituals helped make the Celtic Tiger label "our own" despite its provenance in a report by an American stockbroking firm speaking primarily to an audience of market strategists, and drawing comparisons with south-Asian economies soon recast as "paper tigers". The name retained a fidelity to its origins, becoming metaphorically hinged – from a parish level upwards – to a generalized habitus of wealth accumulation, economic calculation and ostentatious display. But media rituals were crucial in giving the name a wider currency, in generating metaphorical equivalences that took it well beyond the original Morgan Stanley report, in making it the "master signifier" (Coulter & Coleman, 2003, p. 4) of Irish society. The object called "the media" did not do this on its own, of course. A network of economists, stockbrokers, politicians, technocrats, media pundits, journalists, statisticians, trade unionists, financiers, property developers, critical theorists, sociologists, political economists, religious leaders and so on needed to assert their own discursive agency, and they needed to have it consecrated through media visibility. And the cumulative effect was akin to Bourdieu's (1977, p. 72) metaphor of an orchestra without a conductor, as the mediated perspectives of actors in different social fields, even when they diverged and disagreed with each other, helped put the Celtic Tiger at the mythical centre of Irish life.

Transnational mediations

To understand how the Irish case was mediated beyond a national imaginary, it is worth looking more closely at *The Economist*'s cover story tribute of May 1997 alongside a later story from 2004. The 1997 coverage was rich in symbolism. It signified a powerful endorsement of Irish political economy by a leading media advocate of neoliberal reason, read primarily by transnational elites (Starr, 2004).[8] Writing in *The Guardian*, Matthew Engel (1997) quipped – in a piece replete with Irish stereotypes – that "to a small, self-conscious country" like Ireland "this may mean as much as the *Time* story about Swinging London". Engel's *Time* magazine analogy was apt, but not because of the London comparison. Instead, within Irish collective memory, *The Economist* cover page recalled another memorable moment in the country's international mediation: the bestowal of a *Time* magazine cover page in July 1963. Under the title of "Ireland: New Spirit of the Ould Sod", the *Time* (Artzybasheff, 1963) cover marked the consecration of an earlier moment in the trajectory of Irish modernity, when Ireland's previously protected economy was integrated into international capital flows, arguably "piloting and adapting policies which would later be labelled 'neoliberal'" (Kitchin et al., 2012, p. 1306). To the magazine's primarily American readership, this counter-intuitive development was suitably captured in a cover image pairing

Irish Taoiseach Seán Lemass with a leprechaun lifting the curtain on an impressive vista of Irish industrialization.

This wider historical context was not missed in *The Economist*'s May 1997 coverage (written in the magazine's customary anonymous voice). In the more analytical of the two pieces it published, "Green is good" (1997), the magazine departed from the conventional citation of 1987 as the decisive year in the proto-emergence of the Celtic Tiger. Instead, it rearticulated a familiar "repression-modernization dyad" which Cleary (2007) suggests "drastically simplifie[s]" the "trajectory of twentieth century Irish development" (p. 8), emphasizing how "the great turning-point of the past half-century of Irish history came at the end of the 1950s", "when the country abandoned the autarchic social conservatism of Eamon De Valera...and under...Lemass, opened its economy, its society and its politics to the modern world" ("Green Is Good", 1997). Representing the Irish case as more than a one-dimensional victory for post-1980s neoliberalism fitted with the magazine's identification with a particular "meta-narrative" of progress (Starr, 2004, p. 384). Since its establishment in 1843, *The Economist* has propagated the belief that the facilitation of "free markets" and "free trade" are the defining measures of the good society (p. 374). Critically interrogating the magazine's utopian vision of a "world without poverty" (p. 394) enabled by capitalism, Starr argues *The Economist*'s strong pro-globalization message of the 1990s was eager to downplay the disruptive effects of contemporary globalization. Instead of signifying a radical historical break, globalization was framed as "a continuation of trends throughout the modern era", a rational trajectory that started "with the Industrial Revolution and related growth of trade, held down by various things occasionally, but back in full swing now" (p. 384).

As already noted in Chapter 5, *The Economist* affirmed the truth of an elite Irish discourse championing the anti-ideological character of the Celtic Tiger formation, the product of a pragmatic political culture where left/right ideological distinctions "mean nothing" ("Ireland Shines", 1997). Indeed, in keeping with its self-image as a discerning advocate of the free market, the antithesis of an unthinking ideological cheerleader (Starr, 2004), the magazine stresses how Ireland's "experience supports different, indeed contradictory, views of what makes countries grow"; both "statists" and "liberals" can cite different aspects to support their own worldview ("Ireland Shines", 1997).

Nonetheless, *The Economist*'s endorsement of Ireland's "astonishing economic success" enables an emphatic affirmation of a particular model of globalization:

Two things Ireland does show beyond a doubt. First, that small countries on the fringe of rich trading areas can prosper mightily. The curse of the periphery is a myth. Second, "globalisation", taken at the flood, is the fastest course to wealth ("Ireland Shines", 1997).

Irish prosperity symbolizes nothing less than the intellectual victory of the magazine's preferred vision of globalization, because "if any country lends substance to the cliché that the global economy is an opportunity not a threat, it is Ireland". These benefits go beyond the realm of "the economy"; they also facilitate a "deeper" level of "social and cultural change" and "transformations". "As Ireland modernizes", the magazine even predicts that the "illiberalism, anti-individualism and a deep suspicion of economic freedom" that held it back in the past is likely to fade.

The Economist rejected the notion of an easily replicated Irish model in May 1997, insisting "Ireland is more of a special case than its fans abroad realise". However, fast forward to October 2004, the magazine makes this very claim in an article headlined "The Irish Economy: A model of success" (2004), supplemented by the sub-headline "What central Europe can learn from Ireland". The immediate context concerned the May 2004 addition of eight new central European countries into the European Union. This development represented, on the one hand, the assimilation of the new countries into an existing power structure. Yet, on the other, it was shadowed by the contentious question of how the reconfigured Europe might be politically articulated, the tension captured by US Secretary of State Donald Rumsfeld's opportunistic division between "Old Europe" and "New Europe" before the US-led invasion of Iraq in 2003 (and a tension implicit in the antagonistic logic of *The Economist*'s article).

The opening paragraph of the 2004 article immediately distances itself from the simplistic idea that a "model" can be copied from elsewhere to "instantly" produce "similar success". Instead, this childlike view is projected onto the eight new countries that "from Estonia to Slovenia, appear so fascinated with Ireland". They are naïve because, as far as *The Economist* is concerned, they have misread the reasons for Irish success, incorrectly believing that "generous dollops of EU money" was a defining factor.

The new EU members still have something to "learn from Ireland", *The Economist* insists, "but they should be careful to draw the right lessons". And these amount, in short, to a vision of neoliberal internationalism that would only comfort a free-market evangelist like Rumsfeld.

Revisiting the visual metaphor of the May 1997 cover (of a Europe draped in the green of the "Emerald Isle"), the magazine hails the prospect of a "green" Europe that understands "the value of low corporate taxes in helping to attract foreign investment", "labour-market flexibility" and lower taxes, juxtaposed against a Franco-German ("Old Europe") desire for higher "corporate tax rates" and "excessive regulation".[9] To *The Economist*, the key lessons to take from the Irish case essentially affirm the eternal veracity of a liberal economic credo: "For the central Europeans...the road to prosperity is the same as it always was: freer markets, deregulation and smaller government".

Ireland (pre-crash) was not always represented favourably in international media: the excessive cheerleading inevitably invited journalistic speculation about its "dark side". Critical representations were most apparent in left-liberal media outlets, or in regions of the journalistic field(s) closer to the cultural field. For instance, the Celtic Tiger was represented negatively in commentary and culture sections of *The Guardian* between 1997 and 2000, as a signifier for vulgar materialism and the commodification of Ireland.[10] And in the paper's business and economic sections, speculation about the "overheating" of the Irish economy was a familiar theme. Nonetheless, even in a left-liberal publication like *The Guardian*, one could see the outlines of the narrative disseminated in *The Economist*, though the role of the European Union in enabling Irish success was given greater weight. Discourses juxtaposing logics of modernity, progress and liberation with logics of history, failure and repression were a ritual feature of how the Irish story was named and disseminated in international media, *even* when these simple category distinctions and framing schemas were interrogated. These discourses took a straightforward celebratory tone in the elite financial press (Corcoran & Fahy, 2009; Ojala, 2012), which, like *The Economist*, used the story of Irish success to universalize neoliberal prescriptions.

The feel-good Celtic Tiger narrative was still circulating in the transnational media ecology in the years immediately before the collapse of the Irish economy. "The Celtic Tiger is still burning bright", *The Financial Times* reassured us in January 2005 and a year later (Jones, 2005) it was offering a similarly upbeat assessment, quoting, unchallenged, an investment fund manager who determined that "in the current environment, where everyone is searching for value, Ireland is well-placed" (Kelleher, 2006). *Forbes* was hamming up the metaphor in June 2006, insisting the "Celtic Tiger was still roaring onwards" (Monagan, 2006). *Time* magazine was more alert to the dynamics of a "housing boom that...cannot be sustained" in September 2006 (Ledbetter, 2006). Yet, even its most pessimistic assessments of what could go wrong look comparatively gentle in retrospect.

The transnational media circulation of the Celtic Tiger story was, as *The Economist* suggested, also illustrated by Ireland's comparatively frequent citation as a desirable model by politicians and governments in other countries. Scotland, Chile and Iceland were among some of the other countries reportedly intrigued by the Irish economic model. Political and media interest in the Celtic Tiger was periodically heightened by the ritual of Irish political and policy elites touring the world to reveal its secrets, often in tandem with the annual overseas exodus of Irish government ministers to celebrate St Patrick's Day. One example was former Irish Prime Minister John Bruton's appearance on a Television New Zealand current affairs programme in April 2004. The interview invited another retelling of the Celtic Tiger story, with narrative materials that could have been taken directly from *The Economist*'s 1997 profile. Bruton reaffirmed the idea that Irish politicians were not "ideological about economics" (cited in Harman, 2004). Yet, the peculiarity of the post-ideological discourse would have been apparent to many of the watching audience, as he was immediately followed in-studio by – recalling the discussion of Chapter 4 – Roger Douglas, the eponymous political architect of Rogernomics. Douglas had only good things to say about Ireland's low corporate tax regime, like other members of the neoliberal vanguard that reconfigured the New Zealand state in the 1980s and 1990s (see Kerr comments in Riordan, 2000).

However, as if to illustrate the discursive heterogeneity of the Celtic Tiger story, its capacity to be different things to different people, New Zealand enthusiasm for Ireland as an object of fantasy was not confined to an evangelical neoliberal class. The third way incarnation of the New Zealand Labour Party, the party's attempt to reconcile its social democratic heritage with its sponsorship of Rogernomics, may have been tentative about citing the Celtic Tiger when it was the main government party from 1999 to 2008, because of its popularity among political opponents. Yet, when the then opposition finance spokesperson John Key called for New Zealand to adopt Ireland's "low-tax model" in July 2005, he was scorned by serving Finance Minister Michael Cullen, who reproached Key's "startling lack of knowledge" about the importance of EU subsidies, "centralized wage bargaining" and "strong unions" in creating the "Irish economic miracle" (Ruscoe, 2005). The official post-ideological discourse of Irish political elites was effectively globalized. One factor that helped keep the Irish model in circulation in New

Zealand political and media discourse was Tony O'Reilly's ownership of the country's best-selling newspaper, the *New Zealand Herald*. O'Reilly also happened to be Ireland's most powerful media owner; indeed, his *Irish Independent*, Ireland's best-selling daily newspaper, made one of the defining media interventions of the Celtic Tiger period, publishing an unprecedented front-page editorial on the eve of the 1997 election which encouraged readers to vote for the (victorious) Fianna Fáil/Progressive Democrat coalition. O'Reilly's eulogy to the "Irish model" was sometimes deemed a newsworthy story in its own right (O'Riordain, 2000), and *New Zealand Herald* journalists like Bernadette O'Sullivan were reliable cheerleaders. As late as May 2007, the Irish-born business journalist and investment strategist Brian Gaynor (2007) was still underlining the lessons New Zealand needed to take from Irish economic success.

But perhaps the most telling symbol of the Celtic Tiger's international consecration was its flattering citation by US Conservatives and Republicans. The endorsement may have been tinged with political ambivalence at the Irish end, given the poor global reputation of US Republicans during the Bush Junior years. Nonetheless, the endorsements signified a powerful reversal of a historical pattern of Ireland imitating America, even if the Ireland being valorized was a distinctly Americanized one, structurally dependent on American multinational investment. Many of the Reaganite think-tanks of the 1970s and 1980s (see Chapter 2) championed the Irish model, including the Heritage Foundation, The CATO Institute and American Enterprise Institute. And it was directly cited in the campaign rhetoric of, among others, Jeb Bush, Mitt Romney and John McCain (Garofalo, 2010). Illustrating how disconnected appropriations of the Celtic Tiger had become from real economic conditions in Ireland, McCain lauded Ireland's low corporate taxes in one of his televised presidential debates with Barack Obama in October 2008 – in the same week that *The Economist* observed that "the extent of downside risk to the Irish economy is without precedent" ("Tiger Tamed", 2008). The citation was no once-off: a week earlier, McCain had told the Irish-American Fox News host Sean Hannity that his "first overseas trip… might be to Ireland", such were his favourable impressions of the magical things achieved there ("Sean speaks", 2008).

Bodhrans on Wall Street: The privatization of Eircom

The discursive construction of the Celtic Tiger in Irish media and culture was more complex, subtle and manifold: a product of cultural closeness and intimacy. Yet, even ambivalent and ironic representations attested to the centring authority of a celebratory national narrative. This narrative was reproduced in various ways: in media rituals that spoke of "our" economy and "our success"; in the repeated insistence that "we never had it so good"; in discourses of Irish "cool" and sophistication. And it infused the mediated public performance of state and government, as the country's strong fiscal position gave a self-congratulatory aura to policy developments in different spheres. With high budget surpluses matched by significant reductions in personal taxes, it did really seem – within the dominant media-political imaginary – that "the rising tide could lift all boats".

One event became a defining symbol of Celtic Tiger euphoria and hubris: the full privatization[11] of the state-owned telecommunications firm Telecom Eireann (later renamed Eircom) in July 1999 (for further discussion see Phelan, 2007b, 2009). Shorthand descriptions of neoliberalism sometimes define it as an inherently individualist logic, opposed to the logic of the collective. Yet, this misses how neoliberalized formations need their own collectivist dynamics if they are to enable a particular kind of individualism to flourish. Media-political representations of the Eircom privatization showed how a prototypical neoliberal policy could be articulated in a quasi-collectivist and nationalist register. The state company, nominally owned by "the people", was reconstituted into a vehicle for a new kind of national collective, more outward looking, ambitious and monied, heralding the promise of a "shareholder democracy". Buoyed by an extensive pre-floatation advertising campaign that generated considerable media revenues, the media coverage essentially spoke to a new privileged collective of over "half a million" investors (Hearne, 2012), representing an earlier conception of national ownership as an impediment to the development of a modern telecommunications business – an impediment to the image of a modern polity.

The floatation was (and still is) "the biggest privatisation in the history of the Irish State" (*The Irish Times* editorial, 2000, April 22).[12] It was in part a mandated policy response to a European Union directive to member states to liberalize their telecommunications market (Palcic & Reeves, 2011). Within its neoliberalized media representation, it symbolized a moment of national arrival: of "the Irish" asserting their newfound confidence and dynamism on a global capitalist stage. It was, in short, the Ireland of *The Economist* cover story: liberated from its repressive past and assured of its cosmopolitan bearings. The *Irish Independent* editorial published the day after the simultaneous launch of the stock on the New York, London and Dublin stock exchanges captured the heady atmosphere:

On Wall Street yesterday the Minister for Public Enterprise, Mary O'Rourke, looked like a little girl opening her birthday presents. And no wonder. Wall Street, like the Dublin and London markets, had pronounced the Telecom flotation a big success (*Irish Independent* editorial, 1999, July 9).

At the New York launch, culture – everything from the quotidian to the literary – became a resource for a celebration of Irish capitalism. "The beat of the bodhran [a drum used in traditional Irish music] is not a sound often heard on Wall Street", noted *The Irish Times* (O'Sullivan, 1999). "But traders on the world's largest stock market were treated to its singular rhythms yesterday as New York's financial district tuned into things Irish". The paper evoked a spectacle of Irish culture: a building façade "festooned with green, white and orange banners and flags"; "a tent [that] served Barry's tea and Jacob's biscuits"; drummers from the Galway Street theatre company Macnas "accompanied by the outsized heads of James Joyce, Oscar Wilde and Brendan Behan, fittingly sporting a copy of the *Wall Street Journal*"; and the sound of "Irish music blar[ing] out from loud-speakers on the Street". The fusion of culture and economy crystallized in the image of the chairman of the New York Stock Exchange, Richard A. Grasso, looking on, "bodhran in hand", as O'Rourke and Telecom chief executive Alfie Kane rang the bell to signal the start of the day's trading.

The hype surrounding Wall Street's latest dotcom stock soon faded, however. Despite an immediate rise in the company's stock price, it slumped below the flotation price of €3.90 in September 1999 and "within a year of the floatation, the price was down 27%" (Hearne, 2012). And things got a lot worse. The Irish Congress of Trade Unions (2011) later described it "as the biggest single economic mistake made by an Irish Government – until the disastrous blanket bank guarantee of September, 2008" (p. 4). The collapse in the share price, to the dismay of what some media took to calling an "army" of irate shareholders, was only part of the story (Phelan, 2007b). Eircom became the plaything of different venture capitalists, including a consortium led by Tony O'Reilly, the media owner familiar to us from earlier in the chapter. O'Reilly's delisting of the company from the stock market in 2001 – a scenario unanticipated before the floatation – set the course for what followed, as the company was "hollowed out by a series of short-termist owners with zero interest in developing the company and less still in providing the country with a modern telecommunications infrastructure" (Hearne, 2012). Despite paying for the company through a leveraged debt buy-out immediately recorded on Eircom's balance sheet, strangling its capacity to secure future investment capital (Palcic & Reeves, 2011), O'Reilly's Valentia Consortium "made almost €1bn from their three-year involvement" (Hearne, 2013) in the company when it was refloated in 2004 at the dramatically reduced price of €1.55 per share. The company was delisted from the stock exchange for a second time in 2006, before ironically returning to state-owned hands in 2010 – this time in the form of a Singaporese state holding company. "To no one's surprise the company finally went into default in 2012", unable to function because of the burden of the €3.8 billion debt on its balance sheet – in stark contrast to the "virtually debt free" company estimated to be worth "€8.4bn at the time of its privatization" (ICTU, 2011 p. 4). The national legacy has been one of the worst-performing broadband infrastructures in Europe, marked by a combination of slow download speeds, high prices, low levels of investment, regional imbalances and a rural/urban disparity (Palcic & Reeves, 2011). And the ideological logic of the privatization failed on its own terms. Far from the utopian neoliberal image of a new era of vibrant market competition and deregulation, Eircom "continued to dominate the fixed-line market" (p. 161), exploiting its de facto monopoly position to limit "the access of rival firms" to the national network (p. 178). The Irish state was soon forced to re-enter the telecoms market on the grounds of "market failure" (p. 171), as Hearne (2012) puts it, "waving millions of Euro at anyone who would invest [in telecommunications infrastructure] to make up for the Eircom deficit".

Documenting Eircom's abject corporate trajectory – its colonization by the logic of capital – contextualizes the media representation of the initial privatization. In its retrospective assessment, the ICTU (2011) attributes plausible responsibility for the privatization "to [the] ideology of both the FF/PD cabinet and the myriad of 'professional' private advisors" (p. 4). Yet, it misses entirely the role of the Irish media centre in naturalizing the idea that privatizing Eircom was the most obvious and most common-sensical thing to do; in legitimizing the assumption that public ownership of the telecommunications infrastructure was a signifier of an Irish past that must be left behind; and in internalizing a logic of market determinism that presupposed the company had to be fully privatized. Newspaper editorials represented the case in an ideologically homogenous fashion, effectively interchangeable with the logic of the Irish political field (though, of course, some media would later go on to lament the sale, talking about it as if its political legitimization had nothing to do with them!). The privatization was editorially endorsed by six broadsheet newspapers – *Irish Times, Irish Independent, Sunday Independent, Irish Examiner, Sunday Tribune* and *Sunday Business Post* – which taken together comprised the bulk of the weekday and Sunday broadsheet markets in the Republic of Ireland (Phelan, 2007b, 2009). All agreed that the company should be fully privatized. All supported – some more evangelically than others – the idea of greater public participation in the stock market. And all agreed that direct state involvement in a modern telecommunications market is archaic.

Nonetheless, the differences between the papers are interesting because they show how neoliberal logics can be articulated in ways that, through their sheer ordinariness and banality, disavow the impression of ideological commitment (the common-sense assumption being that ideology is always obsessive and fixated, never reasoned and consensual). Even in an atmosphere of ideological closure, the cultivated impression is one of journalistic openness and pluralism. The ICTU's bald claim that the privatization was "the result of an ideology that believes the 'market' will always deliver the best outcome" needs nuancing, because, consistent with the logic of post-ideological neoliberalism (see Chapter 5), some papers explicitly rejected the notion that the market always knows best. Each editorial identity articulated a particular neoliberalized habitus, broadly aligned with their mythical positioning within the Irish journalistic field (Phelan, 2007b). The two O'Reilly-owned Independent group papers, and the *Sunday Business Post*, predictably championed the virtues of privatization, relishing the prospect of a new cultural openness to the stock market. *The Irish Times* insisted that any future privatizations should be decided on a pragmatic "case-by-case basis" (Editorial, 1999, July 17), while affirming the image of a national collective embracing the cosmopolitan world of the stock market. The (now defunct) *Sunday Tribune* articulated vague nostalgia for an era of national collective ownership, recognizing how not everyone has the money to participate in the anticipated shareholder boom. And, as the share price dropped further in late 1999, the *Irish Examiner* articulated the fragments of an anti-neoliberal logic, reproaching the government for its "obsession with selling off state assets" and "its Thatcherite policies" (Editorial, 1999, December 10).

The editorials do not capture the totality of what was said about the Eircom privatization in each newspaper, not to mind its representation in the wider journalistic field. However, they accurately capture an apolitical logic and ideological homogeneity internalized in the institutionalized political field. The level of substantive agreement, even within the elite register of newspaper editorials, was quite remarkable, because modest contrary perspectives on the privatization were far from otherworldly: they were available and at hand *within* a broadly neoliberal imaginary. Palcic and Reeves (2011) note how "one unique aspect" (p. 160) of the Eircom privatization, compared to other EU countries, was the government's decision to sell all its shares at once. Every other state "opted to sell partial stakes in their national operators" and, even when their holding was reduced to a minority share, many states "retained a 'golden share' granting them certain veto rights over decisions in relation to changes in company ownership" (p. 160). Equally puzzling, they suggest, was the Irish government's decision to offload the entire telecommunications network as part of the sale. Not only did it hand over control of a "natural monopoly element" (p. 178) that effectively allowed Eircom to frustrate competitors, it also contradicted the government's grand commitment to creating "an information society" that even its own National Development Plan conceded cannot be secured by "a competitive market alone" (cited in Palcic & Reeves, 2010, p. 161) (though the platitudinal recognition that "the market alone" is inadequate could be described as the (post)ideological principle at the very heart of the official Celtic Tiger imaginary).

When sceptical perspectives on the privatization were articulated in centring media, they sometimes enacted a largely gestural form of opposition. One example was an *Irish Times* article by Pat Rabbitte (1999), the Labour opposition spokesman on enterprise, trade and employment, the day before the floatation. Framed by the headline "They're selling the family silver back to the people who owned it in the first place", the casual reader might have been forgiven for thinking the article offered a defence of the principle of national ownership of Eircom – if not in full, at least in part. Instead, positioning the ruling government coalition as the uniquely ideological ones, Rabbitte voiced concerns about the prospect of wholesale privatizations in the future without proper public or political debate. On the specific privatization, he simply rearticulated the orthodox line that "developments in the international communications industry make strategic partnership essential, and even privatisation desirable".

The Eircom example illustrates a more general phenomenon about how the social logics of the Celtic Tiger formation obscured the logic of the political. The developmental logics and class dynamics of the Irish model were sometimes interrogated in mainstream media representations. And, near the end, the problems in the Irish economy – as conventionally measured – were signalled in some high-profile media interventions. However, the critiques articulated in centring media were often politically ineffectual and weak-willed, cowed by the affective energies objectified in the figure of the Tiger and the strategic capacity of governing elites to offer their own "pre-emptive critique" of the downside of Irish economic success (see Phelan, 2007a). A subsequent moment in Rabbitte's career, when he reflected on his leadership of the defeated Labour Party at the 2007 election, exemplified these internalized constraints. Justifying his decision not to politicize the economy during the election campaign, despite the growing evidence of an imminent economic collapse, Rabbitte insisted:

> "We were never going to be able to fight Fianna Fáil on their platform of the economy", he said. "We couldn't win that debate. Most people think the economy is doing well. Health was genuinely a big issue and that is what we were picking up, but in the last week people went back to Fianna Fáil" (cited in Donohoe, 1997).

Rabbitte's comments typify an anti-political mood, an internalized "policing" (Ranciere, 1999) of economy, deeply inscribed in the imaginary of the Celtic Tiger. His assessment of "what most people think" and took to be the "big issue[s]" not only suggests the choreographed influence of the political marketing paradigm – the data-driven politics of the focus group – that I discussed in Chapter 4; within the mediated logic of the election campaign, it also offers an implicit commentary on how the projection effects of the media centre were part of a culturally sedimented infrastructure that, as he saw it, inhibited his capacity to politicize the economy. Whether Rabbitte had even a back-stage impulse to fight the ruling government on the economy is another matter: his political trajectory, as with most on the third way left, has been one of progressive submission to a regime of market realism, disparaging those who do not follow suit. Nonetheless, his comments capture the immanent rationality of a polity where, as Mitchell suggests, "the economy" takes on a life of its own (see also Chapter 5), becoming a "self-contained structure or totality" (Mitchell, 2005a, p. 127) that, as Rabbitte's casual reification of policy domains suggests, is disembedded from the "health" of society. The "is-ness" of the Celtic Tiger economy became taken for granted: a self-contained object to think and have feelings about, barely politicized beyond the appropriate metaphors of "speeding it up", "slowing it down" and "putting the brakes on". But the economy was made this way not simply by its social disembedding; rather, it needed to be embedded in the representational practices of a diverse network of social actors: economists, bureaucrats, corporations, politicians, employers groups, trade unions and so on.[13] And it needed to be embedded in media rituals that mythically centred the cumulative discursive labour of the Celtic Tiger regime.

Postscript: On the story of Irish recovery

I have thus far examined the interplay of national and transnational logics in the mediated construction of the Celtic Tiger. I focused on the period before its reported collapse, before the Irish story became one of prolonged crisis and, as elsewhere (see Clarke & Newman, 2012), the collapse of the Irish banking system became a crisis of sovereign debt (after the Irish government's September 2008 decision to offer a "blind guarantee for at least €440 billion of bank debt" [Titley, 2013, p. 293]). Any satisfactory analysis of how national, transnational and media logics intersected during the crisis period would need a chapter in its own right. International media representations were an important part of the discursive dynamic shaping the announcement of a "bailout package" for the Irish economy in November 2011. The Irish government's insistence that people not "talk down the economy" found new international targets, to supplement ministerial reproaches of national journalists for their "dangerous" line of questioning (O'Rourke & Hogan, 2014, p. 51).[14] The full trajectory of the Irish crisis cannot be narrated here (see further discussion in Chapter 5). Let us end instead with some fragmentary observations about the present that bring us back to the problematic we began with: the notion of a neoliberal nationalism.

Neoliberal nationalism constitutes a form of nationalism already "locked in" to the logic of neoliberal internationalism. Unlike a liberalism that "takes its primary goal...as the promotion of world peace" (p. 62), Harmes (2012) suggests neoliberal internationalism subscribes to the vision of a "market-preserving federalism" that supports "free trade and international capital mobility...primarily for their ability to promote individual freedom through the creation of an exit option and policy competition at the international level" (p. 69) (the legal fiction being that the main beneficiaries of this regime, transnational corporations, are simply regular individuals). Once enshrined in the regulatory architecture of nation-states and multilateral trade agreements, the internationalist vision mutates into a neoliberal nationalism. States resist forms of transnational governance that threaten this regime, insisting that the relevant policy issues – for example, climate change mitigation policies – are best addressed at a national level. They oppose regulatory "burdens" that undermine their capacity to play the assigned role of the "competition state" (Cerny cited in Kirby, 2002, p. 142), doing all they can to incentivize and retain global capital. Any developments that might jeopardize the coherence of the national "brand" (Jansen, 2008; Volcic & Andrejevic, 2012), within existing market structures, are typically opposed.

Different aspects of the Irish case, even if they inflect its local articulation, do not fit neatly with the logic of an ideal type neoliberal nationalism. We could cite, for instance, a historical national commitment to the internationalism embodied in the United Nations and League of Nations, a general enthusiasm, if waned in recent times, for membership of the European Union, and the post-colonial collective memory of being "a first-world country...with a third-world memory" (Gibbons, 1998, p. 27).[15] In the context of the crisis, the state's formal renunciation of its sovereignty in November 2010 was an abject moment for Irish nationalists. A troika committee of European Union, International Monetary Fund and European Commission officials became the primary ruling authority, symbolized in one instance by its dissemination of a draft of the Irish budget to German politicians ahead of its formal discussion in the Irish Parliament. The pretence of national sovereignty had imploded, though nationalist logics were still crucial. Habermas's (2011) vision of a post-national Europe was eclipsed by the return of a no-nonsense nationalist imaginary that represented the Irish crisis as an *Irish* problem, to be resolved with outside help, but whose costs would ultimately be borne by the "reckless" Irish themselves, the truth of the old colonial stereotypes reinvigorated.[16] The euphoric nationalistic cheerleading of yesteryear backfired; if Irish political elites got to claim credit for the Celtic Tiger in the 1990s and 2000s, in some instances addressing the rest of Europe as if Ireland had solved the problem of the economy, the Irish state and its citizens now had to assume responsibility for its excesses. The subordination of the Irish crisis to the bigger political-technocratic objective of restoring "confidence" in the wider Euro-American banking system was relatively downplayed, along with the culpability of a network of European banks in facilitating the profligate credit regimes of Irish banks. The transnational dynamics of the crisis were hardly invisible, self-evident in the periodic shifting of media attention to Ireland, Portugal, Greece, Iceland and elsewhere. Nonetheless, a more complex media-political articulation of the Irish crisis – its embedding in the logics of a common European financial market, a transatlantic interbank loans market, the global business ambitions of Irish bankers and property developers and the Irish government's decision to guarantee all "deposits, loans and obligations" at the state's six major financial institutions (O'Toole, 2009, p. 208) – could never compete with the simple headline-clarity of the proposition that "Ireland"

and "the Irish" were responsible (a narrative of course partly enabled by the banal nationalist register of different journalistic fields).

The bailout signified a clear moment of national humiliation, captured in news stories that represented it as a de facto return to colonialism less than a century on from the War of Independence. For Fianna Fáil, the party founded by Eamon De Valera, the humiliation was complete in February 2011, when it incurred a record defeat at the general election. However, evaluating the Irish case from the perspective of a *neoliberal* nationalism necessitates a more qualified answer, for the simple reason that the cornerstone policy of its Celtic Tiger articulation, a corporate tax rate of 12.5 per cent, remains in place. Upholding the policy has become the proverbial "line in the sand" for Irish political elites, second now only to the shamrock as a signifier of Irish uniqueness. The policy has been the frequent target of criticism from different European Union member states, especially France and Germany, cited as an exemplary impediment to the development of a federalist fiscal policy (to complement the policy of monetary union). And Ireland's corporate tax regime garnered an unprecedented level of negative media attention in May 2013, after a US Senate report documented how Apple had exploited a loophole in the Irish tax system, using three "ghost companies" technically based in Ireland, but managed from the US, "to avoid paying billions of dollars in US taxes" (Carswell & Lynch, 2013). The companies did not pay taxes in Ireland either (they were "not tax-resident anywhere") because of an "Irish legal concept", known colloquially as the "double Irish" (Keena, 2013), that meant companies "not functionally managed or controlled in Ireland" were excused from paying Irish taxes (Carswell, 2013a). In addition, the report estimated that the Apple subsidiary actually tax-resident in Ireland had "paid a tax rate of 2 per cent or less on $74 billion made on international sales outside North and South America over the past three years" (Carswell, 2013a), allegedly benefitting from a special agreement made with the Irish government when the company established its Irish base in 1980. Different Irish government ministers, including Taoiseach Enda Kenny, were immediately on hand to reassure the world that Ireland had a "totally transparent" tax regime (Minihan & Lynch, 2013), indignant at the depiction of the country as a "tax haven" (the Senate charge ironically led by the same John McCain who lauded Ireland's corporate tax system in 2008). Yet, five months on, Reuters was reporting how the Irish government had since closed only one of the loopholes exploited by Apple, leaving "a bigger loophole" still open (Drawbaugh, 2013). And in February 2014, *The Irish Times* reported how a study by Trinity College finance professor

James Stewart documented how the entire infrastructure of "US multi-nationals" based in Ireland had paid the same 2.2 per cent tax rate paid by Apple in 2011 (O'Brien, 2014).

What's remarkable, if in a predictably unremarkable way, was the relative dearth of critical national introspection on the issue in *The Irish Times* on the immediate week of the Apple revelations. The paper's columnist Vincent Browne (2013) castigated Ireland's "wild west tax haven". But most of the journalistic assessments seemed to spontaneously internalize the finance minister's warning to Irish politicians that they not "jeopardise jobs in their constituencies by joining in unwarranted criticism of Ireland's tax regime" (Noonan cited in Minihan & Lynch, 2013). Much like the Eircom privatization, the dominant register of the coverage illustrated a perfect homology of the journalistic field, political field and corporate field; indeed, to appropriate an unflattering journalistic metaphor, the fact the story had to be uncovered by the US Senate attests to the embedded radar of Irish journalism. The paper's economics editor, Dan O'Brien (2013a), suggested that "it is hard to think of a more important national interest than ensuring that the wealth-creating activities of foreign-owned companies are maintained". An opinion piece by a Dublin-based tax adviser insisted that with corporate "tax avoidance...back on the political agenda" internationally, Ireland needed to come up with "a plan B" to "make sure there is no tax reason not to locate in Ireland" if it wanted to protect itself from corporate restructurings that "would have devastating consequences" (Vale, 2013). The paper was alert to the front-page "negative publicity" being generated elsewhere, noting the "sharp criticism" of Ireland's corporate structures in the *New York Times*, *The Wall Street Journal*, *Washington Post* and *Financial Times* (Carswell, 2013b).

Yet, within the horizon of Irish neoliberal nationalism and its internationalist cheerleaders, the Apple controversy seemed to represent merely a temporary blip in the interminable promotion of "Brand Ireland". For at the annual gathering of the World Economic Forum at Davos in January 2014, the *Irish Independent* (Molloy, 2014) reported how Enda Kenny had taken "the opportunity to reassure Facebook that Ireland's corporate tax rate would not change", Facebook's Sheryl Sandberg reciprocating the goodwill by describing Kenny as the "brilliant leader of a brilliant country". The Davos event represented the latest moment in the ceremonial staging of an Irish recovery story, given further media visibility by the presence of Bono (Molloy, 2014). According to *The Irish Times*, Kenny's Davos appearance "herald[ed] a new spirit of optimism about [the] country's prospects" (Scally, 2014), now that the state had met its deficit reduction targets and formally exited the Troika bailout programme. Like others in the international media, *The Economist* had been anticipating the narrative turn a year earlier. Adapting the original Celtic Tiger story, it maintained "if Ireland succeeds" in its recovery, "all of Europe could celebrate too" ("Celtic metamorphosis", 2013). Once again, Ireland was being touted as a "model" for other countries to follow (Kitchin et al., 2012), the "poster child" of austerity – the "proof that a willingness to take the pain of prolonged austerity will be rewarded in the end" (O'Toole, 2014).

Fintan O'Toole (2014) observes many of the gaps in the "Irish good-news story" in a piece unpatriotically written for *The New York Times*. It obscures the dire condition of the Irish domestic economy "outside the gated community of high-tech multinationals", a world where most people's wages have "dropped sharply", sovereign debt has actually doubled since 2009, unemployment is at 12.8 per cent, mortgage debt has escalated, public services have been severely cut (O'Toole, 2014) and emigration has once again become "a useful safety valve" (Lee, 1989, p. 378) to those in power, dissipating the possibility of a radical political challenge to a deeply consensual political, business and media establishment (Titley, 2013). The story of national revival has been hitched to an economic regime arguably more integrated into the American economy than the Irish domestic one. The logic of neoliberal nationalism becomes increasingly disembedded from the nation, the good-news story circulating elsewhere unrecognizable to many at home, its domestic reception mediated by the wounds of a crisis that has perhaps found its most potent media-political expression in a quintessential neoliberal scapegoating of the "public sector", for "failing to 'share the pain' with a private sector that has been 'taking the pain' and 'shouldering the burden'" (Cawley, 2012, p. 601). Once again, the story has been authored from elsewhere and written for others, the role of "the Irish" essentially scripted by the logic of neoliberal internationalism. Government energy is rechanneled into making the story "our" own – to make everyone proud of "the brand we carry", as Enda Kenny put it so aptly in an interview with *Time* magazine in October 2012 (Mayer, 2012).

If my postscript sounds like nothing more than a derisory commentary on the ideological[17] project of marketing Ireland, I will have short-changed myself – as if it's simply a matter of Irish elites being co-opted by a "false consciousness", as if Kenny's neoliberal nationalism is the product of deep immersion in the "constitutional economics" (Harmes, 2012, p. 66) of Hayek and Buchanan, as if elements of the Irish establishment that wish things were otherwise cannot *see* the structures of their own

domination. For *within* the hegemonic universe of neoliberal internationalism, Kenny's national-salesman posture is an entirely rational one,
one deeply embedded in the material condition of an Irish economy
extraordinarily dependent on multinational capital.[18] The telling question instead, from inside the strategic telos of the neoliberal imaginary,
is what happens to the nation when Kenny's cheery sales talk is out-
flanked by sales pitches from elsewhere? As political-economic systems arguably become neoliberalized like never before (Birch, 2011),
what happens when the logic of the Celtic Tiger model is universalized? And here, as *The Irish Times* recognized (Carswell, 2013c), the politics of the US Senate's investigation of Apple is crucial. Because amidst
the predictable condemnation of its tax affairs, Apple's chief executive
Tim Cook implored US senators to lower US corporate taxes from its
comparatively high rate of 35 per cent. Ireland's tax regime was still
finding some implicit admirers; Carswell's (2013c) report described Tea
Party favourite Senator Rand Paul as a "big fan" of Apple's tax strategy.
Rather than blaming Apple, Paul insisted that US legislators needed to
"look in the mirror and let's make the tax code better, fairer and more
competitive worldwide.... Money goes where it's welcome. Currently,
our tax code makes money not welcome in this country" (Paul cited in
Carswell, 2013c). In a similar vein, one *Washington Post* columnist wondered if there should be "no corporate income tax" at all, before conceding the likely political obstacles (Irwin, 2013). Closer to home, one
reason why the timing of the Apple revelations was "terrible for Ireland"
was because of British Prime Minister David Cameron's plan "to raise
the tax practices of multinationals as a topic of discussion" at the G8
Summit in Northern Ireland (Carswell, 2013c). Six months on, however,
the PR-driven aura of moral reproach was belied by a potentially much
more significant development, when Cameron "announced that the UK
would cut corporation tax to 20%, 'the lowest in the G20'", thereby
directly "copying" the Irish growth model (Blyth, 2013b).

Crouch (2011) cautions against a simple "race to the bottom narrative" of globalization, imagined here as the spectre of a "flight of capital"
from Ireland. "Existing investments in plant, distribution and supplier
networks, as well as social links, are not so easily moved" (p. 127). "It
is...not the case that high-wage, high-tax economies, have always lost
out in competition for direct inward investment" (p. 127). Nonetheless, this regime "still places the initiative" with global corporate firms,
for it is "their market strategy that determines (or at least strongly
affects) whether particular governmental policies will be 'rewarded' with
investment or not" (p. 120). The proposition that global corporations

increasingly set "the rules of the race" (p. 127) will not be news in Ireland; deference to these rules is already internalized in the habitus of political, business and media elites. Yet, by tying the fortunes of the Irish state to the logic of neoliberal nationalism, the boosterism of the Celtic Tiger revival story obscures the possibility of a different kind of Irish polity, one that critically interrogates the role of global corporations in Irish life, one that might give vitality to a different image of nation and a different conception of Irish modernity, one affectively and symbolically embedded in the current Irish presidency of Michael D. Higgins, even within the officially apolitical nature of the office.[19] And it obscures the urgent need for a different kind of transitional polity, one that seriously addresses a wider set of global problems (climate change, environmental destruction, global poverty, transnational migration, grotesque international and intranational inequalities) other than the problems of global capital.

Conclusion: The Possibility of a Radical Media Politics

This book offered a theoretical account of the relationship between neoliberalism, media and the political, supported by empirical analyses from different contexts. I focused on critically understanding the sedimented condition of neoliberalized media regimes, endeavouring to illuminate aspects and dimensions not captured in summary critical narratives about neoliberalism or in summary claims about "the neoliberal media". I emphasized the dialectical interplay between neoliberal logics and other discursive logics, interrogating the image of a monolithic neoliberalism that simply imposes itself on other domains and practices. The strategic intention was to identify the sites of a cultural politics within the immanent rationality of neoliberalized regimes, elucidating objects and logics that might be politically acted on in the name of a radically different kind of media and political culture.

Here I offer some brief reflections on how such a politics might be imagined, broaching strategic and normative concerns largely implicit throughout the rest of the book. But let's start with a brief summary of the different chapters. I began in the introduction by signalling my desire to critique neoliberalism, while also wanting to avoid the kind of totalizing narrative that often shapes critical discussions of the concept. I developed that argument in Chapter 1, prefaced by a review of how the category of neoliberalism is articulated, and disputed, in media research and elsewhere. I formulated a discourse theoretical account of neoliberalism in Chapter 2, alongside a brief history of neoliberalism's variegated political-intellectual trajectories and discursive articulations. A counterpart to Chapter 2, Chapter 3 elaborated on the concept of neoliberal logics, also insisting on Bourdieu's field theory as a necessary supplement to a logics-based approach.

Chapters 4 to 8 recast the argument in different empirical contexts. Chapter 4 looked at the media and political representation of a doctrinaire neoliberal identity in Aotearoa New Zealand in 2011, arguing that the surface impression of an antagonism to neoliberalism obscured the extent to which the country's mediated public culture is embedded in neoliberal logics. Chapter 5 examined the relationship between neoliberalism and the journalistic habitus, culminating in an analysis of how an Irish journalist's construction of the banking crisis was grounded in a realist disposition subordinate to the imperatives of a neoliberal social order. Chapter 6 investigated the mediated construction of the climategate affair, showing how the representation of climate change scientists as self-interested actors was energized by a neoliberalized hatred of politics. Chapter 7 explored the resonances between neoliberal and journalistic accounts of freedom, analysing how the rhetoric of press freedom was articulated in journalistic critiques of the Leveson report in the UK press. Chapter 8 examined the discursive interplay between national, international and neoliberal logics in the mediated construction of the Celtic Tiger, showing how the story of the "Irish model" was used to do similar discursive and ideological work at home and abroad.

The question of a political alternative to neoliberalism can be reformulated in the terms of Laclau and Mouffe: how might we conceptualize a "radical democratic" media politics that intervenes in (Bowman, 2007) the ideological and affective atmosphere of neoliberalized regimes? The notion of a critical intervention can be given different typological articulations, each assuming a different strategic disposition towards the antagonistic condition of the social. Together, they give us a glimpse of how the discursive logics, dispositions and sensibilities documented in the book might be critically interrogated from different perspectives and horizons.

Our first approach would assert a media-political identity in opposition to neoliberalized media norms. Here we have a strategy consistent with Laclau's (2005) theory of populism, necessitating the construction of a clear antagonism between "us" and "them". Mainstream media regimes are opposed because of their political complicity with the existing social order. Radical political energies are directed instead into the material construction of an alternative media infrastructure. This discourse might be articulated as part of an explicit critique of neoliberalism. Or it might be articulated against the capitalist media system. Logics of journalistic neutrality, balance and spectacle are rejected in favour of an explicitly anti-corporate journalism, embedded in a normative commitment to a participatory media democracy. Counter publics are constructed in opposition to the homogenous public of mainstream media (Dahlberg, 2007). The construction of new media spaces becomes, in effect, conterminous with the construction of political antagonisms (Marchart, 2011).

One example of this kind of radical media identity, if dated in some respects, is Indymedia. It embraces a "democratic, open-publishing system" explicitly opposed to the "distortions" of corporate media (Indymedia, 2014). Activist journalists commit to "the creation of radical, accurate, and passionate tellings of the truth" (Indymedia, 2014), far removed from the detached posture of the objective journalist. A more recent, if interlinked, example is the Occupy movement. The construction of an alternative media infrastructure – albeit one built on corporate networks and systems – was central to the initial political construction of a public not adequately captured by the public of mainstream journalism (DeLuca, Lawson & Sun, 2012). The movement articulated a horizontal political identity that did not demand "representation" within the existing political and journalistic infrastructure, because of the latter's capture by the interests of the "1%". Accordingly, Occupy's subsequent visibility in mainstream media spaces became the site of a culture clash, the establishment counter-response of "what do they want?" struggling to make sense of a politics opposed to the existing political architecture.

A second strategic approach would allow for a more fluid interpretation of Laclau's (2005) account of populism. Rather than equating a logic of political antagonism with a blanket hostility to neoliberalized media practices, it would focus on radicalizing journalistic field norms, rather than opposing them wholesale. This approach would still involve the construction of political antagonisms. Yet, its mode of critique might be more agonistic in temper (Connolly, 2000; Mouffe, 2005): establishing clear political borderlines, yet also critically acting on the Other's terrain. Antagonists are named and identified, but reconfigured as agonists: adversaries to be politically and strategically defeated, rather than enemies to be annihilated. The existing social order becomes a terrain to be strategically reconstituted as part of the labour of creating a new hegemonic formation. A militant and critical pluralism disrupts the repressive pluralism of neoliberal regimes, alert to the visceral and affective register of politics (Connolly, 2005) and symbolic violence of neoliberal reason. Discursive antagonisms are staged, but textured by an ethical recognition of the radical contingency of political identity (Glynos & Howarth, 2007).

Imagined from this strategic perspective, many of the logics and objects examined in the book become the potential discursive materials of a sustained antagonism against neoliberalized media regimes. Sedimented discursive logics are rearticulated and combined with heterogeneous elements previously invisible. The logic of individualization highlighted in Chapter 4 is opposed in the name of a collective democratic subject (Chang & Glynos, 2011). But, instead of simply constructing individualism as symptomatic of the ills of neoliberal society, it becomes a social logic to be disarticulated from its hegemonic iteration, disrupting a textbook neoliberal construction of the interests of the individual and the collective as antithetical, and a third way tendency to represent them as magically harmonious. Likewise, the political marketing paradigm (see Chapter 4) becomes a set of logics and idioms to be worked on, politicizing the hegemonic authority of marketing logics and metaphors in public communication.

The rhetorical appeal to "realism" is disarticulated from its market realist bearings (see Chapter 5), resignified to highlight the necessity of radically rethinking how we organize economy and society. The appeal to the unitary public of journalism (see Chapter 5) is confronted by a dissensual conception of the public, radically democratizing the ethical and political comportment of journalistic spaces (Markham, 2014; Muhlmann, 2010). The pejorative representation of politics is politicized and challenged (see Chapter 6), but liberated from the anti-political and moralizing premise that the given order of politics is the only politics possible. The concepts of the public good and common good are reclaimed (see Chapters 6 and 7), their inherently political nature affirmed rather than disavowed. The construction of "accountability" and "transparency" (see Chapter 6) as inherently democratic logics is contested, illuminating their role in governmentality mechanisms that repress the autonomy of different social fields. The "libertarian impulses" (Newman, 2011b, p. 239) in neoliberal thought are rechanneled into a critique of bureaucracy and audit regimes (Fisher, 2009), turning the neoliberal critique of "big government" into a critique of neoliberal governance. The rhetoric of the "free press" becomes the object of a sustained hegemonic labour to reimagine media freedom (see Chapter 7), building on Leveson's recognition of the inadequacy of a one-dimensional market discourse. The repetition of an ideological antagonism between market and state in debates about the political economy of media is interrupted, enabling a new configuration of state, market and civil society logics opposed to the logics of profit and corporatization (see Chapter 7). The neoliberalization of the nation becomes the site of a cultural and media politics to rearticulate the nation (Chapter 8) while rejecting the insularity of narrow nationalist appeals. The project becomes the springboard of a new internationalism and globalism, enabling forms of mediated transnational community and solidarity that cannot be articulated in a neoliberal imaginary.

Our final strategic approach might, if we excise the word's pejorative connotations, be described as more "reformist" in orientation, part of a transitional strategy (Connolly, 2008) of moving towards a different kind of mediated polity. This approach would focus on the possibility of political contestation within the existing social order, against the simplistic image of an entirely closed politics (see Bloom & Dallyn, 2011). Here social agents seek to strategically disturb, by reappropriating and rearticulating, the constitutive logics and performative idioms of neoliberalized regimes. A journalistic projection of self-interested motivation is projected back on to journalists themselves, politicizing a habitus normally taken for granted. The knowing reduction of representations to the interests behind them is questioned, even at the risk of seeming naïve in the symbolically violent and individualistic cultures that naturalize these assumptions. Or the language of individual freedom is used to represent the market, rather than the state, as the instrument of collective enslavement. Such micro-political strategies are not incompatible with the organized construction of political antagonisms. But the approach imagined here would emphasize the potential for fragmentary enactments of the political within a mediated world of politics as usual, sometimes having energizing effects that go beyond the particular event or moment. One obvious contemporary referent is the phenomenon of the viral video as a mechanism of quickly bringing public visibility to particular social and political issues, however fleeting the attention span.

Much more could be said about these strategic questions: I can only offer the fragments of a critical media politics here. However, let us conclude by coming back to a strategic concern considered at the outset of the book: the political and analytical consequences that come from privileging neoliberalism as an object of critique. It is not just a scholarly question: indeed, one of the legacies of the financial crisis seems to be the increasing media visibility of neoliberalism as a named antagonist. I positioned my own approach against a critical tendency to invoke the concept in a subsumptive fashion. I highlighted the problems with over-relying on appeals to a catch-all neoliberalism, obscuring the messy and paradoxical condition of neoliberalized formations. The concept potentially becomes an analytical fetish, locking critique into a repetitive telling of the same neoliberal story. Political openings are obscured rather than illuminated by the image of a unitary neoliberalism.

Yet, critiquing how the term operates as a conceptual and analytical device does *not* preclude its strategic deployment as a "summary label" (Peck, 2010, p. xii) in political rhetoric. The political victories of the Chavez regime and others in Latin America showed how neoliberalism could be productively constructed as an antagonist. Naming an antagonist invariably simplifies: there will always be an excess; there will always be discursive elements not captured. However, names that simplify are an absolutely central part of the discursive work of politics. They give definition and clarity to the failings in the existing social order and mobilize support for the idea that another order might be possible. Once again, we can learn from the neoliberals. Naming the post-World War II conjuncture as "collectivist" helped centre the neoliberal project, enabling different identities to see what they had in common. Moreover, Hayek, Friedman and others strengthened their arguments by engaging with the political rationality of their antagonists; in Mouffe's (2005) terms, the antagonist was an adversary. Perhaps the name "neoliberal" can perform a similar energizing role today, so long as we also critically engage with the political rationality of neoliberals. Certainly, they will not be defeated with moralizing narratives of our own.

Whether constructing neoliberalism as *the* antagonist can energize a popular desire for a different kind of society is a strategic question that will be answered differently in different contexts, and responsive to the particular audience. However we name our antagonists and adversaries, we will need to engage in the slow labour of transfiguring them into rhetorical forms that work politically and persuade others (Aune, 1994; Finlayson, 2012; Seymour, 2013), constructing modes of political identification and disidentification that resonate with – by disrupting – people's experiences of "everyday neoliberalism" (Mirowski, 2013, p. 89). We will need to act on a domain of subjectivity and intersubjectivity not easily grasped and moved by the logic of naming (Bourdieu, 2000). And our talk of antagonisms will need to be embedded in an affirmative and creative politics of our own, if it is to really feel like there are alternatives.

Notes

Introduction

1   All citations of "neoliberalism" hyphenated in the original text have been changed in the book.
2   Mirowski (2013) notes how those associated with neoliberal "doctrine did call themselves 'neoliberals' for a brief period lasting from the 1930s to the early 1950s, but then they abruptly stopped the practice" (p. 38).
3   Hayek's quote recalls Keynes's famous aphorism: "the ideas of economists and political philosophers, both when they are right and when they are wrong, are more powerful than is commonly understood" (cited in Krugman, 2011).
4   Laclau (1990) argues the traditional Marxist understanding of false consciousness equates ideology with the masking or obscuring of "a positive essence" (p. 92): people's capacity to see what is really going on in the world is concealed by an ideological representation. His problem with this can be simply stated: the positive essence does not exist, because all identities are marked by their structural failure to constitute themselves as fully positive forms. Laclau retains the concept of ideology and the concept of false consciousness, but he does so by flipping the false consciousness thesis around (Glynos, 2008). Instead of involving "the misrecognition of a positive essence", false consciousness consists of the failure to recognize the "precarious character" of any positive identity (Laclau, 1990, p. 92). Thus ideology is enacted in the assumption that something objectively *is* the case, without recognizing the conditions of possibility that enable the "something" to be in the first place. Ideology therefore becomes an inevitable feature of social life, because to perpetually interrogate the conditions of possibility of each and every social practice would, as Laclau and Mouffe (2001) suggest, be to enter the universe of the "psychotic" (p. 112) – like the driver of a car who cannot decide which side of the road he should be driving on, because he keeps questioning the arbitrariness of the particular social norm.
5   Dahlberg's (2011) discussion of the critical nature of discourse theory captures how critique is understood in this book. Emphasizing the affinities between Laclau and Mouffe and the critical theory of the Frankfurt School, he suggests critique "involves highlighting and explaining, using hegemonic logics...the occluded power relations, closures, and exclusions that accompany social systematicity" (p. 43). For specific reflections on the critique of neoliberalism, see Chapter 1. For further discussion of discourse theory, see Chapter 2.
6   Ranciere's (1999) distinction between politics and the police echoes Mouffe's (2005) distinction between the political and politics, though he does not follow her by making the argument in explicitly ontological terms.
7   My conception of radical democracy takes direction from Laclau and Mouffe (2001). Instead of disparaging liberal democratic institutions, they call for a

left politics that seeks to radically transform them. As they put it, the "project of 'radical and plural democracy' [is] conceived as a new stage in the deepening of the 'democratic revolution', as the extension of the democratic struggles for equality and liberty to a wider range of social relations" (p. xv). For further discussion of radical democracy, see Tønder and Thomassen (2006).

8 In researching this book, it was striking to note how often mainstream media were named as "neoliberal" in alternative media and blogs. Within a mainstream media culture, we might point to the high-profile journalism of someone like Paul Mason (2013), the former economics editor of BBC2's *Newsnight* and now the culture and digital editor of Channel 4 news. His willingness to critically interrogate the structural condition of neoliberal societies in his reporting of the financial crisis offers a marked contrast to some of the journalism analysed in this book (see, for example, the discussion of Stephen Collins's journalism in Chapter 5).

9 This is not to suggest such work is without value or entirely alien from the approach pursued here. For further discussion of the similarities and differences between the critical discourse analysis paradigm and the discourse analytical tradition informed by Laclau and Mouffe, see Carpenter and De Cleen (2007); Dahlberg and Phelan (2011).

Chapter 1

1 The concept of articulation is examined more fully in Chapter 2 as part of the discussion of post-Marxist discourse theory. For now, it is enough to note how the meaning of a concept is contingent on its discursive relationship with other concepts.

2 For example, one recent anthology of the political economy literature (Wasko, Murdock & Sousa, 2011) belies the impression of a field fixated on "neoliberalism". The term has only two index entries and does not feature in any of the 26 article titles (though the term is cited elsewhere in the book).

3 Hall's critique of an "economistic" Marxism needs to be put in historical context; his critique of Marxist theory should not be simplistically projected onto contemporary Marxist analyses that sometimes draw on him as a source (Dyer-Witheford & Compton, 2012). Hall's strategy was one of deliberately interrogating blind spots within Marxist theory then dominating the radical wing of the British Labour Party and which he saw as an ineffectual counterpoint to Thatcher. His analysis of capitalism was still broadly Marxist in character (see also Hall, 2011), a point sometimes obscured in the theoretical antagonism between cultural studies and political economy.

4 Critically assessing Flew's assessment of Freedman's book is beyond my focus. But it is worth noting that Freedman (2008) attaches similar caveats to the term: "there is a danger...that, in providing long lists of its negative tendencies, neoliberalism is itself flattened and homogenized, that it comes to be an umbrella term for all that is wrong with a commercially minded society" (p. 37).

5 Here I directly transpose Laclau and Mouffe's (2001) conception of society as an impossible object, implying any discursive articulation of society will always fail to capture the totality of the relations and processes potentially attributable to society. Peck (2010) makes an analogous point about the

impossibility of the neoliberal project itself, arguing it "possesses a progressive, forward-leaning dynamic by virtue of the very *unattainability* of its idealized direction" (p. 7).

Chapter 2

1   As a counterpoint, Best (2014) suggests "no one, witnessing the ongoing global impact of decades of hegemonic neoliberalism, would dispute that class is a 'special' – as in, especially invisible and especially insidious in its invisibility – modality of power and domination" (p. 272).

2   Laclau/Laclau and Mouffe's work is commonly named as "discourse theory" or "discourse analysis". Laclau has pursued the refinement of discourse theory concepts most purposefully, though others have made important contributions. For further discussion, see Dahlberg and Phelan (2011) and Howarth (2000).

3   Parts of this section were adapted from Phelan (2003).

4   The Beveridge Report published in December 1942, though "'not acted upon before 1945" (Cockett, 1995, p. 63), was a comprehensive survey of social insurance schemes in Britain and contained the blueprint for the subsequent expansion of the Welfare State (p. 59).

5   Peck (2010) suggests this episode has been omitted from most "received histories of the neoliberal counter-revolution", because of the "Mont Pelerinians ambivalence" about "the subsequent mutation of the German 'social model', which by the 1980s would be understood as an institutionalized *alternative* to neoliberalism" (p. 5).

6   *National Review*, the magazine founded by William J. Buckley Jr., offers a good indicator of Mont Pelerin's place in the canon of neoliberal and conservative political thought. The magazine included four books written by those present at the inaugural meeting in its top ten non-fiction books of the 20th century: Hayek's *Road To Serfdom* (No. 4) and *The Constitution of Liberty* (No. 9), Popper's *The Open Society and Its Enemies* (No. 6) and Friedman's *Capitalism and Freedom* (No. 10) (National Review, 2005).

7   Rand's "objectivist" philosophy famously shaped the thinking of the young Alan Greenspan. She was name-dropped, more recently, by US Republican congressman and former vice-presidential candidate Paul Ryan.

8   Laclau (2005) therefore conceptualizes discursive antagonisms as, following Derrida, both "impossible and necessary" (p. 71). They are "necessary" because all discourses and identities need an antagonistic element to ensure their representational coherence, to mark one discourse as different from others. However, they are also "impossible" because if the heterogeneous elements were articulated, they could potentially undermine the coherence of the antagonistic representation. The coherence of the antagonism would be called into question because of the articulation of discursive elements previously excluded. For further discussion of how Laclau's use of the impossibility/possibility couplet is informed by Derrida's deconstructionism, see Thomassen (2005).

9   My distinction in one sense simplifies, because Laclau uses the category of antagonism in two distinct senses – to signify both an explicitly named enemy, but also to signify a more radical "outside" and "lack": an ontological

condition of antagonism, essentially synonymous with the category of heterogeneity (Laclau, 2005; Thomassen, 2005). Thanks to Lincoln Dahlberg for pushing me on this point.

Chapter 3

1   Glynos and Howarth (2007) describe radical contingency as referring to "the inherent (as opposed to accidental) stability of an object's identity" (p. 109). This contingency is "ontological", because it highlights how all positive identities are structurally precarious and vulnerable to dislocation (pp. 109–110). For more on Laclau's account of radical contingency and dislocation, see Dahlberg and Phelan (2011), Howarth (2000), Laclau (1990), Laclau (2005) and Thomassen (2005).

2   This dual emphasis on the rules and grammar of a practice, and the conditions governing its constitution, draws on Heidegger's distinction between ontic-level and ontological-level social analysis (Glynos & Howarth, 2007, p. 208; see also Marchart, 2007). An ontic-level analysis examines everyday interpretations of a practice, typically working with taken-for-granted understandings of how the practice is signified and empirically understood. In contrast, an ontological-level perspective would explore the practice's conditions of possibility/impossibility; it asks *how* the practice is made possible.

3   The literature on mediation and mediatization would offer a useful platform for exploring this question (Meyer, 2002; Livingstone, 2009; Strömbäck, 2008), building on Altheide and Snow's (1979) concept of "media logic" and its deployment in the work of other media scholars (Berglez, 2011). Media and journalistic logics are most obviously conceptualized as a subset of Glynos and Howarth's (2007) category of "social logics", since they are a central element in the banal reproduction of the official social order. But media and journalistic logics are also potentially "political logics", since they can enable public contestation of the social order, and "dislocations" in the social order need to be made publicly visible and dramatized in the media (Owen, 2012). Media logics also clearly play a constitutive role in the production of fantasmatic logics: think about the "fantasy of stardom" underpinning talent shows like *The X Factor* (Gilbert, 2011, p. 95). Or consider the fantasmatic dimensions underpinning the journalist's desire to "speak truth to power". Whether these resonances justify a supplement to Glynos and Howarth's typology needs more than a quick answer. If media scholars might be inclined to see the need for a supplementary category, the relative parsimony of Glynos and Howarth's schema has its attractiveness and clarity.

4   As Glynos and Howarth (2007) recognize, the concept of subsumption has a distinct connotation within Marxist theory, emphasizing the "real subsumption" of social life to the logic of capital.

5   Exploring how the concept of neoliberal governmentality might overlap with the concept of neoliberal logics is beyond my focus here, even if there are clearly resonances. For an overview of the relationship between Laclau/Laclau and Mouffe and Foucault, see Howarth (2000).

6   My understanding of the term "regimes" follows Glynos and Howarth (2007), who use it to describe how a particular system of social logics has been ordered and institutionalized.

7 The Bourdieu quote highlighted by Hilgers (2013) captures the point well. Contrary to the functionalist stereotypes sometimes projected onto his work, Bourdieu is alert to how culture "is not just a common code, or even a common repertoire of answers to common problems, or a set of particular and particularised forms of thought, but rather a whole body of fundamental schemes, assimilated beforehand, which generate, according to an art of invention similar to that of musical writing, an infinite number of particular schemes, directly applied to particular situations" (Bourdieu [2005] cited in Hilgers, 2013, p. 78).

Chapter 4

1 The moment reinscribed a simplistic view of neoliberalism as an anti-statist project, failing to "recognize that, in practice, neoliberals too are statists (just different *kinds* of statists)" (Peck, 2010, p. 277).
2 Laclau's (1990) account of the political would interrogate Meyer's sharp distinction between media and political logics. Nonetheless, Meyer's distinction suggests an obvious affinity with Bourdieu's distinction between the journalistic field and the political field.
3 The qualitative selection of media texts was based on an initial sample of articles about the Brash coup sourced from the Newztext database. Unsurprisingly, given the corporatized nature of the New Zealand media system (Hope, 2012), the sample includes a large amount of recycled articles across newspaper titles. Many of the articles attributed to particular titles here were also published elsewhere.
4 Two of the policies identified by Brash (2011), which National had previously criticized in opposition, were the policy of interest-free student loans and the Working for Families Scheme – a system of tax-credit support for families with dependent children.
5 New Zealand print journalists now work for corporations, rather than individual titles, for owners and shareholders primarily based in Australia and as far away as Ireland (see Chapter 8). The recycling of content across papers within the same corporate structure is partly made possible by the regional character of the newspaper market. The condition of broadcasting is also indicative. After an abortive failure to rearticulate itself as a public service broadcaster under the third way formation of the early 2000s, the state-owned television broadcaster Television New Zealand (TVNZ) has now been hyper-commercialized, exemplified by a commercial deal with Sky TV where archived content, originally made under a public service remit, is now broadcast on a subscription basis only (Thompson, 2012). The neoliberalized character of the media system is often most tellingly captured in mundane news reports of TVNZ's annual profits, reported in the business pages as if it was just another commercial corporation. Normative arguments about the role of a public service broadcaster are passed over in silence or dismissed as the concerns of "elitist" academics.
6 My conception of dialectical processes follows Laclau's deconstructionist understanding of the dialectic, which emphasizes the constitutive failure underpinning any attempt to fully reconcile dialectically opposed identities (for further discussion, see Dahlberg & Phelan, 2011).

7 These political energies were evident in the 2012 and 2013 construction of a popular antagonism against the government's plan to sell different state assets, even if the protests saw no change in policy.

8 The initial enthusiasm for Shearer is now quite ironic given his subsequent resignation as party leader in August 2013, after failing to register any significant impact in public opinion polls. His leadership abilities were consistently questioned in 2012 and 2013, much of it coming from the same journalists and pundits who initially raved about his "back story" (Shearer had previously worked for the United Nations in different conflict zones).

Chapter 5

1 In interrogating discourses that dismiss journalistic agency, I am not proposing that we accept a journalistic tendency to exaggerate agency, as if journalists really are the heroic and autonomous figures valorized in journalistic mythologies. Rather, I am suggesting journalists' own interpretations of their practices need to be worked through analytically, rather than dismissed.

2 My argument here could perhaps be accused of imagining a strawman, since few would claim that mainstream and alternative media spaces are entirely autonomous from each other; most would emphasize the relational contestation between both domains. That said, I think the claim does capture a certain contemporary mood that Gilbert and Fisher (2013) link to the one-dimensional enthusiasm for anarchist ideas among many in the Occupy movement. As Fisher suggests: "an anarchist fatalism is the other side of capitalist realism. According to this logic, both Parliament and mainstream media are irredeemably corrupt, and we should totally disengage from them. This is given extra force by the appeal to networks and new technology, which allegedly make the mainstream media (or MSM) and the state irrelevant. I think these arguments should be rejected *tout court*" (Fisher in Gilbert & Fisher, 2013, p. 97).

3 Muhlmann's (2010) argument is a subtle one. Her appeal to democracy does not rely on some tired appeal to the "fourth estate" and "free press" as the alpha and omega of journalists' democratic credo. Rather, she appeals to a dissensual conception of the public, against the unified public of liberal democracy. The spirit of her critique resonates with Ranciere (2004), who likewise interrogates Bourdieu's suspicion of "mere" appearances, exemplified in a tendency to see "all recognition [as] misrecognition, [and] all unveiling [as] veiling" (p. 170).

4 Aune's critique of the "realist style" is grounded in a defence of the concept of rhetoric against the pejorative connotations normally associated with the term. Instead of its dominant media connotation as a synonym for "bullshit" and exaggerated speech, Aune and others (see Finlayson, 2012; Laclau, 2005) emphasize how rhetoric is constitutive of social practice.

5 Rather than formally referencing each Collins article, I have included dates when specific quotes are cited.

6 The term is articulated in a complimentary way in three instances, two authored by a journalist, Mark Brennock, filling in for Collins while on holidays. Brennock deploys the term in a context far removed from the immediate Irish one, to pay homage to the powerful "rhetoric" of Martin Luther King.

7 Populism is another signifier regularly Othered by Collins, another emblem of unreasonable and overblown political demands.

8 Of course, Collins articulates a particular logic of fairness that could be contested. Yet, his appeal to a moral economy (Clarke & Newman, 2012) at least avoids the kind of moralizing excesses and scapegoating strategies documented by Tyler (2013) in the UK. Denouncing "vested interests" seems comparatively tame when juxtaposed with an all-out attack against what Wacquant (2007) calls the "phony concept" of "the underclass" (p. 8).

9 Fisher's description of "capitalist realism" captures the affinities well. "Capitalist realism isn't the direct endorsement of neoliberal doctrine; it's the idea that, whether we like it or not, the world is governed by neoliberal ideas, and that won't change. There's no point fighting the inevitable" (cited in Fisher & Gilbert, 2013, p. 90).

10 To describe Collins's position as anti-political does not mean he is hostile to politicians or the world of "politics as usual". On the contrary, he spends much of the time in his columns defending politicians against what he sees as populist discourses. But he is hostile to the political as conceived by Laclau and others, because of his desire to repress fundamental questioning about the nature of the social order.

11 Collins's positioning of the Irish media as hostile to austerity recalls a familiar neoliberal move. His self-image might be that of the reasonable, fourth-estate journalist. Yet, his obsession with a media opposed to his own worldview bears a striking similarity to the rhetorical strategies of the climate change sceptics analysed in Chapter 6. We might counter Collins's claim by factually pointing out how austerity policies have been represented in the Irish media (Mercille, 2013a). And we might note the irony of a senior journalist at Ireland's most prestigious paper talking about "the media" as if it was somehow discrete from himself; indeed, there is a double irony in that journalists usually (and justifiably) dislike these kinds of catch-all denunciations, as if there were not different kinds of media – as if there was not a journalistic field with its complex geography of relational positionings and logics. But perhaps another response would be to suggest that Collins's claim is not simply self-serving, and that his perception does capture an atmosphere of "disaffected consent" (Gilbert cited in Clarke & Newman, 2012, p. 309) texturing the Irish media construction of the crisis. Critical attention is therefore focused on the discursive work of Collins and others in repressing the capacity of that popular disaffection to be transfigured into a strategically effective politics – in constructing antagonism as an aberration of the political, rather than a constitutive feature.

12 For example, the first comment on a June 2013 piece claiming the Irish media portrayal of the crisis is exaggerated, asked: "Is there anybody connected with the *Irish Times* even the slightest embarrassed with this nonsense that is repeated now almost on a weekly basis by Stephen Collins – this is now propaganda, plain and simple". Another commenter on the same article named Collins's stance as "neoliberal", suggesting "this...piece is so deluded and lacking perspective, in fact, that it is akin to Marie Antoinette telling the poor to eat cake". And a third wondered if they had "stumbled on the government press home page" such was their incredulity "about this ludicrous article".

Chapter 6

1 I feel a certain ambivalence about recycling the name "climategate", because it risks affirming the "scandal" narrative I set out to interrogate. It is hard to escape the social and discursive power of the initial naming; when talking about this chapter with others, climategate was usually the best memory trigger.

2 I am interested in exploring the cultural politics of climate change as it relates to the core problematic of the book. I make no claim to competency in assessing the scientific aspects of the issue.

3 For my purposes here, rational choice theory and public choice theory are treated as interchangeable.

4 Connolly (2008) captures this multi-modal political subjectivity in his description of Fox News anchor Bill O'Reilly: "the poster boy of the right expresses its temper in his facial expressions, vocal timbre, insistent interruptions, demand for unquestioned authority, and accusatory style" (p. 49).

5 The MPs expenses scandal was a major political and media event, following revelations by *The Daily Telegraph* that politicians from different parties had manipulated their expenses allowances for self-serving ends. Chang and Glynos (2011) suggest the "MPs' expenses scandal became a lightning rod for people's growing frustration with the economic and political system, signalling for many a new nadir in the public's trust toward institutions as such" (p. 110). The scandal had a domino effect elsewhere, inspiring a less dramatic local version in countries like New Zealand.

6 Chang and Glynos's (2011) discussion of fantasmatic logics is also suggestive in the context of climategate. Drawing on a psychoanalytically inflected discourse theoretical approach, they identify two main fantasies in the tabloid coverage of the MPs expenses scandal: a fantasy of individual "self-sufficiency" and a fantasy of state "paternalism" – the first the exemplar of a neoliberal subjectivity, the second its defining antagonist. Those identifying with the fantasy of individual self-sufficiency treated the scandal as entirely predictable, because "of course" politicians and others will seek to "sponge" off the state. An analogous version of this fantasy energized the media representation of climategate, articulated in assessments that affected little surprise at the notion that scientists might "manipulate" data to support their generous funding regimes. The fantasy of state paternalism speaks to a more redemptive image of the state, a belief in its capacity "to do right" by its citizens. However, it is a fantasy neoliberals have often skilfully disrupted, rechanneling its disappointments into a generalized critique of the state's capacity to serve the public good. Indeed, interpreted in the context of the parallel financial crisis, the media hype and excesses of the MPs expenses scandal can be seen as emblematic of a strategy of neoliberal distraction – once again constructing the state and politicians as "the problem" despite the much greater financial significance of the banking scandals (Clarke & Newman, 2012; Fisher, 2009).

7 If my argument interrogates public discourses that *reduce* representations to the interests behind him, invoking Bourdieu would suggest that I am hardly indifferent to the interested nature of social practices. Although he is sceptical about the possibility of a disinterested social practice (see Bourdieu & Eagleton, 1994) Bourdieu (1998a, 2005) was equally critical of neoclassical economics and rational choice theory for normalizing a simplistic conception of interest.

8 All comments taken from both blogs are republished in their original form.
9 Using the general search term "University of East Anglia", I found 223 stories on the Factiva database between November 17 and November 24, most of which were about the hacked emails. The term "climategate" produced 883 articles for 2009 and an additional 2016 in 2010.
10 To interrogate journalists' appeal to accountability and transparency is not to suggest that these logics cannot be put to emancipatory and democratizing ends. Rather, it is to recognize how these logics can also legitimize symbolically violent regimes that repress the autonomy of other social fields (Birchall, 2011). For a rich analysis of how an aggressive journalistic posture acting in the name of the "taxpayer" can undermine the autonomy of the visual arts field, see Bernanke (2013).
11 The point can only be noted here. But the Chomsky example does prompt the question of how the truth effects of rational choice projections might be replicated in left-wing discourses that, as we noted in Chapter 5, are similarly inclined to reduce representation to the interests behind them.

Chapter 7

1 Contrary to the impression that the Leveson (2012) report constituted a radical definition of the relationship between state and media, the report was clearly authored from within the discourse of the fourth estate, praising the press's general capacity to "hold power to account" (p. 5). The corrosive influence of the commercial news environment was discussed extensively at the Inquiry, and the published report included a chapter on plurality and media ownership. However, the recommendations steered away from any systematic assessment of the political economy of the UK media system. Freedman and Schlosberg (2013) characterize the issue of "concentrated media ownership" as the "real elephant in the room", given that "the gap between the problem as laid out [in the report] and the solutions proposed is so vast".
2 The distinction between positive and negative liberty was originally formulated by Isaiah Berlin (see Gray, 1980, 1986). I use the categories of freedom and liberty interchangeably in this chapter. For a critical discussion of the limits of the positive/negative liberty binary, see Connolly (2013).
3 Hayek was partly attempting to reclaim a classical liberty tradition from what he and others saw as John Stuart Mill's impurification of liberalism with socialist ideas. Caldwell's (2008) discussion of an unpublished paper of Hayek's on Mill suggests Hayek explained Mill's turn to socialism in crude gendered and biographical terms, essentially blaming Mill's wife, Harriet Taylor Mill, for enfeebling his character.
4 To underline his point, Hayek (1944) describes the Nazi Sate as more "moral" than the liberal state because the former "imposes on its members its views on all moral questions" (p. 57).
5 The importance of the intellectual as an antagonist in neoliberal thought was recognized by the Institute of Economic Affairs' republication of the condensed version of *The Road to Serfdom* in 2005, supplementing it with Hayek's 1949 essay "The Intellectuals and Socialism". The condensed version of the

book was originally published in the *Readers Digest* in 1945, selling in the "hundreds of thousands" and giving Hayek an unprecedented public profile (Cockett, 1995, p. 100).

6 Contra Hayek's notion of an "impersonal market", the coercive potential of market actors has been quite literally personified in the legal rights of corporations – in the fiction of the corporation as a person with legal rights.

7 Hanretty (2013) makes a similar argument against the establishment of the Leveson Inquiry itself, reading it as symptomatic of a political culture where "difficult decisions involving normatively sensitive issues are systematically turned over to judges" (p. 10).

8 Australia had its own version of Leveson in the Finklestein Inquiry, which convened in September 2011. The power of the Murdoch press was at the centre of the Inquiry, and enacted in a "vitriolic and defensive" media representation of the Inquiry's recommendations, again asserted in the name of "press freedom" (Lidberg & Hirst, 2013, p. 114).

9 This rival proposal became a central part of the stand-off in the lead-up to the ratification of the Royal Charter. At the time of writing, the industry is still planning to establish its own system of self-regulation in parallel with the Royal Charter regulator.

10 Hume would not be the first on the libertarian left to identity with Hayekian ideas. See, for instance, Griffith's (2011) discussion of how Hillary Wainwright, the left-wing journalist and founder of *Red Pepper* magazine, explicitly appropriated Hayek's critique of the state.

11 For a critical, yet not dismissive, assessment of Hayek's critique of an abstracted rationalism, see Connolly (2013). For a discussion of how Hayek's account of tacit knowledge has been developed by those on the libertarian-left, see Griffiths (2011).

12 Incidentally, the connection to Hirschman was noted by a poster called "Alan" in the comment thread on Lashmar's article in *openDemocracy*.

13 The actor Hugh Grant was a member of the Hacked Off campaign.

Chapter 8

1 Framing the chapter as a conjunctural analysis is informed by Grossberg's (2010) attempt to renew cultural studies's focus on "context(s) as the real object of study of cultural studies", a "context...generally understood as a conjuncture" (p. 40). In a Deleuzian spirit, he captures the dynamic movement between objects and contexts that my analysis seeks to grasp: "a conjuncture is constituted by, at, and as the articulation of multiple, overlapping, competing, reinforcing, etc, lines of force and transformation, destabilization and (re-)stabilization, with differing temporalities and spatialities, producing a potentially but never actually chaotic assemblage or articulations of contradictions and contestations" (p. 41).

2 Couldry (2003b) formally defines media rituals as "formalized actions organized around key media-related categories and boundaries whose performance frames, or suggests a connection with, wider media-related values" (p. 29). He cites as a mundane example the everyday articulation of a distinction between "ordinary people" and "people in the media" (p. 102), the power

dynamics of which are evident in the standard practice of not naming the latter in journalistic vox-pops.

3   A similar argument informs Billig's (1999) analysis of Freud (for further discussion, see Phelan, 2012). Billig questions the tendency to conceptualize repression as a "mysterious inner process" (p. 1), something internal to the individual mind and psyche. Departing from a Lacanian reading of the unconscious as a "deep structure" (p. 81), homologous to the structure of language, Billig emphasizes instead how repression works through mundane linguistic practices and storytelling. "Language is inherently expressive and repressive" (p. 1), he argues, and the act of remembering something is simultaneously an act of forgetting elements that might disturb the coherence of the narrated memory. In his view, repression is something that is "socially, rather than biologically, constituted" – or, as he puts it, repression is "ideologically constituted, for ideologies concern what people in a particular historical epoch do not talk of" (p. 10).

4   Mitchell's claim seems, prima facia, implausible, even for those of us with only a patchy grasp of the history of political economy. He recognizes that foundational figures like Adam Smith talked about economy. Yet, when Smith uses the term, Mitchell (2005a) argues "the word carries the older meaning of frugality or the prudent uses of resources" (p. 128), quite distinct from its modern usage.

5   Mitchell (2005a) recognizes that Polanyi (see further discussion in Chapter 7) was an "important figure in the creation of the concept of the economy in the 1940s" (p. 130). Yet he argues Polanyi's (1944) analysis of the capitalist transformations of the early 19th century projected a contemporary use of the term "onto a period a century before the word was used" (p. 130) in the modern sense claimed by Mitchell.

6   Because of my limited familiarity with Mitchell's work, I emailed him directly to check if he had researched media elsewhere (Personal correspondence, 2013).

7   For a general discussion of how the political economy of media systems has been entangled in the trajectory of neoliberal political economy, see Dyer-Witheford and Compton's (2012) discussion of "slump media".

8   Starr (2004) describes *The Economist*'s readership as "an elite group of highly educated readers with interests in business, finance, economics, and politics...[that are] overwhelmingly male (91%). Its publicity highlights that it circulates in the highest echelons of decision makers, including 'some impressive names from among the world's opinion leaders' – a point that is illustrated by a photo of US president George W. Bush reading *The Economist* on board a plane" (p. 379).

9   *The Economist*'s antagonistic division between two models of political economy recalls the "Boston versus Berlin" debates of Irish elites (Allen, 2003) over the appropriate development trajectory and model for Ireland. Should the country embrace the free-market, entrepreneurial culture of the US? Or should it embrace the corporatist and social democratic ethos of European countries like Germany? To its critics, the debate was not much of a debate at all, offering little more than a choice between the doctrinaire neoliberalism of the US and the ordoliberal institutions of the German state. Nonetheless, the desire of some senior government ministers to align Ireland with Boston

rather than Berlin shaped an Irish elite condescension towards Europe during the Celtic Tiger years, articulated in flattering comparisons of the dynamism of the Irish economy with the sluggish condition of continental Europe.

10 For instance, *The Guardian* published a long feature-length article in December 1999 "investigat[ing] the mire behind the smiling face of the Celtic Tiger" (Cooney, 1999). Similarly, an August 2000 piece documented how the "fabled Celtic success story conceals a harsh reality of corruption, poverty and racism" (O'Mahony, 2000).

11 The company had been already part privatized in 1996, when a 20 per cent stake was sold as part of a strategic alliance with a consortium consisting of the Swedish and Dutch national telecom companies (Palcic & Reeves, 2011).

12 The editorials cited in this section are referenced in-text only. For further details, see Phelan (2007b).

13 The economy takes the paradoxical form of what Grossberg (2010), in an explicit engagement with Mitchell, calls an "embedded disembeddedness" (p. 147): simultaneously "experienced as something outside of, greater than, and even in control of the social and, at the same time, as the very medium of our lived reality" (p. 150).

14 The government's attempt to deflect blame for the crisis was clearly opportunistic. However, it would go entirely against the grain of my argument if I were to disparage the focus on "mere" talk. If we subscribe to Laclau's conception of representations as constitutive of social reality, or side with Mitchell's (2005a) view of a corporate-driven economy as "one formed more and more out of sociotechnical processes concerned with the manufacture of images and management of representations" (p. 140), the government's strategic concerns about the truth effects of representations (and not just *media* representations – think of the representational power of credit ratings agencies) were entirely justified.

15 For a discussion of the post-colonial dynamics of Irish neoliberalism, see Kitchin et al. (2012).

16 Priyadharshini (1999) offers an interesting take on the generalized phenomenon of the "Tiger" economy, observing how the epithet is typically applied to ex-colonies. The metaphor embodies a subtle form of neocolonial Othering, she argues, animalizing the counter-intuitive economic success of identities historically represented as "wild beasts" (p. 9). To run with the argument, we might say the collapse of the Celtic Tiger revitalized an old colonial stereotype of Irish stupidity and fecklessness, rendering the development consistent with what we have known about "the Irish" all along. This intersects with an Irish fixation on the "Irishness" of the crisis, amplifying a narcissistic national tendency to cast ourselves as the "most oppressed people in the world ever" (what Kennedy [1997] dubbed the MOPE syndrome). Justified public anger towards the Irish political establishment is simultaneously depoliticized, embodied in Irish people's own fatalism about a national capacity to stuff things up. The line of argument is clearly impressionistic, based on my own assessment of the Irish crisis from afar and my own encounters with these colonial projections. However, these thematics were clearly discernible in some of the comment threads on Irish news websites during the crisis, sometimes given particularly galling expression in the cosmopolitan emigrant's relief to be done with the place.

17   The question of ideology has obviously been a central concern throughout this book. My scepticism here is directed against a residual tendency to see ideological matters as relatively superficial – something that camouflages social "reality", rather than a general feature of social orders (Finlayson, 2012). I also draw on Bourdieu's discussion of how the charge of ideology can "itself becom[e] an instrument of symbolic domination" (cited in Bourdieu & Eagleton, 1994, p. 265).

18   To cite just one stark statistic, O'Brien (2013a) notes how "of the €77 billion earned from exports" in 2012, "90 per cent was generated by non-Irish companies".

19   An intellectual, poet and former government minister, Higgins has explicitly critiqued neoliberalism in a number of political speeches since coming to office, prompting criticism from some in the journalistic police that he is going beyond the merely "ceremonial" nature of the office (see O'Brien, 2013b). McCaffery correctly notes how Higgins's intellectual reflections are regarded with some condescension from the market realists in government – commended for their worthiness, but demarcated from the universe of policy making (cited in Lynch, 2013).

References

Abercrombie, N., Hill, S. & Turner, B. S. (1980). *The dominant ideology thesis.* London: George Allen and Unwin.

Ahern apologizes for suicide remark (video file). (2007, July 4). Retrieved from http://www.rte.ie

Allen, K. (2003). Neither Boston nor Berlin: Class polarization and neo-liberalism in the Irish Republic. In C. Coulter & S. Coleman (Eds.), *The end of Irish history: Critical reflections on the Celtic Tiger* (pp. 56–73). Manchester: Manchester University Press.

Altheide, D. L. & Snow, R. P. (1979). *Media logic.* Thousand Oaks, CA: Sage.

Amadae, S. M. (2003). *Rationalizing capitalist democracy: The cold war origins of rational choice liberalism.* Chicago: University of Chicago Press.

Ampuja, M. (2012). Globalization theory, media centrism and neoliberalism: A critique of recent intellectual trends. *Critical Sociology, 38*(2), 281–301.

Anderson, B. (1991). *Imagined communities: Reflections on the origin and spread of nationalism* (Revised edition). London: Verso.

Andersson, L. (2012). There is no alternative: The critical potential of alternative media for challenging neoliberal discourse. *tripleC: Communication, Capitalism & Critique, 10*(2): 752–764.

Andrejevic, M. (2008). Theory review: Power, knowledge, and governance. *Journalism Studies, 9*(4), 605–614.

Andrejevic, M. (2010). Decision markets and vernacular postmodernism. *Journal of Communication Inquiry, 34*(4), 403–416.

Armstrong, J. (2011, May 7). Elements of farce to Brash's outsider status. *The New Zealand Herald.* Retrieved from http://www.nzherald.co.nz

Artzybasheff, B. (1963, July 12). *Prime Minister Sean Lemass* (cover illustration). *Time.* Retrieved from http://www.time.com

Atkinson, J. (2010, August 17). Joe Atkinson: Politics as comedy. *The New Zealand Herald.* Retrieved from http://www.nzherald.co.nz

Aune, J. A. (1994). *Rhetoric and Marxism.* Boulder, CO: Westview Press.

Aune, J. A. (2001). *Selling the free market: The rhetoric of economic correctness.* New York: Guilford Press.

Aune, J. A. (2008). Democratic style and ideological containment. *Communication and Critical/Cultural Studies, 6*(3), 482–490.

Banning, M. E. (2009). When poststructural theory and contemporary politics collide—The vexed case of global warming. *Communication and Critical/Cultural Studies, 6*(3), 285-304.

Barnett, C. (2003). *Culture and democracy: Media, space and representation.* Edinburgh: Edinburgh University Press.

Barnett, C. (2005). The consolations of neoliberalism. *Geoforum, 36*(1), 7–12.

Barnett, C. (2006). Temporality and the paradoxes of democracy. *Political Geography, 24*(5), 641–647.

Barnett, C. (2008). Political affects in public space: Normative blind-spots in non-representational ontologies. *Transactions of the Institute of British Geographers, 33*(2), 186–200.

Barnett, S. (2013a). Leveson past, present and future: The politics of press regulation. *The Political Quarterly, 84*(3), 353–361.

Barnett, S. (2013b, April 3). Three-D Issue 20: Oh what tangled webs they weave: A response to Paul Lashmar. *Media, Communication and Cultural Studies Association.* Retrieved from http://www.meccsa.org.uk

Barnhurst, K. G. (2011). The new "media affect" and the crisis of representation for political communication. *The International Journal of Press/Politics, 16*(4), 573–593.

Barry, A. (2002). The anti-political economy. *Economy and Society, 31*(2), 268–284.

Beaud, M. & Dostaler, G. (1997). *Economic thought since Keynes: A history and dictionary of major economists.* London: Routledge.

Benson, R. (2007, August). *After Habermas: The revival of a macro-sociology of media.* Paper presented at the American Sociological Association Annual Conference, New York.

Benson, R. & Neveu, E. (2005). *Bourdieu and the journalistic field.* Cambridge: Polity.

Berglez, P. (2006). *The materiality of media discourse.* Orebro: Orebro University Press.

Berglez, P. (2011). Inside, outside, and beyond media logic: Journalistic creativity in climate reporting. *Media Culture & Society, 33*(3), 449–465.

Berglez, P. (2013). *Global journalism: Theory and practice.* New York: Peter Lang.

Berglez. P. & Olausson, U. (2014). The post-political condition of climate change: An ideology approach. *Capitalism Nature Socialism, 25*(1), 54–71.

Bernanke, J. (2013). *Interfield antagonisms: An examination of the New Zealand journalistic and visual arts fields in the case of the mainstream media coverage of et. al. and the 2005 Venice Biennale* (Doctoral dissertation). Retrieved from WorldCat. (847519031)

Best, B. (2004). Speculating without hedging: What Marxian political economy can offer Laclauian discourse theory. *Critical Discourse Studies, 11*(3), 272–287.

Billig, M. (1995). *Banal nationalism.* London: Sage.

Billig, M. (1999). *Freudian repression: Conversation creating the unconscious.* Cambridge: Cambridge University Press.

Billig, M. (2003). Critical discourse analysis and the rhetoric of critique. In G. Weiss & R. Wodak (Eds.), *Critical Discourse Analysis: Theory and interdisciplinarity* (pp. 35–46). London: Palgrave Macmillan.

Birch, K. (2011). Have we ever been neoliberal? (Working Paper). Retrieved from http://www.iippe.org/wiki/images/c/cd/Working_Paper_Ever_Neoliberal.pdf

Birch, K. & Mykhnenko, V. (Eds.). (2010). *The rise and fall of neoliberalism: The collapse of an economic order?* London: Zed Books.

Birch, K. & Tickell, A. (2010). Making neoliberal order in the United States. In K. Birch & V. Mykhnenko (Eds.), *The rise and fall of neoliberalism: The collapse of an economic order?* (pp. 42–59). London: Zed Books.

Birchall, C. (2011). Transparency, interrupted. *Theory, Culture & Society, 28*(7–8), 60–84.

Bloom, P. & Dallyn, S. (2011). The paradox of order: Reimagining ideological domination. *Journal of Political Ideologies, 16*(1), 53–78.

Blumler, J. & Coleman, S. (2010). Political communication in freefall: The British case – and others? *The International Journal of Press/Politics, 15*(2), 139–154.

Blumler, J. & Kavanagh, D. (1999). The third age of political communication: Influences and features. *Political Communication, 16*(3), 209–230.

Blyth, M. (2013a). *Austerity: The history of a dangerous idea*. Oxford: Oxford University Press.

Blyth, M. (2013b, November 15). Eternal austerity makes complete sense – if you're rich. *The Guardian*. Retrieved from http://www.theguardian.com

Bourdieu, P. (1977). *Outline of a theory of practice*. Cambridge: Cambridge University Press.

Bourdieu, P. (1990). *Homo academicus*. Cambridge: Polity.

Bourdieu, P. (1991). *Language and symbolic power*. Cambridge: Polity.

Bourdieu, P. (1998a). *Acts of resistance: Against the new myths of our time*. Cambridge: Polity.

Bourdieu, P. (1998b). *On television and journalism*. London: Pluto.

Bourdieu, P. (2000). *Pascalian meditations*. Cambridge: Polity.

Bourdieu, P. (2005a). The political field, the social science field, and the journalistic field. In R. Benson & E. Neveu (Eds.), *Bourdieu and the journalistic field* (pp. 29–47). Cambridge: Polity.

Bourdieu, P. (2005b). *The social structures of the economy*. Cambridge: Polity.

Bourdieu, P. & Eagleton, T. (1994). Doxa and common life: An interview. In S. Žižek (Ed.), *Mapping ideology* (pp. 265–277). London & New York: Verso.

Bourdieu, P. & Wacquant, L. (1992). *An invitation to reflexive sociology*. Chicago: University of Chicago Press.

Bourdieu, P. & Wacquant, L. (2001). NewLiberalSpeak: Notes on the new planetary vulgate. *Radical Philosophy, 105*(Jan/Feb), 2–5.

Bowman, P. (2007). *Post-Marxism versus cultural studies: Theory, politics and Intervention*. Edinburgh: Edinburgh University Press.

Boykoff, M. T. (2013). Public enemy no. 1? Understanding media representations of outlier views on climate change. *American Behavioral Scientist, 57*(6), 796–817.

Bradley, R. (2012, June 11). The green road to serfdom (web log post). Retrieved from http://www.thegwpf.org/robert-bradley-geen-road-serfdom/

Brady, C. (2005). *Up with the Times*. Dublin: Gill & Macmillan Ltd.

Brash, D. (2011). Letter to John Key. *Scoop*. Retrieved September 10, 2011 from http://www.scoop.co.nz/stories/PO1105/S00186/letter-to-john-key.htm

Brash "Too Extreme" for Key (2011, April 30). *Taranaki Daily News*. Retrieved from http://www.newstext.com.au

Brenchley, F. (1996, August 5). Ireland builds success on input from all sides. *The Australian Financial Review*. Retrieved from http://www. factiva.com

Brenner, N. & Theodore, N. (2002). Cities and the geographies of "actually existing neoliberalism". *Antipode 34*, 349–79.

Brown, W. (2003). Neo-liberalism and the end of liberal democracy. *Theory & Event, 7*(1).

Browne, H. (2006, May). Irish Times. *The Dubliner*. Retrieved May 2007 from http://www.thedubliner.ie

Browne, V. (2013, May 22). Government zealously guards our wild west tax haven. *The Irish Times*. Retrieved from http://www.irishtimes.com

Buchanan, J. M. (1989). Post-Reagan political economy. In J. M Buchanan (Ed.), *Reaganomics and after* (pp. 21–39). London: Institute of Economic Affairs.

Burke, K. (1969). *A rhetoric of motives*. Los Angeles: University of California Press, original.

Caldwell, B. (2008). Hayek on Mill. *History of Political Economy, 40*(4), 689–704.

Cappella, J. N. & Jamieson, K. H. (1997). *Spiral of cynicism: The press and the public good*. New York: Oxford University Press.

Carey, J. W. (1997a). Afterword: The culture in question. In E. S. Munson & C. A. Warren (Eds.), *James Carey: A critical reader* (pp. 308–339). Minneapolis: University of Minnesota Press.

Carey, J. W. (1997b). The dark continent of American journalism. In E. S. Munson & C. A. Warren (Eds.), *James Carey: A critical reader* (pp. 144–188). Minneapolis: University of Minnesota Press.

Carey, J. (1997c). A Republic, if you can keep it: Liberty and public life in the age of Glasnost. In E. S. Munson & C. A. Warren (Eds.), *James Carey: A critical reader* (pp. 207–27). Minneapolis: University of Minnesota Press.

Carpentier, N. & De Cleen, B. (2007). Bringing discourse theory into media studies. *Journal of Language and Politics, 6*(2), 265–293.

Carswell, S. (2013a, May 22). Apple defends use of Irish subsidiaries as tax strategy comes under scrutiny. *The Irish Times*. Retrieved from http://www.irishtimes.com

Carswell, S. (2013b, May 23). US Senate hearing generates negative publicity for Ireland. *The Irish Times*. Retrieved from http://www.irishtimes.com

Carswell, S. (2013c, May 24). Fallout from Apple could be serious for Ireland. *The Irish Times*. Retrieved from http://www.irishtimes.com

Carswell, S. & Lynch, S. (2013, May 21). Government denies facilitating Apple tax avoidance. *The Irish Times*. Retrieved from http://www.irishtimes.com

Carswell, S., Lynch, S. & Beesley, A. (2013, May 22). Ireland labelled a "tax haven" as US Senate investigates Apple's offshore strategies. *The Irish Times*. Retrieved from http://www.irishtimes.com

Carvalho, A. (2007). Ideological cultures and media discourses on scientific knowledge: Re-reading news on climate change. *Public Understanding of Science, 16*(2), 223–243.

Castree, N. (2006). From neoliberalism to neoliberalisation: Confusions, consolations and necessary illusions. *Environment and Planning, 38*(1), 1–6.

Cawley, A. (2012). Sharing the pain or shouldering the burden? News-media framing of the public sector and the private sector in Ireland during the economic crisis, 2008–2010. *Journalism Studies, 13*(4), 600–615.

Celtic Tiger roars with good news (1996, December 11). *The Daily Mirror*. Retrieved from http://www. factiva.com

Celtic metamorphosis (2013, January 12). *The Economist*. Retrieved from www. economist.com

Chakravartty, P. & Schiller, D. (2010). Global financial crisis: Neoliberal newspeak and digital capitalism in crisis. *International Journal of Communication, 4*, 670–692.

Chambers, S. A. & Finlayson, A. (2008). Ann Coulter and the problem of pluralism: From values to politics. *Borderlands, 7*(1). Retrieved from http://www.borderlands.net.au

Champagne, P. & Marchetti, D. (2005). The contaminated blood scandal: Reframing medical news. In R. Benson & E. Neveu (Eds.), *Bourdieu and the journalistic field* (pp. 113–134). Cambridge: Polity.

Chang, W. & Glynos, J. (2011). Ideology and politics in the popular press: The case of the 2009 UK MPs' Expenses Scandal. In L. Dahlberg & S. Phelan (Eds.),

Discourse theory and critical media politics (pp. 106–127). London: Palgrave Macmillan.

Cho, Y. (2008). We know where we're going, but we don't know where we are: An interview with Lawrence Grossberg. *Journal of Communication Inquiry, 32*(2), 102–122.

Chouliaraki, L. & Fairclough, N. (1999). *Discourse in late modernity: Rethinking critical discourse analysis.* Edinburgh: Edinburgh University Press.

Clarke, J. (2008). Living with/in and without neo-liberalism. *Focaal, 51*(Summer), 135–47.

Clarke, J. (2010). Of crises and conjunctures: The problem of the present. *Journal of Communication Inquiry, 34*(4), 337–354.

Clarke, J. & Newman, J. (2012). The alchemy of austerity. *Critical Social Policy, 32*(3), 299–319.

Cleary, J. (2007). *Outrageous fortune: Capital and culture in modern Ireland.* Dublin: Field Day Publications.

Cloud, D. L. (1994). The materiality of discourse as oxymoron: A challenge to critical rhetoric. *Western Journal of Communication, 58*(1), 141–163.

Cockett, R. (1995). *Thinking the unthinkable: Think-tanks and the economic counter-revolution, 1931–1983.* London: Fontana Press.

Cohen, N. (2008). The valorization of surveillance: Towards a political economy of Facebook. *Democratic Communiqué, 22*(1), 5–22.

Coleman, M. (2014). Coleman biography abstract. Retrieved from http://www.marccoleman.ie

Collier, S. J. (2012). Neoliberalism as big leviathan, or...? A response to Wacquant and Hilgers. *Social Anthropology, 20*(2), 186–195.

Comrie, M. (2012). Politics, power and political journalists. In M. Hirst, S. Phelan & V. Rupar (Eds.), *Scooped: The politics and power of journalism in Aotearoa, New Zealand* (pp. 114–128). New Zealand: AUT Media.

Conboy, M. (2004). *Journalism: A critical history.* London: Sage

Connolly, W. E. (2005). *Pluralism.* Durham, NC: Duke University Press.

Connolly, W. E. (2008). *Capitalism and Christianity, American style.* Durham, NC: Duke University Press.

Connolly, W. E. (2013). *The fragility of things: Self-organizing processes, neoliberal fantasies, and democratic activism.* Durham, NC: Duke University Press.

Coole, D. (2005). Rethinking agency: A phenomenological approach to embodiment and agentic capacities. *Political Studies, 53*, 124–142.

Cooney, P. (1999, December 4). Dirty dealings. *The Guardian.* Retrieved from http://www.theguardian.com

Corcoran, F. & Fahy, D. (2009). Exploring the European elite sphere: The role of the *Financial Times. Journalism Studies, 10*(1), 100–113.

Corner, J. (1999). [Review of the book *On television and journalism,* by P. Bourdieu]. *European Journal of Communication, 14*(2), 251–253.

Corner, J. (2003). Mediated persona and political culture. In J. Corner & D. Pels (Eds.), *Media and the restyling of politics* (pp. 67–85). London: Sage.

Cottle, S. (2006). Mediatized rituals: Beyond manufacturing consent. *Media, Culture & Society, 28*(3), 411–432.

Couldry, N. (2003a). Media meta-capital: Extending the range of Bourdieu's field theory. *Theory and Society, 32*(5–6), 653–677.

Couldry, N. (2003b). *Media rituals: A critical approach.* London: Routledge.

Couldry, N. (2008a). Media discourse and the naturalisation of categories. In R. Wodak & V. Koller (Eds.), *Handbook of communication in the public sphere* (Vol. 4) (pp. 67–88). Berlin and New York: Mouton de Gruyter.

Couldry, N. (2008b). Actor network theory and media: Do they connect and on what terms? In A. Hepp, F. Krotz, S. Moores & C. Winter (Eds.), *Connectivity, networks and flows: Conceptualizing contemporary communications* (pp. 93–110). Cresskill, NJ: Hampton Press.

Couldry, N. (2009). Does "the media" have a future? *European Journal of Communication, 24*(4), 437–449.

Couldry, N. (2010). *Why voice matters: Culture and politics after neoliberalism.* London: Sage.

Coulter, C. & Coleman, S. (Eds.). (2003). *The end of Irish history: Critical reflections on the Celtic Tiger.* Manchester: Manchester University Press.

Crouch, C. (2011). *The strange non-death of neoliberalism.* Cambridge: Polity.

Cubitt, S. (2011). *Time to live.* Paper presented at the 17th International Symposium for Electronic Art, Istanbul, Turkey. Retrieved September 2013 from http://isea2011.sabanciuniv.edu/paper-list

Curran, J. (2002). *Media and power.* London: Routledge.

Cushion, S. (2012). *Television journalism.* London: Sage.

Dahlberg, L. (2007). Rethinking the fragmentation of the cyberpublic: From consensus to contestation. *New Media & Society, 9*(5), 827–847.

Dahlberg, L. (2011). Discourse theory as critical media politics? Five questions. In L. Dahlberg & S. Phelan (Eds.), *Discourse theory and critical media politics* (pp. 41–63). Basingstoke: Palgrave Macmillan.

Dahlberg, L. & Phelan, S. (2011). *Discourse theory and critical media politics.* Basingstoke: Palgrave Macmillan.

Dahlgren, P. (2004). Theory, boundaries and political communication: The uses of disparity. *European Journal of Communication, 19*(1), 7–18.

Darras, E. (2005). Media consecration of the political order. In R. Benson & E. Neveu (Eds.), *Bourdieu and the journalistic field* (pp. 156–173). Cambridge: Polity.

Dawes, S. (2013). Press freedom, privacy and the public sphere. *Journalism Studies, 15*(1), 17–32.

Deacon, D., Pickering, M., Golding, P. & Murdock, G. (2007). *Researching communications: A practical guide to methods in media and cultural analysis.* London: Bloomsbury Publishing.

Dean, J. (2001). Publicity's secret. *Political Theory, 29*(5), 624–650.

Dean, J. (2009). *Democracy and other neoliberal fantasies: Communicative capitalism and left politics.* Durham, N.C.: Duke University Press.

Defty, A. (2013, April 11). More Thatcherite than Thatcher? Iron lady's real legacy is sitting in the House of Commons. *The Lincolnite.* Retrieved from http://www.thelincolnite.co.uk

Delingpole, J. (2009a, November 20). Climategate: The final nail in the coffin of Anthropogenic global warming (web log article). Retrieved from http://blogs.telegraph.co.uk

Delingpole, J. (2009b, November 21). Climategate: How the MSM reported the greatest scandal in modern science (web log article). Retrieved from http://blogs.telegraph.co.uk

Delingpole, J. (2009c, November 26). Climategate: This is our Berlin Wall moment! (web log article). Retrieved from http://blogs.telegraph.co.uk

Delingpole, J. (2009d, December 9). Watching the climategate scandal explode makes me feel like a proud parent. *The Spectator*. Retrieved from http://www.spectator.co.uk

Delingpole, J. (2011). *Watermelons: The Green movement's true colours* (Kindle version). Retrieved from http://www.amazon.com.

Delingpole, J. (2014). *About James*. Retrieved from http://www.jamesdelingpole.com/about

Deluca, K. M., Lawson, S. & Sun, Y. (2012). Occupy Wall Street on the public screens of social media: The many framings of the birth of a protest movement. *Communication, Culture & Critique, 5*(4), 483–509.

Deuze, M. (2005). What is journalism? Professional identity and ideology of journalists reconsidered. *Journalism, 6*(4), 442–464.

Doherty, B. (1995). Best of both worlds: Milton Friedman reminisces about his career as an economist and his lifetime "avocation" as a spokesman for freedom. *Reason*, (June). Retrieved from reason.com

Donohoe, M. (2007, May 26). Labour ponders why it did not work out. *The Irish Times*. Retrieved from http://www.irishtimes.com

Douglas, R. (1993). *Unfinished business*. Mississauga, ON: Random House of Canada.

Drawbaugh, K. (2013, October 15). Measured praise from U.S. senators on Irish tax loophole change. *Reuters*. Retrieved from http://www.reuters.com

Duncan, G. (2007). *Society and politics: New Zealand social policy* (2nd ed.). Auckland: Pearson Education.

Dyer-Witheford, N. & Compton, J. (2012, October). *Prolegomenon to a Theory of Slump Media*. Paper presented at the European Sociological Association conference, Bilbao, Spain.

Eagleton, T. (1991). *Ideology: An introduction*. New York: Verso.

Eaton, G. (2013, April 8). How public spending rose under Thatcher. *New Statesman*. Retrieved from http://www.newstatesman.com

Editorial: National may find ACT very different (2011, May 5). *The Dominion Post*. Retrieved from http://www.newstext.com.au

Edwards, B. [Brian] (2011). I risk arrest by speculating on what was in the English Breakfast tea. And how John Key's life could have been in danger. *Brian Edwards Media* 15 November (web log post). Retrieved June 20, 2012 from http://brianedwardsmedia.co.nz/2011/11/i-risk-arrest-by-speculating-on-what-was-in-the-english-breakfast-tea-and-how-john-and-johns-lives-could-have-been-in-danger/

Edwards, B. [Bryce] (2011). NZ Politics Daily: 4 July (web log post). Retrieved October 15, 2011 from http://liberation.typepad.com/liberation/2011/07/nz-politics-daily-4-july.html

Ekström, M. (2003). Epistemologies of TV journalism: A theoretical framework. *Journalism: Theory, Practice and Criticism, 3*(3), 259–282.

Electoral Commission (2008). Official Count Results – Overall Status. Retrieved October 20, 2011 from http:www.electionresults.govt.nz/electionresults 2008/partystatus.html

Ellis, G. (2011). Recalibrating news media ownership. *Australian Journal of Communication, 38*(3), 17–30.

Engel, M. (1997, June 5). Any old rider for the Celtic Tiger. *The Guardian*. Retrieved from http://www.theguardian.com

Fahy, D., O'Brien, M. & Poti, V. (2010). From boom to bust: A post-Celtic Tiger analysis of the norms, values and roles of Irish financial journalists. *Irish Communications Review, 12,* 5–20.

Fairclough, N. (2000). *New Labour, new language.* London: Routledge.

Fairclough, N. (2002). Language in new capitalism. *Discourse & Society, 13*(2), 163–166.

Fenton, N. (2006). Bridging the mythical divide: Political economy and cultural studies approaches to the analysis of the media. In E. Devereux (Ed.), *Media studies: Key issues and debates* (pp. 7–27). London: Sage.

Fenton, N. (Ed.). (2010). *New media, old news: Journalism and democracy in the digital age.* London: Sage.

Fenton, N. (2011). Deregulation or democracy? New media, news, neoliberalism and the public interest. *Continuum, 25*(1), 63–72.

Fenton, N. (2013). Cosmopolitanism as conformity and contestation. *Journalism Studies, 14*(2), 172–186.

Ferguson, J. (2010). The uses of neoliberalism. *Antipode, 41*(s1), 166–184.

Fine, B. (2010). Zombieconomics: The living death of the dismal science. In K. Birch & V. Mykhnenko (Eds.), *The rise and fall of neoliberalism: The collapse of an economic order?* (pp. 53–70). London: Zed Books.

Finlayson, A. (2003). *Making sense of New Labour.* London: Lawrence & Wishart.

Finlayson, A. (2012). Rhetoric and the political theory of ideologies. *Political Studies, 60*(4), 751–767.

Fisher, M. (2009). Capitalist realism: Is there no alternative? London & New York: Zed Books.

Fisher, M. & Gilbert, J. (2013). Capitalist realism and neoliberal hegemony: A dialogue. *New Formations: A Journal of Culture/Theory/Politics, 80–81,* 89–101.

Flew, T. (2008). A game of two halves [Review of *The politics of media policy,* by D. Freedman]. *Australian Journalism Review, 30*(2), 127–129.

Flew, T. (2009). The cultural economy moment? *Cultural Science, 2*(1), Retrieved from http://culturalscience.org/journal/index.php/culturalscience/article/view/23/79

Flew, T. & Cunningham, S. (2010). Creative industries after a decade of debate. *The Information Society, 26*(2), 113–123.

Flinders, M. V. (2012). The demonisation of politicians: Moral panic, folk devils and MPs' expenses. *Contemporary Politics, 18*(1), 1–17.

Flynn, R. (2009). Republic of Ireland PLC – testing the limits of marketisation. In D. Ging, M. Cronin & P. Kirby (Eds.), *Transforming Ireland: Challenges, critiques, resources* (pp. 89–106). Manchester: Manchester University Press.

Foss, S. K., Foss, K. & Trapp, R. (1990). *Contemporary perspectives on rhetoric* (2nd ed.). Long Grove, IL: Waveland Press.

Foucault, M. (2007). *Security, territory, population: Lectures at the College de France 1977–1978.* New York: Picador.

Foucault, M. (2008). *The birth of biopolitics: Lectures at the Collège de France, 1978–1979.* Basingstoke: Palgrave Macmillan.

Frank, T. (2000). *One market under God: Extreme capitalism, market populism and the end of economic democracy.* London: Secker & Warburg.

Franklin, B. (2012). The future of journalism. *Journalism Studies, 13*(5–6), 663–681.

Freakonomics book abstract. (2014). Retrieved January 25, 2014 from http://freakonomics.com/books/freakonomics/

Freedland, J. (2013, October 11). The secret state is just itching to gag the press. *The Guardian*. Retrieved from http://www.theguardian.com/

Freedman, D. (2008). *The politics of media policy*. Cambridge: Polity.

Freedman, D. (2012). The phone hacking scandal: Implications for regulation. *Television & New Media, 13*(1), 17–20.

Freedman, D. & Schlosberg, J. (2013). Leveson: The real "elephant in the room" is concentrated ownership (web log post). Retrieved November 1, 2013 from http://inforrm.wordpress.com/2013/01/12/leveson-the-real-elephant-in-the-room-is-concentrated-ownership-des-freedman-and-justin-schlosberg

Freespeech Network (2014). About page. *Free Speech Network*. Retrieved from http://freespeechnetwork.org.uk

Friedman, M. (1962). *Capitalism and freedom*. Chicago: University of Chicago Press.

Friedman, M. & Friedman, R. (1990). *Free to choose: A personal statement*. Orlando, FL: Harcourt.

Fuchs, C. (2012, January 18). Call for papers: Communication, crisis, and critique in contemporary capitalism. Retrieved from http://www.fuchs.uti.at/777/

Fukuyama, F. (1989). The end of history? *National Interest* (Summer). Retrieved February 1 2014 from http://ps321.community.uaf.edu/files/2012/10/Fukuyama-End-of-history-article.pdf

Gaber, I. (2012). Rupert and the "three card trope" – what you see ain't necessarily what you get. *Media, Culture & Society, 34*(5), 637–646.

Galtung, J. & Ruge, M. (1965). The structure of foreign news: The presentation of the Congo, Cuba and Cyprus crises in four Norwegian newspapers. *Journal of International Peace Research, 1*, 64–91.

Garland, C. & Harper, S. (2012). Did somebody say neoliberalism? On the uses and limitations of a critical concept in media and communication studies. *tripleC – Cognition, Communication, Co-operation, 10*(2), 413–424. Retrieved from http://www.triple-c.at/index.php/tripleC/article/view/396/369

Garnham, N. (2011). The political economy of communications revisited. In J. Wasko, G. Murdock & H. Sousa (Eds.), *The handbook of political economy of communications* (pp. 41–61). West Sussex: Wiley-Blackwell.

Garofalo, P. (2010, December 2). Before bankruptcy, conservatives touted Ireland as model for U.S. *Think Progress*. Retrieved from http://www.thinkprogress.org

Gaynor, B. (2007, May 12). Exports help Emerald Isle rise and shine. *The New Zealand Herald*. Retrieved from http://www.nzherald.co.nz

George, S. (1997). How to win the war of ideas: Lessons from the Gramscian right. *Dissent Magazine*, (Summer), 47–53.

Geras, N. (1987). Post-Marxism? *New Left Review, 163*(May–June), 40–82.

Gibbons, L. (1998). Ireland and the colonization of theory. *Interventions, 1*(1), 27.

Giddens, A. (2000). *The third way and its critics*. Cambridge: Polity.

Gilbert, G. (2012). *Mediation, regulation, critique: Mapping the relationship between cultural meanings and political responses to poverty, 1970–2010* (Doctoral dissertation). Retrieved from WorldCat. (818685540).

Gilbert, J. (2008). *Anti-capitalism and culture: Radical theory and poplar politics*. Oxford: Bloomsbury.

Gilbert, J. (2011). What does democracy feel like? Form, function, affect, and the materiality of the sign. In L. Dahlberg & S. Phelan (Eds.), *Discourse theory and critical media politics* (pp. 82–105). Basingstoke: Palgrave Macmillan.

Gilligan, A. (2013). The truth – about Hacked Off's media coup; Andrew Gilligan uncovers the intriguing connections between Leveson and left-wing ideology. *The Telegraph*. Retrieved from www.telegraph.co.uk

Giroux, H. (2010). *Zombie politics and culture in the age of casino capitalism*. New York: Peter Lang.

Glynos, J. (2008). Ideological fantasy at work. *Journal of Political Ideologies, 13*(3), 275–296.

Glynos, J. & Howarth, D. (2007). *Logics of critical explanation in social and political theory*. London: Routledge.

Goodwin, I., Lyons, A. & McCreanor, T. (2014). Ending up online: Mediated youth drinking cultures. In A. Bennett & B. Robards (Eds.), *Mediated youth cultures: The internet, belonging and new cultural configurations* (pp. 59–74). Basingstoke: Palgrave Macmillan.

Grantham, B. & Miller, T. (2010). The end of neoliberalism. *Popular Communication, 8*(3), 174–176.

Gray, J. (1980). On negative and positive liberty. *Political Studies, 28*(4), 507–526.

Gray, J. (1986). *Liberalism*. London: Open University Press.

Gray, J. (1998a). *False dawn: The delusions of global capitalism*. London: Granta.

Gray, J. (1998b). *Hayek on liberty* (3rd ed.). London: Routledge.

Green, D. & Shapiro, I. (1994). *Pathologies of rational choice theory: A critique of applications in political science*. Binghamton: Yale University Press.

Green is good (1997, May 15). *The Economist*. Retrieved from http://www.economist.com

Greenslade, R. (2012, November 30). Leveson report: What the national newspapers say.... (web log post). Retrieved from www.guardian.com

Griffiths, S. (2011). Pluralism, neo-liberalism and the "all-knowing" state. *Journal of Political Ideologies, 16*(3), 295–311.

Grossberg, L. (2010). *Cultural studies in the future tense*. Durham, NC: Duke University Press.

Grundmann, R. (2013). "Climategate" and the scientific ethos. *Science, Technology, & Human Values, 38*(1), 67–93.

Grusin, R. (2010). *Premediation: Affect and mediality after 9/11*. Basingstoke and New York: Palgrave Macmillan.

Habermas, J. (1989). *The structural transformation of the public sphere*. Cambridge: Polity.

Habermas, J. (2011, November 10). Europe's post-democratic era: The monopolisation of the EU by political elites reducing a sense of civic solidarity that's crucial to the European project. *The Guardian*. Retrieved from http://www.theguardian.com

Hager, N. (2006). *The hollow men*. Wellington: Craig Potton.

Hall, S. (1980). Encoding/decoding. In S. Hall, D. Hobson, A. Lowe & P. Willis (Eds.), *Culture, media, language: Working papers in cultural studies, 1972–1979* (pp. 128–138). London: Routledge in association with the Centre for Contemporary Cultural Studies.

Hall, S. (1988). *The hard road to renewal: Thatcherism and the crisis of the left*. London: Verso.

Hall, S. (2001). Foucault: Power, knowledge and discourse. In M. Wetherell, S. Taylor & S. Yates (Eds.), *Discourse theory and practice: A reader* (pp. 72–81). London: Sage.

Hall, S. (2011). The neo-liberal revolution. *Cultural Studies, 25*(6), 705–728.

Hall, S. (2013, April 24). The Kilburn manifesto: Our challenge to the neoliberal victory. *The Guardian.* Retrieved from http://www.theguardian.com

Hall, S., Critcher, C., Jefferson, T., Clarke, J. & Roberts, B. (2013). *Policing the crisis: Mugging, the state and law and order* (35th anniversary ed.). Basingstoke: Palgrave Macmillan.

Hallin D. C. (1992). The passing of the "high modernism" of American journalism. *Journal of Communication, 42*(3), 14–25.

Hallin, D. C. (2005). Field theory, differentiation theory, and comparative media research. In R. Benson & E. Neveu (Eds.), *Bourdieu and the journalistic field* (pp. 224–243). Cambridge: Polity.

Hallin, D. C. (2006). The passing of the high modernism of American journalism revisited. *Political Communication Report, 16*(1).

Hallin, D. C. (2008). Neoliberalism, social movements and change in media systems in the late twentieth century. In D. Hesmondhalgh & J. Toynbee (Eds.), *The media and social theory* (pp. 45–58). London: Routledge.

Hallin, D. C. & Mancini, P. (2004). *Comparing media systems: Three models of media and politics.* Cambridge: Cambridge University Press.

Hames, T. & Feasey, R. (1994). Anglo-American think tanks under Reagan and Thatcher. In A. Adonis & T. Hames (Eds.), *A conservative revolution? The Thatcher-Reagan decade in perspective* (pp. 215–237). Manchester, UK: Manchester University Press.

Hanitzsch, T., Hanusch, F., Mellado, C., Anikina, M., Berganza, R., Cangoz, I., Coman, M., Hamada, B. & Hern, M. E. (2011). Mapping journalism cultures across nations. *Journalism Studies, 12*(3), 273–293.

Hanretty, C. (2013). Leveson Inquiry: Letting the judges take the hard decisions?. *Political Insight, 4*(1), 8–11.

Hanusch, F. (2013, May 19). Whose views skew the news? Media chiefs ready to vote out Labor, while reporters lean left. *The Conversation.* Retrieved from http://www.theconversation.com

Harcup, T. (2012). Questioning the "bleeding obvious": What's the point of researching journalism? *Journalism, 13*(1), 21–37.

Harcup, T. & O'Neill, D. (2001). What is news? Galtung and Ruge revisited. *Journalism Studies, 2*(2), 261–280.

Harman, R. (Producer) (2004, July 17). *Agenda* [Television broadcast]. Transcript retrieved from http://agendatv.itmsconnect.-com/default.aspx?tabid1/4200

Harmes, A. (2012). The rise of neoliberal nationalism. *Review of International Political Economy, 19*(1) 59–86.

Harvey, D. (2005). *A brief history of neoliberalism.* Oxford: Oxford University Press.

Harvey, D. (2009, March 13–15). Is this really the end of neoliberalism? *Counterpunch.* Retrieved from http://www.counterpunch.org/2009/03/13/is-this-really-the-end-of-neoliberalism/

Harvey, D. (2010). *The enigma of capital: And the crises of capitalism.* London: Profile.

Hay, C. (1996). Narrating crisis: The discursive construction of the "Winter of Discontent". *Sociology, 30*(2), 253–277.

Hay, C. (2001). What place for ideas in the structure-agency debate? Globalisation as a process without a subject (web log post). Retrieved from http://www.raggedclaws.com/criticalrealism/archive/cshay_wpisad.html

Hay, C. (2002). *Political analysis: A critical introduction*. Basingstoke & New York: Palgrave Macmillan.

Hay, C. (2004). The normalizing role of rationalist assumptions in the institutional embedding of neoliberalism. *Economy and Society, 33*(4), 500–527.

Hay, C. (2007). *Why we hate politics*. Cambridge: Polity.

Hay, C. & Stoker, G. (2009). Revitalising politics: Have we lost the plot? *Representation, 45*(3), 225–236.

Hayek, F. A. (1944). *The road to serfdom*. London: Routledge

Hayek, F. A. (1960). *The constitution of liberty*. London: Routledge.

Hayek, F. A. (1982). *Law, legislation and liberty: A new statement of the liberal principles of justice and political economy*. London: Routledge.

Hayek, F. A. (1991). *The fatal conceit: The errors of socialism*. Chicago: University of Chicago Press.

Hearn, A. (2008). Meat, mask, burden: Probing the contours of the branded self. *Journal of Consumer Culture, 8*(2), 197–217.

Hearne, J. (2012, April 2). End of the line for Eircom dream. *The Irish Examiner*. Retrieved from http://www.irishexaminer.com

Heath, J. (2000). Ideology, irrationality and collectively self-defeating behavior. *Constellations, 7*(3), 363–371.

Herman, E. S. & McChesney, R. W. (1997). *The global media: The new missionaries of corporate capitalism*. London: Cassell.

Hesmondhalgh, D. (2008). Neoliberalism, imperialism and the media. In D. Hesmondhalgh & J. Toynbee (Eds.), *The media and social theory* (pp. 95–111). Abingdon and New York: Routledge.

Higgins, M. (2008). *Media and their publics*. New York: Open University Press.

Hilgers, M. (2013). Embodying neoliberalism: Thoughts and responses to critics. *Social Anthropology, 21*(1), 75–89.

Hirschman, A. O. (1991). *The rhetoric of reaction: Perversity, futility, jeopardy*. Cambridge: Belknap Press.

Hirst, M. (2012). The cultural politics of journalism: Quotidian intellectuals and the power of media capital. In M. Hirst, S. Phelan & V. Rupar (Eds.), *Scooped: The politics and power of journalism in Aotearoa New Zealand* (pp. 48–64). Auckland: AUT Media.

Holborow, M. (2012a). Neoliberal keywords and the contradictions of an ideology. In D. Block, J. Gray & M. Holborow (Eds.), *Neoliberalism and applied linguistics* (pp. 33–55). New York: Routledge.

Holborow, M. (2012b). What is neoliberalism? Discourse, ideology and the real world. In D. Block, J. Gray & M. Holborow (Eds.), *Neoliberalism and applied linguistics* (pp. 14–32). New York: Routledge.

Holliman, R. (2011). Advocacy in the tail: Exploring the implications of "climategate" for science journalism and public debate in the digital age. *Journalism, 12*(7), 832–846.

Hope, W. (1999). Ideology, communication and capitalist crisis: The New Zealand experience. In A. Calabrese & J. Burgelman (Eds.), *Communication, citizenship, and social policy: Rethinking the welfare state* (pp. 91–112). Lanham, MD: Rowman & Littlefield.

Hope, W. (2012). New thoughts on the public sphere in Aotearoa/New Zealand. In M. Hirst, S. Phelan & V. Rupar (Eds.), *Scooped: The politics and power of journalism in Aotearoa/New Zealand* (pp. 27–47). Auckland: AUT Media.

Howarth, D. (2000). *Discourse*. Buckingham: Open University Press.

Howarth, D. (2004). Hegemony, political subjectivity, and radical democracy. In S. Critchley & O. Marchart (Eds.), *Laclau: A critical reader* (pp. 256–276). London: Routledge.

Hubbard, A. (2011, December 4). Waiting in the wings. *Sunday Star Times*. Retrieved from http://www.sundaystartimes.co.nz

Hume, M. (2012a, September 28). Why "free the press" should be the battle cry for today. *Spiked*. Retrieved from http://spiked-online.com

Hume, M. (2012b, December 27). What's left of press freedom? *Spiked*. Retrieved from http://spiked-online.com

Indymedia (2014). About Indymedia. Retrieved from indymedia.org

Ireland shines. (1997, May 15). *The Economist*. Retrieved from http://www.economist.com

Irish Congress of Trade Unions (2011). *Privatization: Learning from the Eircom debacle* (Brochure). Dublin: Irish Congress of Trade Unions.

The Irish economy: A model of success (2004, October 14). *The Economist*. Retrieved from http://www.economist.com

Irish premier calls for single Irish market (1994, September 19). *Reuters News*.

The Irish Times (1994, September 24). Editorial: Roar of "Celtic Tiger" muted on dole queues – economic performance. *The Irish Times*. Retrieved from factiva.com

The Irish Times (2005, December 31). Irish Times appointment. Retrieved from http://www.irishtimes.com

The Irish Times (2014). Dan O'Brien biography abstract. Retrieved from http://www.irishtimes.com

Irish workforce a prime incentive for US investment, says President (1994, October 26). *The Irish Times*. Retrieved from http://www.irishtimes.com

Irwin, N. (2013, May 21). Five things we learned from Tuesday's big Apple tax hearing. *The Washington Post*. Retrieved from http://www.washingtonpost.com

Jansen, S. (2008). Designer nations: Neo-liberal nation-branding – Brand Estonia. *Social Identities*, *14*(1), 121–142.

Jessop, B. (2010). From hegemony to crisis?: The continuing ecological dominance of neo-liberalism. In K. Birch & V. Mykhenko (Eds.), *The rise and fall of neoliberalism: The collapse of an economic order?* (pp. 177–187). London: Zed Books.

Jones, M. (2005, January 29). Rooms with an Atlantic view. *The Financial Times*. Retrieved from http://www.ft.com

Jutel, O. (2013). American populism and the new political economy of the media field. *The Political Economy of Communication*, (1), 26–42. Retrieved from http://www.polecom.org

Karppinen, K. (2008). Media and paradoxes of pluralism. In D. Hesmondhalgh & J. Toynbee (Eds.), *The media and social theory* (pp. 27–42). New York: Routledge.

Karppinen, K. (2013). Uses of democratic theory in media and communication studies. *Observatorio (OBS*) Journal*, *7*(3), 1–17.

Keena, C. (2013, May 24). Ireland caught in crossfire as firms exploit US tax loophole. *The Irish Times*. Retrieved from http://www.irishtimes.com

Kelleher, E. (2006, March 17). Gartmore stalks Celtic Tiger. *The Financial Times*. Retrieved from http://www.ft.com

Kelsey, J. (1997). *The New Zealand experiment: A world model for structural adjustment?* Auckland: Auckland University Press with Bridget Williams Books.

Kennedy, L. (1997). *Colonialism, religion and nationalism*. Belfast: The Institute of Irish Studies.

Kinsella, S. (2012). Is Ireland really a role model for austerity? *Cambridge Journal of Economics, 36*(1), 223–235.

Kirby, P., Gibbons, L. & Cronin, M. (Eds.). (2002). *Reinventing Ireland: Culture, society and the global economy*. London: Pluto Press.

Kirby, P. (2002). *The Celtic Tiger in distress: Growth with inequality in Ireland*. New York: Palgrave Macmillan.

Kitchin, R., O'Callaghan, C., Gleeson, J., Keaveney, K. & Boyle, M. (2012). Placing neoliberalism: The rise and fall of Ireland's Celtic Tiger. *Environment and Planning, 44*(6), 1302–1326.

Krugman, P. (2011, May 5). Op-Ed; Madmen in authority: An update. *The New York Times*. Retrieved from http://www.nytimes.com

Labour Party (2011). Key/Brash extreme team will hurt mainstream New Zealand (Press release). Retrieved from http://www.scoop.co.nz/stories/PA1104/S00515/keybrash-extreme-team-will-hurt-mainstream-new-zealand.htm

Lacher, H. (1999). Embedded liberalism, disembedded markets: Reconceptualising the Pax Americana. *Political Economy, 4*(3), 343–360.

Laclau, E. (1990). *New reflections on the revolution of our time*. London: Verso.

Laclau, E. (1996). *Emancipation(s)*. London: Verso.

Laclau, E. (2000). Identity and hegemony. In J. Butler, E. Laclau & S. Žižek (Eds.), *Contingency, hegemony and universality* (pp. 44–89). London: Verso.

Laclau, E. (2004). Glimpsing the future. In S. Critchley & O. Marchart (Eds.), *Laclau: A critical reader* (pp. 279–328). London, Routledge.

Laclau, E. (2005). *On populist reason*. London: Verso.

Laclau, E. (2006). Ideology and post-Marxism. *Journal of Political Ideologies, 11*(2), 103–114.

Laclau, E. & Bhaskar, R. (1998). Discourse theory vs. critical realism. *Journal of Critical Realism, 1*(2), 9–14.

Laclau, E. & Mouffe, C. (1990). Post-Marxism without apologies. In E. Laclau (Ed.), *New reflections on the revolution of our time* (pp. 97–132). London: Verso.

Laclau, E. & Mouffe, C. (2001). *Hegemony and socialist strategy* (2nd ed.). London: Verso.

Lahsen, M. (2013). Climategate: The role of the social sciences. *Climatic Change, 119*(3–4), 547–558.

Lane, J. F. (2006). *Bourdieu's politics: Problems and possibilities*. New York: Routledge.

Larner, W. (2003). Neoliberalism? *Environment and Planning: Society and Space, 21*(5), 509–512.

Lashmar, P. (2013, March 27). The path to hell...an investigative journalist's view of Leveson. *openDemocracy*. Retrieved from http://www.opendemocracy.net

Latour, B. (2004). Why has critique run out of steam? From matters of fact to matters of concern. *Critical Inquiry, 30*(Winter), 225–248.

Layton, L. (2010). Irrational exuberance: Neoliberal subjectivity and the perversion of truth. *Subjectivity, 3*(3), 303–322.

Ledbetter, J. (2006, September 18). Ireland has become the economic darling of Europe, but how long can the Celtic Tiger keep its roar? *Time*. Retrieved from http://www.time.com

Lee, J. (1989). *Ireland 1912–1985*. Cambridge: Cambridge University Press.

Leiserowitz, A., Maibach, E. W., Roser-Renouf, C., Smith, N. & Dawson, E. (2013). Climategate, public opinion, and the loss of trust. *American Behavioral Scientist, 57*(6), 818–837.

Lentin, A. & Titley, G. (2011). *The crisis of multiculturalism: Racism in a neoliberal age*. London: Zed Books.

Leveson Inquiry. (2012, November). *An Inquiry into the Culture, Practices and Ethics of the Press: Executive Summary*. Retrieved from http://www.official-documents.gov.uk/document/hc1213/hc07/0779/0779.asp

Leveson Vote: No cause for hyperventilating (2013, March 17). *The Guardian* [Editorial]. Retrieved from www.guardian.com

Lidberg, J. & Hirst, M. (2013). In the shadow of phone hacking: Media accountability inquiries in Australia. *The Political Economy of Communication, 1*(1), 111–121. Retrieved from http://www.polecom.org/index.php/polecom/index

Lilleker, D. G. (2006). *Key concepts in political communication*. New York: Sage.

Linehan, H. (1996, July 13). Let the games begin. *The Irish Times*. Retrieved from http://www.irishtimes.com

Linnane, C. (1994, November 15). Irish FinMin says transfer pricing declining. Reuters News.

Livingstone, S. (2009). On the mediation of everything: ICA presidential address 2008. *Journal of Communication, 59*(1), 1–18.

Louw, E. (2005). *The media and political process*. London: Sage.

Luck of the Irish. (1994, September 24). *Investors Chronicle*, p. 26.

Luckhurst, T. (2010). [Book review: N. Fenton (Ed.), *New Media, Old News: Journalism and Democracy*]. *European Journal of Communication, 25*(4), 424–427.

Luckhurst, T. (2012). *Responsibility without power: Lord Justice Leveson's constitutional dilemma*. Suffolk: Abramis Academic Publishing.

Luckhurst, T. (2013, January 14). Self-regulation without statutory underpinning is possible and desirable (web log post). Retrieved from http://www.cfom.org.uk/2013/01/new-tim-luckhurst-writes-that-self-regulation-without-statutory-underpinning-is-possible-and-desirable/

Lynch, R. (2013, December 9). Inspiration, intellectuals & iconoclasts on the internet: Interview with Colum McCaffery. *Village: Ireland's Political Magazine*. Retrieved from http://www.villagemagazine.ie

MacLeavy, J. (2010). Remaking the welfare state: From safety net to trampoline. In K. Birch & V. Mykhnenko (Eds.), *The rise and fall of neoliberalism: The collapse of an economic order?* (pp. 133–150). London: Zed Books.

Maibach, E., Leiserowitz, A., Cobb, S., Shank, M., Cobb, K. M. & Gulledge, J. (2012). The legacy of climategate: Undermining or revitalizing climate science and policy? *WIREs Climate Change, 3*(3), 289–295.

Malpass, L. (2011, May 3). Brash's "extremist" policies seen as sensible in Australia. *The Dominion Post*. Retrieved from http://www.cis.org.au/media-information/opinion-pieces/article/2857-brashs-extremist-policies-seen-as-sensible-in-australia

Manning, P. (2013). Financial journalism, news sources and the banking crisis. *Journalism: Theory, Practice and Criticism, 14*(2), 173–189.

Mansell, R. (2011). New visions, old practices: Policy and regulation in the internet era. *Continuum: Journal of Media and Cultural Studies, 25*(1), 19–32.

Marchart, O. (2007). *Post-foundational political thought*. Edinburgh: Edinburgh University Press.

Marchart, O. (2011). Mediatic (counter-)apparatuses and the concept of the political in communication studies. In L. Dahlberg & S. Phelan (Eds.), *Discourse theory and critical media politics* (pp. 64–81). Basingstoke: Palgrave Macmillan.

Markham, T. (2014). Journalism and critical engagement: Naiveté, embarrassment, and intelligibility. *Communication and Critical/Cultural Studies, 11*(2), 158–174.

Mason, P. (2013, April 26). Why it's still kicking off everywhere (web log post). *New Left Project*. Retrieved from http://www.newleftproject.org

Mayer, C. (2012, October 15). The Irish answer. *Time* magazine. Retrieved from http://www.time.com

McCarthy, A. (2007). Reality television: A neoliberal theatre of suffering. *Social Text, 25*(4), 17–42.

McChesney, R. W. (1998). Introduction. In N. Chomsky, *Profit over people: Neoliberalism and global order* (pp. 6–13). New York: Seven Stories Press.

McChesney, R. W. (2012). Farewell to journalism: Time for a rethinking. *Journalism Studies, 13*(5-6), 682–694.

McGrath, B. (1994a, September 2). Morgan Stanley eyes Irish market. The *Irish Times*. Retrieved from http://www.irishtimes.com

McGrath, B. (1994b, September 3). Market surges on lack of bad news. *The Irish Times*. Retrieved from http://www.irishtimes.com

McGrath, S. (2007, September 13). Ayn Rand. *The New York Times*. Retrieved from http://www.nytimes.com

McGuigan, J. (2006). [Review of Hartley, J. (Ed.), *Creative industries*]. *Global Media and Communication, 3*(2), 372–374.

McLennan, G. (2004). Travelling with vehicular ideas: The case of the third way. *Economy and Society, 33*(4), 484–499.

McNair, B. (2004). PR must die: Spin, anti-spin and political public relations in the UK, 1997–2004. *Journalism Studies, 5*(3), 325–338.

McQuail, D. (2013). *Journalism and society*. London: Sage.

Menz, G. (2005). Making Thatcher look timid: The rise and fall of the New Zealand model. In S. Soederberg, G. Menz & P. G. Cerny (Eds.), *Internalizing globalization: The rise of neoliberalism and the decline of national varieties of capitalism* (pp. 49–68). Basingstoke: Palgrave Macmillan.

Mercille, J. (2013a). The role of media in fiscal consolidation programmes: The case of Ireland. *Cambridge Journal of Economics, 38*(2), 281–300.

Mercille, J. (2013b). The role of media in sustaining Ireland's housing bubble. *New Political Economy*. DOI: 10.1080/13563467.2013.779652

Meyer, T. (2002). *Media democracy: How the media colonize politics*. Cambridge: Polity.

Miller, D. (2003, November). System failure: It's not just the media, it's the whole bloody system. In *Can't vote, won't vote: Are the media to blame for political disengagement?* Seminar conducted at Goldsmiths College, University of London.

Miller, D. (2010). How neoliberalism got where it is: Elite planning, corporate lobbying and the release of the free market. In K. Birch & V. Mykhnenko (Eds.), *The rise and fall of neoliberalism: The collapse of an economic order?* (pp. 23–41). London: Zed Books.

Miller, T. (2010). How the media biopoliticized neoliberalism; or, Foucault meets Marx. *Revista Galaxia* (20), 22–31.

Minihan, M. & Lynch, S. (2013, May 23). Noonan rejects special Apple tax deal claim. Ireland will not become the "whipping boy" of US senate, says Minister. *The Irish Times*. Retrieved from http://www.irishtimes.com

Mirowski, P. (2013). *Never let a serious crisis go to waste: How neoliberalism survived the financial meltdown.* London & Brooklyn: Verso.

Mitchell, T. (2002). *Rule of experts: Egypt, techno-politics, modernity.* Oakland: University of California Press.

Mitchell, T. (2005a). Economists and the economy in the twentieth century. In G. Steinmetz (Ed.), *The politics of method in the human sciences: Positivism and its epistemological others* (pp. 126–141). Durham, NC: Duke University Press.

Mitchell, T. (2005b). The work of economics: How a discipline makes its world. *European Journal of Sociology, 46*(2), 297–320.

Mitchell, T. (2008). Rethinking economy. *Geoforum, 39*(3), 1116–1121.

Molloy, T. (2014, January 24). Facebook chief praises our "brilliant leader", Enda Kenny. *The Irish Times.* Retrieved from http://www.irishtimes.com

Monagan, D. (2006, June 19). When Irish eyes are buying. *Forbes.* Retrieved from http://www.forbes.com

Monbiot, G. (2003, December 9). Invasion of the entryists. *The Guardian.* Retrieved from http://www.theguardian.com

Montgomery, M. (2008). The discourse of the broadcast news interview. *Journalism Studies, 9*(2), 260–277.

Morley, D. & Chen, K. H. (Eds.). (1996). *Stuart Hall: Critical dialogues in cultural studies.* London: Routledge.

Mosco, V. (2009). *The political economy of communication* (2nd ed.). London: Sage.

Mouffe, C. (2005). *On the political.* London: Routledge.

Muhlmann, G. (2010). *Journalism for democracy.* Cambridge: Polity.

Mullin, C. (2009). Fear and loathing in tabloid Britain. *British Journalism Review, 20*(3), 45–50.

Nerlich, B. (2010). "Climategate": Paradoxical metaphors and political paralysis. *Environmental Values, 19*(4), 419–442.

Neveu, E. (2005). Bourdieu, the Frankfurt School, and cultural studies: On some misunderstandings. In R. Benson & E. Neveu (Eds.), *Bourdieu and the journalistic field* (pp. 195–213). Cambridge: Polity.

Newman, S. (2011a). The libertarian impulse. *Journal of Political Ideologies, 16*(3), 239–244.

Newman, S. (2011b). Postanarchism: A politics of anti-politics. *Journal of Political Ideologies, 16*(3), 313–327.

Nimmo, K. (2007, May 6). Climate change: An inconvenient globalist scam (web log post). Retrieved from http://www.infowars.net

Nolan, D. (2006). Media, citizenship, and governmentality: Defining "the public" of public television broadcasting. *Social Semiotics, 16*(2), 225–242.

The non-fiction 100. (2005, October 19). *National Review.* Retrieved from http://www.nationalreview.com

Norval, A. (2007). *Aversive democracy: Inheritance and originality in the democratic tradition.* Cambridge, UK: Cambridge University Press.

Nuki, P. (1994, November 6). Speculators pile in as Celtic Tiger roars. *The Sunday Times.* Retrieved from http://www.thesundaytimes.co.uk

O'Brien, C. (2014, February 11). US firms paid effective tax rate of 2.2% in 2011. *The Irish Times.* Retrieved from http://www.irishtimes.com

O'Brien, D. (2013a, May 24). Clampdown on tax avoidance could get nasty. *The Irish Times.* Retrieved from http://www.irishtimes.com

O'Brien, D. (2013b, September 20). Presidency ill-served by economic partnership. *The Irish Times*. Retrieved from http://www.irishtimes.com

O'Mahony, J. (2000, August 19). Saturday review – A tiger by the tail. *The Guardian*. Retrieved from http://www.theguardian.com

Ojala, M. (2012, August). *Mediating the political imaginary of governance: Global elites and the Financial Times*. Paper presented at the Finish Conference of Communication Research. Jyvaskyla, Finland.

Oksala, J. (2010). Foucault's politicization of ontology. *Continental Philosophy Review, 43*(4), 445–466.

O'Rourke, B. & Hogan, J. (2014). Guaranteeing failure: Neoliberal discourse in the Irish economic crisis. *Journal of Political Ideologies, 19*(1), 41–59.

O'Sullivan, J. (1999, July 9). Telecom charms the Big Apple to bodhran's beat. *The Irish Times*. Retrieved from http://www.irishtimes.com

O'Toole, F. (2009). *Ship of fools: How stupidity and corruption sank the Celtic Tiger*. London: Faber and Faber Ltd.

O'Toole, F. (2014, January 10). Ireland's rebound is European blarney. *The New York Times*. Retrieved from http://www/nytimes.com

Ouellette, L. & Hay, J. (2008). *Better living through reality TV: Television and post-welfare citizenship*. Malden, MA: Blackwell.

Owen, T. (2012). *Patents, pills, the press and the poor: Discourse and hegemony in news coverage of the global "Access to Medicines" dispute, 1997–2003* (Unpublished doctoral dissertation). Massey University, Wellington, New Zealand.

Palcic, D. & Reeves, E. (2011). *Privatisation in Ireland: Lessons from a European Economy*. Basingstoke and New York: Palgrave Macmillan.

Pallister, D., Vidal, J. & Maguire, K. (2000, July 7). Life after Living Marxism: Fighting for freedom – to offend, outrage and question everything. *The Guardian*. Retrieved from http://www.theguardian.com

Pearce, F. (2010). *The climate files: The battle for the truth about global warming* (Kindle version). Retrieved from http://www.amazon.com.

Peck, J. (2010). *Constructions of neoliberal reason*. Oxford: Oxford University Press.

Peck, J. (2006). Why we shouldn't be bored with the political economy versus cultural studies debate. *Cultural Critique, 64*(Fall), 92–125

Peters, J. D. (2005). *Courting the abyss: Free speech and the liberal tradition*. Chicago: University of Chicago Press.

Petley, J. (2012). The Leveson inquiry: Journalism ethics and press freedom. *Journalism, 13*(4), 529–538.

Phelan, S. (2003). *The influence of neo-liberal assumptions on media treatment of political economy in Ireland*. (Unpublished doctoral dissertation). Dublin City University, Dublin, Ireland.

Phelan, S. (2007a). The discourses of neoliberal hegemony: The case of the Irish republic. *Critical Discourse Studies, 4*(1), 29–48.

Phelan, S. (2007b). The discursive dynamics of neo-liberal consensus: Irish broadsheet editorials and the privatisation of Eircom. *Journal of Language and Politics, 5*(3), 7–28.

Phelan, S. (2009). Irish neoliberalism, media, and the politics of discourse. In D. Ging, M. Cronin & P. Kirby (Eds.), *Transforming Ireland: Challenges critique, and resources* (pp. 73–88). Manchester: Manchester University Press.

Phelan, S. (2011a). The media as the neoliberalized sediment: Articulating Laclau's discourse theory with Bourdieu's field theory. In L. Dahlberg & S. Phelan (Eds.),

Discourse theory and critical media politics (pp. 128–153). Basingstoke: Palgrave Macmillan.

Phelan, S. (2011b). Media critique, agonistic respect the (im)possibility of a "really quite pretentious" liminal space. *Journalism Practice, 5*(3), 272–286.

Phelan, S. (2012). Media power, journalism and agency. In M. Hirst, S. Phelan, & V. Rupar (Eds.,) *Scooped: The politics and power of journalism in Aotearoa New Zealand* (pp. 80–95). Auckland: AUT Media.

Phelan, S. (2014). Critiquing neoliberalism: Three interrogations and a defence. In L. Lievrouw (Ed.), *Challenging communication research* (pp. 27–42). New York: Peter Lang.

Pickard, V. (2007). Neoliberal visions and revisions in global communications policy from NWICO to WSIS. *Journal of Communication Inquiry, 31*(2), 118–139.

PM not dispelling Brash (2011, April 26). *Marlborough Express*. Retrieved from http://www.newstext.com.au

Polanyi, K. (1944). *The great transformation*. Boston: Beacon.

Power, M. (1997). *The audit society: Rituals of verification*. Oxford: Oxford University Press.

Preston, P. (2012, September 22). Making trouble is the greatest press freedom of all. *The Guardian*. Retrieved from http://www.theguardian.com

Priyadharshini, E. (1999, July). *The rhetoric of otherness in the discourse of economics: A postcolonial critique*. Paper presented at the annual Critical Management Studies conference, Manchester, England.

Rabbitte, P. (1999, July 8). They're selling the family silver back to the people who owned it in the first place. *The Irish Times*. Retrieved from http://www.irishtimes.com

Ramsay, G. (2013, March 21). How the press has failed to represent the public mood over Leveson. *New Statesman*. Retrieved from http://www.newstatesman.com/.

Ranciere, J. (1999). *Disagreement: Politics and philosophy*. Minneapolis: University of Minnesota Press.

Ranciere, J. (2004). *The philosopher and his poor*. Durham, NC: Duke University Press.

Ranciere, J. (2009). *The emancipated spectator*. London: Verso.

Raphael, T. (1998, December 30). Irish economy creates a pot of gold. *The Wall Street Journal*. Retrieved from http://www.wsj.com

Ravetz, J. R. (2011). "Climategate" and the maturing of post-normal science. *Futures, 43*(2), 149–157.

Richardson, K. (1998). Signs and wonders: Interpreting the economy through television. In A. Bell & P. Garret (Eds.), *Approaches to media discourse* (pp. 220–250). Oxford: Oxford University Press.

Riordan, D. (2000, September 22). Business leaders consider the Irish model. *The New Zealand Herald*. Retrieved from http://www.nzherald.co.nz

Roar of Celtic Tiger muted on dole queues (1994, September 24). *The Irish Times*.

Rodgers, D. T. (2011). *Age of fracture*. Cambridge: Belknap Press.

Rose, N. (1993). Government, authority and expertise in advanced liberalism. *Economy and Society, 22*(3), 283–299.

Rose, N., O'Malley, P. & Valverde, M. (2006). Governmentality. *Annual Review of Law and Social Science, 2*, 83–104.

RTÉ (2010, December 4). Aprés Match – The EU/IMF bailout (Video file). Retrieved from http://www.youtube.com

Ruscoe, K. (2005, July 21). Cullen scorns Nats' Celtic Tiger plans. *The Dominion Post*. Retrieved from http://www.stuff.co.nz/dominion-post/

Rustin, M. (1988). Absolute voluntarism: Critique of a post-Marxist concept of hegemony. *New German Critique, 43*(Winter), 146–173.

Rustin, M. (2010, May 19). From the beginning to the end of neo-liberalism in Britain. *openDemocracy*. Retrieved from http://www.opendemocracy.net/ourkingdom/mike-rustin/after-neo-liberalism-in-britain

Ryghaug, M. & Skjolsvoid, T. M. (2010). The global warming of climate science: Climategate and the construction of scientific facts. *International Studies in the Philosophy of Science, 24*(3), 287–307.

Savigny, H. (2008). *The problem of political marketing*. London: Continuum.

Scally, D. (2014, January 23). Kenny expects further concessions on legacy debt. *The Irish Times*. Retrieved from http://www.irishtimes.com

Scannell, P. (1998). Media-language-world. In A. Bell & P. Garrett (Eds.), *Approaches to media discourse* (pp. 251–267). Oxford: Blackwell.

Schudson, M. (2005). Autonomy from what? In R. Benson & E. Neveu (Eds.), *Bourdieu and the journalistic field* (pp. 214–223). Cambridge: Polity.

Sean speaks with John and Cindy McCain aboard the campaign plane. (2008, October 9). *Hannity & Colmes*. (Television News Program). Retrieved from http://www.foxnews.com

Segbers, K. (2012). Debating Flinders. *Contemporary Politics, 18*(1), 24–26.

Sen, A. K. (1999). *Development as freedom*. Oxford: Oxford University Press.

Sender, K. (2006). Queens for a day: Queer eye for the straight guy and the neoliberal project. *Critical Studies in Media Communications, 23*(2), 131–151.

Seymour, R. (2013, June 12). Where next for the left? (web log post). *The Northstar*. Retrieved from http://www.thenorthstar.info

Shore, C. (2008). Audit culture and illiberal governance: Universities and the politics of accountability. *Anthropological Theory, 8*(2), 278–299.

Silke, H. & Preston, P. (2011). Market 'realities': De-coding neoliberal ideology and media discourses. *Australian Journal of Communication, 38*(3), 47–64.

Skeggs, B. (2014). Values beyond value? Is anything beyond the logic of capital. *The British Journal of Sociology, 65*(1), 1–20.

Small, V. (2011, January 26). John Key reveals plan for asset sales. *Stuff*. Retrieved from http://www.stuff.co.nz/national/politics/4582922/John-Key-reveals-plan-for-asset-sales

Small, V., Watkins, T. & Mccammon, B. (2011, April 26). Banks would beat Hide, leaked poll shows. *Stuff*. Retrieved from http://www.stuff.co.nz/national/politics/4926196/Banks-would-beat-Hide-leaked-poll-shows

Smith, N. (2005). *Showcasing globalization? The political economy of the Irish Republic*. Manchester: Manchester University Press.

Spencer, R. W. (2009, November 21). Spencer on elitism in the IPCC climate machine. *Watts Up With That*. Retrieved from https://wattsupwiththat.com

Springer, S. (2012). Neoliberalism as discourse: Between Foucauldian political economy and Marxian poststructuralism. *Critical Discourse Studies, 9*(2), 133–147.

Stäheli, U. (2004). Competing figures of the limit: Dispersion, transgression, antagonism and indifference. In S. Critchley & O. Marchart (Eds.), *Laclau: A critical reader* (pp. 226–240). London: Routledge.

Stanyer, J. (2007). *Modern political communication*. Cambridge: Polity.

Starr, M. A. (2004). Reading The Economist on globalization: Knowledge, identity, and power. *Global Society, 18*(4), 373–95.

Steel, J. (2012). *Journalism and free speech*. London: Routledge.

Stiglitz, J. E. (2008, July 7). The end of neo-liberalism? *Project Syndicate*. Retrieved from http://www.project-syndicate.org

Street, J. (2001). *Mass media, politics and democracy*. Basingstoke: Palgrave Macmillan.

Street, J. (2012). Do celebrity politics and celebrity politicians matter? *The British Journal of Politics & International Relations, 14*(3), 346–356.

Strömbäck, J. (2008). Four phases of mediatization: An analysis of the mediatization of politics. *The International Journal of Press/Politics, 13*(3), 228–246.

Sussman, G. & Galizio, L. (2003). The global reproduction of American politics. *Political Communication, 20*(3), 309–328.

Swartz, D. (1997). *Culture & power: The sociology of Pierre Bourdieu*. Chicago, IL: University of Chicago Press.

Thomassen, L. (2005). Antagonism, hegemony and ideology after heterogeneity. *Journal of Political Ideologies, 10*(3), 289–309.

Thompson, D. (2010, November 12). Telegraph blogger James Delingpole wins Bastiat Prize for online journalism (web log article). Retrieved from http://blogs.telegraph.co.uk

Thompson, J. B. (1995). *The media and modernity: A social theory of the media*. Stanford, CA: Stanford University Press.

Thompson, P. A. (2012). Last chance to see? In M. Hirst, S. Phelan & V. Rupar (Eds.), *Scooped: The politics and power of journalism in Aotearoa New Zealand*. Auckland: AUT Media.

Thussu, D. (2007). *News as entertainment: The rise of global infotainment*. London: Sage.

The tiger tamed (2008, November 20). *The Economist*. Retrieved from http://www.economist.com

Titley, G. (2013). Budgetjam! A communications intervention in the political-economic crisis in Ireland. *Journalism, 14*(2), 292–306.

Tønder, L. & Thomassen, L. (Eds.) (2006). *Radical democracy: Politics between abundance and lack*. Manchester: Manchester University Press.

Topper, K. (2005). *The disorder of political inquiry*. Cambridge: Harvard University Press.

Trotter, C. (2011a, May 13). One people anthem for dismantling welfare state. *The Dominion Post*. Retrieved from http://www.stuff.co.nz/dominion-post/

Trotter, C. (2011b, November 18). John, Brash will be gone by morning tea. *Taranaki Daily News*. Retrieved from http://www.stuff.co.nz/taranaki-daily-news/

TSB Bank (2013, April 11). TSB Bank/bank better – TV commercial (Video file). Retrieved from http://www.youtube.com

TVNZ (2011, November 27). Post-Election interviews on Q and A. *Scoop*. Retrieved from http://www.scoop.co.nz

Tyler, I. (2013). The riots of the underclass? Stigmatisation, mediation and the government of poverty and disadvantage in neoliberal Britain. *Sociological Research, 18*(4). Retrieved from http://www.socresonline.org.uk/18/4/8.html

Ungar, R. (2012, May 24). Op-Ed; Who is the smallest government spender since Eisenhower? Would you believe it's Barack Obama? *Forbes*. Retrieved from http://www.forbes.com

Vale, P. (2013, May 22). Ireland must devise plan B as seismic shift in global tax likely. *The Irish Times*. Retrieved from http://www.irishtimes.com

Volcic, Z. & Andrejevic, M. (2011). Nation branding in the era of commercial nationalism. *International Journal of Communication, 5*(1), 598–618.

Wacquant, L. (2004). Pointers on Pierre Bourdieu and democratic politics. *Constellations, 11*(1), 3–15.

Wacquant, L. (2007). *Urban outcasts: A comparative sociology of advanced marginality.* Cambridge: Polity.

Wacquant, L. (2012). Three steps to a historical anthropology of actually existing neoliberalism. *Social Anthropology, 19*(4), 66–79.

Wasko, J., Murdock, G. & Sousa, H. (2011). *The handbook of political economy of communications.* Oxford: Wiley-Blackwell.

Watkins, T. (2011a, May 5). Brash steamroller powering ahead. *The Dominion Post*. Retrieved from http://www.stuff.co.nz/dominion-post/comment/columnists/4945920/Brash-steamroller-powering-ahead

Watkins, T. (2011b, December 2). Key-like qualities give Shearer the edge. *The Dominion Post*. Retrieved from http://www.stuff.co.nz

Watkins, T. & Small, V. (2011, April 26). Hide has the numbers: ACT President. *Stuff*. Retrieved from http://www.stuff.co.nz/national/politics/4925084/Hide-offered-me-Epsom-says-Don-Brash

Watts, A. (2009, November 19). Breaking news story: CRU has apparently been hacked – hundreds of files released (web log post). Retrieved from http://wattsupwiththat.com/2009/11/19/breaking-news-story-hadley-cru-has-apparently-been-hacked-hundreds-of-files-released/

Wittgenstein, L. (1973). *Philosophical investigations.* Oxford: Blackwell.

Wodak, R. (2009). *The discourse of politics in action: Politics as usual.* Basingstoke: Palgrave Macmillan.

Wood, H. & Skeggs, B. (2011). *Reality television and class.* Basingstoke: Palgrave Macmillan.

Wring, D. (2012). "It's just business": The political economy of the hacking scandal. *Media, Culture & Society, 34*(5), 631–636.

Zelizer, B. (2004). *Taking journalism seriously: News and the academy.* London: Sage.

Index

Lightning Source UK Ltd.
Milton Keynes UK
UKOW05f2217131216
289862UK00017B/56/P